Compensation
and
Motivation

COMPENSATION and MOTIVATION

Maximizing Employee Performance With Behavior-Based Incentive Plans

Thomas J. McCoy

American Management Association

Library of Congress Cataloging-in-Publication Data

McCoy, Thomas J.
  Compensation and motivation : maximizing employee performance
with behavior-based incentive plans / Thomas J. McCoy.
    p.   cm.
  Includes bibliographical references and index.
  ISBN 0-8144-5029-6
  1. Compensation management. 2. Employee motivation.
3. Incentives in industry. I. Title.
  HF5549.5.C67M36   1992
658.3'225—dc20   *91-40021*
                                                            CIP

Printing number

10   9   8   7   6   5

To my father,
Edmund T. McCoy,
who taught me by example

Contents

Acknowledgments

The comments obtained for the case histories in this book are all from personal interviews. The people who were actively involved in variable compensation programs were candid, open, and enthusiastic about sharing their experiences and knowledge. Perhaps they gained this attitude from working with a process in which "sensitive information" is shared with all employees, in which everyone comes to realize that real power comes from working together. Whatever the reason, the experience was wonderfully refreshing.

I appreciate the time and participation of these people. Their experiences are each unique and educational. Without them, this book would not be nearly as interesting as it is. My special thanks and sincere wishes for a continuing relationship go to Wayne Hilgers, Claude Sullivan, David Engelman, David Halleck, and Phillip Cooke.

Because this book is the direct result of my professional experiences and observations it is only appropriate that I thank those gentlemen who provided me the opportunities to gain these insights: Ralph Mueller and Keith Hughes.

Of course, my wife Cathy and my sons Logan and Mitchell deserve special thanks for their understanding and for giving me the time and support necessary to complete this task. I could not have done it without them.

Special thanks go to my editor, Adrienne Hickey of AMACOM Books, and to Mary Lou Motl of Custom Editorial Productions for sharing their understanding of the publishing process and for their sincere encouragement.

Compensation
and
Motivation

Introduction

This is a book of both philosophies and methods of tapping into the source of human potential. It will show you that to tap into this source it is necessary to understand what constitutes the resource that is being dealt with. Just as engineers need to understand the molecular structure of the resources they use to build a solid, lasting structure, so too is it necessary for compensation professionals to understand the emotional structure of the human resources that are used to build a solid, lasting organization.

This being the case, it will be necessary to expand our understanding beyond the numerical world of matrix design into other, more amorphous disciplines of human behavior. For many, this will be an uncomfortable and stressful period of change. Some will refuse to make the change. To those who elect to move forward into the future, the following perspective is provided: There is no singular "right" way to progress. Behavior-based incentive compensation is a combination of art and science. Each organization will develop its own solution based on its culture and management style. Indeed, some will change their culture and management style as a result.

Whichever approach your organization will take, do not be afraid to start. With open communications and the proper employee preparation, you will find a fertile and receptive field to plant the seeds of performance improvement. Make it fun—everyone responds well to that approach. Above all, realize that the plan design will not be perfect the first time out. Using the material provided in this book, your experience will give you the results on which to build the next generation of employee involvement: behavior-based incentive compensation.

Visualize yourself in the following situation: The marketplace has changed dramatically during the eighteen months since this year's business plan was developed. Competition has increased, and costs have escalated. You are in the third quarter of the fiscal year, and the organization will not meet plan unless the pace of business picks up.

The compensation department's mission statement reads "To be the foremost leader in the design and development of reward systems that drive performance." In an effort to improve the organization's position, senior management has requested a plan that will utilize the compensation process to motivate the employees to increase productivity and reduce costs.

A performance-improvement incentive program would seem to be in order. But on what should the incentive be focused, and to whom should it be directed? Are the support employees or the operations employees more important? Should the program be team-oriented or individual-based? What about the issue of equity among employees? Is it sensible to change the current system, which took so much effort to develop in the first place?

What should be used as the incentive, cash or some noncash alternative? What will be effective in motivating the employees?

How will the compensation plan be structured? Should it be open-ended or closed-ended? What are the objectives, and how will they be measured? How big should the budget be, and how will the funds be allocated? Should a sweepstakes be utilized in an effort to minimize the cost, or should everyone be compensated based on their individual contributions? If everyone earns, should this be an add-on or at-risk design? How will the program be administered?

What will be the impact on the rest of the organization's initiatives, such as empowerment, total quality management, training, just-in-time inventory management, and organizational development? Are there adequate communication systems in place? Can performance data be captured to provide a real picture of improvement? Who can improve performance results? Should efforts be focused on the management level or on the nonexempt employees?

Management wants action, and time is of the essence. But it will take a minimum of three weeks just to develop and produce communications materials for any new program. And there are all these unanswered questions. Where can you turn for assistance and information?

This book has been written as a reference guide to incentive compensation as it is applied to the general employee population. It is designed to help the reader through the planning and implementation process so that the resulting employee performance incentive program plan will be on target, fair, motivational, results-oriented, and within budget.

But this book is more than just another technical manual on compensation. It goes beyond the standard presentation to deal with the relationship of compensation to motivation. It shows how a relatively new concept, behavior-based incentive compensation, can be utilized to attract, retain, and motivate all levels of employees. In a human resources environment that is becoming increasingly competitive, this could be a valuable program for many organizations.

What Is Behavior-Based Incentive Compensation?

Behavior-based incentive compensation (BBIC) differs from traditional compensation in three significant areas:

1. The plan design requires a high degree of consideration of human resources as well as of finances.
2. BBIC is contingent upon performance.
3. It is extremely flexible in its ability to produce improvement in any area of organizational need.

Let's look at these three basic features associated with behavior-based incentive compensation.

1. *Human resources.* As employees are being called upon to perform in new, different, and more resourceful ways in response to the organization's needs, so, too, the organization must respond to their special needs as well. What this means is that satisfying employees' needs has become an important element in compensation plans that are designed to drive performance. Fortunately, there exists a scientific discipline, behavioral psychology, that can be of great help in the development of these programs.

2. *Finances.* This is the traditional element of incentive compensation that deals with the payout and performance criteria. Normally, a behavior-based incentive compensation plan is a self-funding process—the gains of improvement provide the incentive compensation budget. Therefore, in a behavior-based incentive compensation plan, the financial element also deals with the performance improvement required to generate the funds that will be used to pay the incentive compensation.

3. *Flexibility of design.* The unique beauty of behavior-based incentive compensation is the fact that it can be designed to emphasize financial issues, operational issues, human resources issues, or any combination thereof, based on the situation and current needs of the organization. The term *current needs* is key here; business conditions change quickly. Thus, this approach can change compensation systems permanently or just on a temporary basis, in a broad spectrum or in one targeted business issue.

No compensation system meets all needs, but the unique flexibility of behavior-based incentive compensation allows it to be applicable in a wide variety of business environments and on all levels of an organization. Thus, it is quickly developing among the manufacturing and service companies of North America as an attractive alternative to traditional base compensation practices.

Incentive compensation means many things to many people, depending on the situation. One point that everyone agrees on: Incentives change compensation systems and the way employees relate to them.

The flexibility of this system also makes it difficult to grasp the specifics of its varied applications: It can be approached from a great many different perspectives. In addition, including behavioral psychology as another factor in the design plan increases the number of elements to consider.

This book organizes the thought process surrounding behavior-based incentive compensation so that you can successfully apply it to your needs. It explains how to utilize a process and a system that will help you:

1. Identify your organization's needs.
2. Choose the right behavioral and compensation elements that will address those needs.
3. Combine these elements in the proper proportions into an incentive compensation plan that will maximize performance results and provide the best return on both compensation dollar and management effort.

The concept of behavior-based incentive compensation is broadly applicable on all levels of an organization, throughout industry and the service sector. It is applicable and effective wherever people are utilized to accomplish tasks.

It appears to be revolutionary rather than evolutionary. A certain degree of knowledge is required to effectively design and implement such a plan, but this is nothing to shy away from. In response to rising compensation and benefits costs, increased demand for skilled employees, and competitive pressures in the marketplace, many organizations are already using this compensation technology with a high degree of success. This success is reflected in their profit and loss statements. In fact, as you will see, all the broad social and economic trends indicate that this will be the compensation strategy of the competitive future.

Changing Needs/Changing Practices

Compensation is entering a sophisticated and exciting age where program design can have a measurable impact on bottom line results.

Data from a nationwide survey sponsored by the American Productivity and Quality Center in conjunction with the American Compensation Association indicate that approximately 15 percent of U.S. manufacturing and service companies have some form of group or team reward systems in addition to their base compensation plans.[1] A survey of nontraditional reward systems conducted in 1990 by the consulting firm of Towers Perrin shows that over half of the lower-level-employee incentive compensation plans found at 144 companies had been developed since 1987.[2]

From another quarter comes the observation that, as organizations move toward decentralized decision making, responsibility is being allocated to the lowest appropriate level. In response, field managers are developing "bonus" plans to help power the process. Incentive compensation programs are even easing into the nonsales environment. This is a natural side effect not only of the pressure put on line management for results but also of the support staff's desire to participate in the types of programs that they see the sales force enjoying. These incentive programs are usually "bootleg" programs, quickly designed in the field. As a result, they are almost always an add-on to base compensation as rewards for improved performance that is within the position description. They are brought into existence by front-line profit and loss accountability and by the need to be competitive and responsive to the customer.

Behavior-based incentive compensation programs arise out of an increasing need to utilize compensation as a tool to manage performance. It is the responsibility of the compensation department to contain and control these various programs. It is also the compensation department's responsibility to service this legitimate customer need by developing quality compensation products, on a timely basis, that respond to changing economic and human resources environments.

The material that is discussed in this book has application in both large and small organizations. A smaller organization may find more benefit in the discussion of psychology as it pertains to employee motivation and rewards, while a larger organization may find interest in the specific techniques that help create a common focus and sense of shared destiny. Whatever the size of your organization, this book is meant to provide you with the depth and level of detail necessary to improve the effect that pay has on performance. It will help you understand the ingredients of an effective incentive compensation plan design. Perhaps more importantly, it offers a process and a system that you can utilize to accomplish this. The case examples will assist you in translating theory into actual practice as you design and implement your own plans.

Behavior-based incentive compensation plans will achieve extraordinary results because they tap into the pure source of human potential. These plans, tied as they are to performance, will draw out additional employee contributions in a win-win situation for the employee, for the organization, and for you.

Notes

1. Carla O'Dell and Jerry McAdams, *People, Performance, and Pay,* a report on the American Productivity Center/American Compensation Association national survey of nontraditional reward practices, American Productivity and Quality Center, 1987.
2. *Achieving Results Through Sharing: Group Incentive Survey Report,* Towers Perrin, April 1990.

1

The Formula for Tapping Human Potential

Compensation is changing, and it will never be the same. Fortunately, it is changing in a planned, organized way. The underlying fundamentals of this change can be documented and arranged into a design that will address the specific performance needs of an organization. This book was written for that purpose.

Since its fundamental purpose of attracting, retaining, and motivating employees remains the same, why do we say that the area of compensation is changing? The answer is that the basic structures of business and industry are all changing at the same time. The business environment is so different from what it was only a few years ago that traditional compensation philosophies no longer fill the expanded role that compensation is beginning to play.

New compensation strategies include the element of human dynamics in their designs as a method of tapping the wealth of potential that exists in an organization's human resources. Behavioral psychology is coming into play as a key tactical element in the business strategy.

A Change in Priorities

Not all of the issues predominant in today's business landscape can be addressed by technological advances. Service, now a major element in the business equation, requires the creation of value without necessarily creating a tangible product. As such, it depends primarily on the skills, attitudes, and abilities of employees, not on technology.

Product quality is of increased importance, too. Customer demand has driven quality to the point where it provides a competitive edge for the organizations that can deliver it. Problems with quality, created as a result of the variability inherent in any production process, require a high degree of human involvement to control. We

7

see that quality, like service, depends primarily on the skills, attitudes, and abilities of the employees.

A new generation of employees with different expectations is now in the workplace. They are better educated, aspire to a higher standard of living, and have different expectations compared with previous generations. As we will see, they will soon be in a position to demand that their expectations be met.

The cumulative result of all these changes is that the pendulum has swung to the point where a company's most important resource leaves at 5 P.M. each day. Now, both technology and the employees must be considered in the business equation.

Compensation as a Tool

Over the years, many tools have been developed to manage technological resources. Now business is in the process of developing tools to manage its human resources effectively. One key tool that is being redesigned to manage human resources is the compensation process. This is a unique and subtle change in the perspective of capital investment that the more progressive companies are beginning to recognize and utilize in order to gain a competitive edge.

The organizations of the 1990s will need to be leaner and more responsive than they have been in the past in order to survive and prosper. The traditional approach to rewarding tenure through promotion is no longer economically feasible. Companies are turning to other methods to maintain and encourage the loyalty and involvement of their employees. Dual-career–path planning and systems like skill-based pay, exempt overtime, lump-sum payments, gainsharing, key-contributor programs, group performance-based incentive compensation, and profit-sharing programs are just a few approaches that have developed as tools to manage human resources.

Many leading companies are organizing their employees around small work groups in a successful effort to increase involvement, provide more interesting work, and cross-develop skills. Fundamental to the success of this approach in the long term is the use of compensation incentives, tied to performance, in lieu of promotion or merit increases.

Broad-Based Incentive Compensation

Incentive compensation is effective because it creates a "superordinate" goal that provides an overall reason for employees to function successfully. In a team environment it encourages synergy because, as employees share the gains of improvement, they develop a vested interest in cooperatively reaching a successful outcome. Redesigning compensation to align it more closely with performance and the gains of improvement is arguably the strongest and most far-reaching of all human resources tools currently available or on the horizon.

Let's look at how compensation systems are being redesigned by comparing a traditional compensation strategy to a strategy where nonexecutive employees such as managers, professionals, technicians, and nonexempt employees receive incentive compensation based on their performance. This comparison will provide a clear understanding of the forces at work in the business environment.

Compensation Comparisons

In general terms, traditional compensation strategy is job-based. It is a method of managing a labor budget to keep costs to a minimum. The administrative thinking that supports this strategy relies on the market practices of companies that a given organization competes with for human resources talent. Compensation opportunities are based on job ranking determined by a job-evaluation process. Differences in compensation among employees are determined by an annual performance evaluation. The whole process is driven by a merit increase budget that establishes and defines all the parameters.

On the other hand, incentive compensation, applied across the organization, operates outside the constraints of the merit increase budget. The controlling parameters applied on this scale are based on the expansive and optimistic vision of "shared gains."

Instead of a closed view of competitive equity, broad-based incentive compensation presents a business strategy of competition not only for labor but for the customer. Focusing on outward growth, it makes the statement to all employees that "we need to grow in the marketplace, and when we do, we will share the benefits of that growth with those employees who help make it happen"—a unique approach for compensation to take.

Changing this approach to compensation changes the relationship between all employees: exempt, nonexempt, managerial, and individual contributor. All now become partners, bringing a whole new set of psychological elements into play. These elements are the motivational tools that separate incentive compensation from traditional compensation.

The combination of behavioral psychology's motivational tools and incentive compensation's reward mechanisms results in this new type of compensation system that we call behavior-based incentive compensation (BBIC). The reward mechanisms tie compensation to performance, and the psychological elements provide the motivation to get involved with the job. The basis for such a radical approach to compensation is the need today to make better use of the total human resources available to an organization. The potential for employees to affect overall performance is the single largest competitive asset a company has. We have entered the age of the Human Potential Revolution, which, like the Industrial Revolution, will have a significant global impact.

The Human Potential Revolution

How can we be so sure that megachanges will take place as a result of tapping the human potential of our employees? Personal observation has shown us that the day-to-day performance of employees improves when they assume, and are given, responsibility for results. Employees assume responsibility for results when the following three elements are present:

1. *Focus.* Employees understand, agree with, and have the capacity to comply with the intent of the organization.
2. *Empowerment.* Employees are held accountable for, and have control over, the results.
3. *Positive reinforcement.* The results are tied to a strong reward system.

Let us focus on positive reinforcement for a moment. Webster's *Ninth New Collegiate Dictionary* defines an *incentive* as "that which is stimulating, something that has a tendency to incite to determination or action." In the context of this discussion, a reward that is contingent upon results could be considered an incentive. That sounds appropriate for our needs as they relate to the competitive environment of the 1990s.

The purpose of behavior-based incentive compensation is to link employee performance with an established reward system and to use that system to encourage employees to take action. The degree and quality of action they take will be a function of the linkage between the elements of behavioral psychology and incentive compensation.

An article on quality and continual improvement in the October 1989 issue of the *Training and Development Journal* states that business as a whole has learned a lot about what it takes to create the proper environment for quality improvement. Programs and systems such as motivational incentives, supervisory development, and career opportunities are listed as critical elements. The article then makes the observation that the potential of these programs remains underutilized even in the best organizations as a result of lack of faith on the part of senior management.[1]

It could be that this lack of faith results from a lack of knowledge and understanding. In order to accept and embrace the process and system of behavior-based incentive compensation, it is first necessary to understand *why* these elements cause employees to respond.

Maximize the BBIC Program's Potential

Behavior-based incentive compensation incorporates both technical and psychological elements. In order to maximize the potential of a BBIC program, it is necessary to understand both *what* to include in the way of compensation plan design and *why* the combined elements will be effective.

Understanding the why will allow the proper selection of whats, thus increasing the accuracy of plan design and the effectiveness of the plan. Both the what and the why will be examined in detail in this book, with emphasis placed on their interdependent relationship.

The advent of providing incentive compensation opportunities to all levels of employees will require compensation professionals to become knowledgeable in psychology as well as in compensation. Only then will it be possible to combine this knowledge in the application of a leading-edge form of compensation strategy, a strategy that taps into the source of human potential.

Features and Benefits

Incentive-based compensation plans, properly designed and implemented, are effective because they tap into the basic desire to participate and contribute that exists in each of us. BBIC is unique because it consciously focuses on the needs of the individual and, by addressing those needs, provides motivation.

In the workplace, motivation can take a variety of forms. It can mean the satisfaction of doing something interesting or challenging, of performing work that has value. It can mean job security or the opportunity to become involved in decision making. It can mean recognition from one's peers or supervisor. It can mean financial rewards. Behavior-based incentive compensation, because of its flexibility, has the power to identify and address each and all of these needs.

Behavior-based incentive compensation is a better way of distributing compensation funds because it is based on performance improvement and is contingent upon results. It is a reward system that pays for results and pays in proportion to the improvement. Because of this, it is an excellent method of communicating performance objectives. It can be designed on an individual or team basis, can be permanent or temporary, and can be changed as business conditions dictate.

Behavior-based incentive compensation is a means of placing under a single umbrella a myriad of employee performance programs, such as employee involvement, just-in-time asset management, statistical process control, cycle-time analysis, and total quality. It is the central focal point that unifies all the programs. Tying compensation to these programs makes it obvious to the employees how they relate to the business strategy, and how the business strategy, in turn, relates to their personal objectives. It provides a strong reason to participate actively because it permits a high level of self-interest.

Behavior-based incentive compensation is a balance of two elements: organizational needs and individual needs.

1. *Organizational needs* are the traditional economic reasons for implementing any compensation strategy. Behavior-based incentive compensation provides a measurable return on investment and thus has a major impact on an organization's performance. With that kind of an effect on an organization, with the ability to link company or stockholder interests to employee rewards, the role of the compensation professional is significantly increased.

2. *Individual needs* are the basic emotional elements in all of us. Behavior-based incentive compensation fulfills these needs in an agreement with the employees that their contributions will be valued and that their efforts will be rewarded in proportion. Part of this compensation strategy requires that employees know what goals to strive for and how well they are performing as a result of measured feedback. They must also be empowered to change performance, systems, procedures, resources, and capabilities as a result of what the feedback has told them. All this provides a sense of control and added value to the employees' work.

Balancing the organization's needs and the employees' needs will determine the design and focus of the plan.

Behavior-based incentive compensation is both static and dynamic. On the static side is a compensation technique that must incorporate a specific financial rationale and certain well-defined motivational elements in order to be effective. On the dynamic side are the psychological elements that make the day-to-day implementation of the plan exciting and even fun for all employees.

Behavior-based incentive compensation is good news for the organization and for the employees. And, because of the impact it has on the organization's performance, it's good news for the customer, too. Any marketing executive knows that good news is an opportunity for promotion and celebration. This opportunity is what breathes life into the compensation plan and gives it energy.

Are you beginning to see a pattern develop, a pattern that includes promotion, communication, information sharing, and performance feedback? BBIC draws back the veil of secrecy that normally shrouds the compensation process and reveals to all employees the incentive opportunities that are available to them.

We Are Not Alone

Broad-based incentive compensation is a growing compensation philosophy. According to *Success* magazine, in 1985 U.S. business spent $10 billion energizing workers with incentives and elaborate profit-sharing plans. Five years before, it was one half that amount.[2] In a survey of 1,600 companies sponsored by the American Productivity and Quality Center and the American Compensation Association, over 75 percent of the companies reported installing new methods of distributing compensation.[3]

There are more and more seminars being offered on this subject by a number of organizations, including the American Compensation Association, the American Productivity and Quality Center, and the American Management Association. Compensation consulting firms such as Hay Group, Hewitt, and Mercer are exploring the topic as a new growth frontier for their organizations.

Broad-based incentive compensation is becoming an important competitive strategy—witness the list of companies that are piloting the approach and enjoying the results. The United Auto Workers and Ford Motor Company negotiated a plan in the early 1980s, and in 1988 more than 170,000 hourly employees shared over $600 million as a result. In the same year, IBM spent $70 million on awards to employees. Companies like Kodak, Pacific Bell, and PepsiCo are also focusing their attention on this area of employee performance improvement. The question isn't whether or not behavior-based incentive compensation is the wave of the future—it is. The question is how to maximize return on investment in compensation. BBIC is the answer.

Incentive compensation is often overlooked as an integral part of the total quality management movement that is sweeping the United States. A good example is Motorola, where the focus on quality provides employees with psychic rewards for participating. The company does this so effectively that it has won national and international awards for quality. Motorola has begun investigating the use of incentive compensation as the necessary next step—necessary because the company's management is beginning to understand the importance of including both the psychological and material needs of the employees in any effort to improve the organization's performance.

Behavior-based incentive compensation is a marriage made in the income statement because it is focused on improving profitability. It encourages all employees to focus on strategic issues and translate these issues into areas that they can impact, including new-product cycle time, customer service, productivity, quality, and expenses.

BBIC builds on its traditional compensation foundation as a strategy to attract, retain, and motivate *the best* employees. The Associates Financial Services, currently a division of Ford Motor Company, utilizes behavior-based incentives for its 3,500 employees involved in consumer lending. In a competitive recruiting environment, the branch managers promote this aspect of the compensation package to attract the best candidates.

A Shortage of Qualified Candidates

Behavior-based incentive compensation is also a strategy to motivate the average employee to exceptional performance. It's a means of doing better with what you have—and this is exceptionally important. One of the problems faced by businesses in North America is that the qualified workforce is shrinking because overall population growth has slowed. A Hudson Institute study, *Workforce 2000*, commissioned by the U.S. Labor Department, reports that by the year 2000 the sixteen- to twenty-four-year-old age group will drop 8 percent under current levels. It also indicates most of the job growth during the 1990s will be in jobs that require advanced skills in reading, language, and math—and that there will be a shortage of people with these skills.[4] What it comes down to is that the U.S. economy is creating about one million more jobs a year than there are qualified workers. Experts are pointing to a labor shortage that is estimated to last into the turn of the century.

Endangered Standard of Living

Workforce 2000 also predicts that the majority of jobs created in the 1990s will be in the service industries. The impact of this on the labor force will be shrinking wages, a result of the service industry's low productivity. This fact of economic life will be in direct conflict with the employees' desire to maintain a standard of living that is at least equal to what they have experienced in the past. Behavior-based incentive compensation provides a perfect opportunity for management to provide their employees with the means to maintain and even improve their standard of living by tying pay to performance and sharing the gains of improved results. An employer who is working toward filling the employees' needs will certainly be viewed as the employer of choice.

The American Productivity and Quality Center's report on *People, Performance, and Pay* found that the more competition an organization faced, the more likely it was to utilize a nontraditional form of compensation to motivate its employees.[5] Other national survey data show that only about half of middle managers and one-third of professionals feel that their pay is linked to their performance. In effect, these people have been given no reason to excel. Behavior-based incentive compensation, on the other hand, will improve the organization's competitive position by turning compensation cost into a performance-improvement tool.

Dueling Needs

As the workforce ages (data show the average age will be thirty-nine by the year 2000), organizations will need extra stimuli to encourage productivity, flexibility, and the willingness to change and learn. This goes hand in hand with the employees' desire for rewarding work. Data gathered during the 1970s showed that the number-one motivator in the workplace was the satisfaction of doing interesting work—that is to say, work that provides a sense of accomplishment to the employee. While rewarding work is still very high on the list of priorities, data gathered during the late 1980s by various compensation consulting firms show that materialism is on the rise. This can be verified by personal observation: Just spend an hour in front of the television during prime time. Pay special attention to the programs and advertisements that are directed toward youth and young adults.

During the 1980s, there was a significant shift in U.S. workforce demographics. Dr. George Wilkinson, president and senior fellow of the United Way Strategic Institute, presents the profile of a qualified employee as one who has high expectations, who is better educated than the previous generation, and who has (or aspires to) a higher standard of living. These employees have different values, too: They value people over institutions. They value individualism over conformity. They need self-esteem, developed through challenge, responsibility, growth, and reward. They want to make a contribution. They will resist a mandate, yet get actively involved if they feel they have ownership. They expect to be consulted about business decisions, and they value the ability to make a difference.

With limited amount of time and multiple demands upon that time, the workers of the 1990s will respond most favorably to the environment that supports them from a holistic standpoint, addressing both their intrinsic needs and their extrinsic (material) needs.

Going forward, probably the most significant challenge and opportunity for management will be to link employees' performance to the fulfillment of their expectations, needs, and values. Behavior-based incentive compensation places strong emphasis on behavioral psychology and the psychic rewards it can provide. From the viewpoint of the employee, this can be perceived as intrinsic reward. The presence of intrinsic reward in conjunction with financial or extrinsic reward is a powerful force for fulfilling employee needs.

The Formula for Tapping Employee Potential

Management, charged with the responsibility of designing and implementing a system that will prove both motivational and results-oriented, will have a perspective of the formula for tapping human potential that looks like this:

$$\frac{\text{Behavioral}}{\text{psychology}} + \frac{\text{incentive}}{\text{compensation}} = \frac{\text{performance}}{\text{improvement}}$$

Figure 1-1 exhibits the relationship between the formula for tapping human potential and the BBIC Fishbone diagram. This diagram can be used to apply the concepts of the formula and will be a valuable tool to assist you in developing your program structure analysis and design capabilities. Both formula and diagram will be used in this book to maintain an organized thought process as we proceed to combine two such diverse disciplines as compensation and psychology into the concept of behavior-based incentive compensation.

The Fishbone diagram will also function as a template for compensation plan design. By following the basic rules of the formula, the output (the resulting plan) will be a function of the balance you have established between the two key elements, compensation and psychology. In this way, you will find it possible to design a behavior-based incentive compensation plan that is targeted to address specific business issues. Herein lies the power of BBIC.

In the Fishbone diagram, behavioral psychology in the form of incentive compensation is represented on one side of the "backbone" and tangible rewards in the form of extrinsic compensation are represented on the other side. The key factors of each of these

Figure 1-1. Relationship between the BBIC formula and the Fishbone.

Behavioral Psychology + Incentive Compensation = Performance Improvement

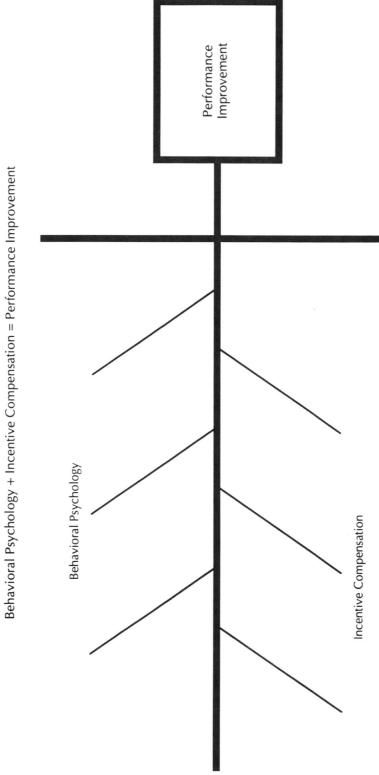

disciplines will provide the Fishbone structure. As we progress through this book, we will add specific elements to both sides of the diagram until it is complete. You will see how the techniques of prioritization and relationship identification will be major tools for use in the development of the most effective behavior-based incentive compensation plan.

The extrinsic incentive compensation side of the BBIC formula is based on the concept of sharing the gains of improved results. This does not include only productivity or cost improvement, as is commonly thought under the term *gainsharing*, but includes all of the gains that result when the employees contribute more of their discretionary time, energy, and creative thought to the business at hand. This is the materialistic element of the formula. By offering to share the gains, management provides the employees with a reason to be proactive. Contained in the extrinsic incentive compensation side are two familiar concepts:

1. The person closest to the job knows it best.
2. Human assets are most fully utilized when both hands and mind are employed.

The behavioral psychology side of the formula is the softer side. It deals with human emotions and perceptions and the need for intrinsic rewards associated with the job. These rewards are contained in such elements as the opportunity to perform meaningful work, the opportunity to complete cycles of work and thus achieve closure, the opportunity to see a finished product, to experience variety, and receive performance feedback. Intrinsic compensation is based on the human needs for social acceptance and personal esteem. These needs add a major new element to the concept of compensation in a format that can be applied in a practical manner.

Shakespeare wrote, "He is well paid that is well satisfied." Inasmuch as satisfaction is a matter of perception on the part of the recipient, the behavioral side of the formula has a great potential to satisfy. The hidden strength of behavior-based incentive compensation is its ability to provide the input that perceptions are made of.

It's Not So New

By now you have recognized this compensation philosophy. In fact, it's probably in use now in your company in the sales force and executive ranks. Sales incentive compensation and executive incentive compensation fit the formula as it applies to those particular groups.

Based on what we know so far, we may see that they are usually less than fully effective.

If you were to evaluate these compensation plans utilizing the BBIC formula as a template, you would probably find the formula unbalanced, with an overemphasis on the incentive compensation side and an underemphasis on the behavioral psychology side.

What's the Holdup?

Consciously or not, the effectiveness of the concept of incentive compensation has proven itself in the form of sales incentive compensation and contests for over fifty years. If it works so effectively in sales, why hasn't this approach to compensation been applied in other areas?

What barriers are resisting the spread of this powerful motivational technique? Are nonsales employees so different from sales employees that they fail to respond to the same motivational influences? The data do not seem to reflect this. Incentive compensation has been incorporated at the executive level, and even though its effectiveness has been less measurable than that of sales incentive compensation, in many situations it has slowly permeated through the ranks to the senior manager level. So we see that extrinsic reward systems exist in almost every organization. What about intrinsic reward systems?

The two factors of the formula, the two sides of the Fishbone, exist in almost every organization. The intrinsic reward factors normally are found in the form of employee-recognition programs, such as those that give awards for safety, service, and top performer. Unfortunately, these two types of programs, intrinsic compensation and extrinsic compensation, were generally unrelated in the compensation philosophy of the 1980s. Combining these two factors into a common strategy will result in broad-based compensation programs that will drive the performance of all employees. So why hasn't this been done? Why do executive incentive compensation plans focus almost solely on the extrinsic reward factors, and why do all-employee programs focus almost solely on the intrinsic reward factors?

There appear to be three forces at work that have historically slowed the integration of these factors and thus the application of this concept to all employees. These forces are not very strong, and once identified, they can be easily overcome. The first force is environment. Nonsales employees historically have functioned in a closely supervised environment where routine and stability are highly valued. A manager or supervisor responsible for maintaining the status quo would have no need for, and would vigorously oppose, a compensation strategy that would energize the workforce. This type of environment has pretty much passed from the business world. Environmental resistance is no longer an issue because, as we have seen, the business environment has gone from being static to being dynamic. Flexible, empowered employees are proving to be a major asset in the struggle for profitability.

The second force is the concept of employee profile and job function as it relates to the administration of the compensation philosophy. In most organizations, there seems to be a stratification of job function above which the skills of organization, conceptualization, and decision making are the key criteria. Below this stratification, the job function criteria tend to emphasize individual contribution. Under this concept, certain jobs require an employee profile that emphasizes certain skills and personal attributes. It is possible for an individual to be overqualified as well as underqualified for the position.

What appears to happen below the senior manager level is a shift in employee profile and job function to a degree so significant that the design elements of an incentive compensation plan must differ greatly from those of an executive incentive plan.

A successful behavior-based incentive compensation plan requires the proper balance of intrinsic and extrinsic rewards as they relate to the target audience. The reward factors that underlie the executive incentive compensation plans are inappropriate for the nonexecutive audience and must be adjusted. Until now there have been few tools to assist in the accurate development of such a design. With the use of the BBIC formula and the Fishbone diagram, this becomes a well-defined task.

The third force is one of measurement. The employee profile and work-related responsibilities at a level below senior manager are such that the objectives must be specific and meaningful for incentive compensation to be effective. Performance measurement must be more precise and relate more closely to performance than in plans for executives. Performance feedback must be more timely, too, and the reward must be more immediate. The business issues remain essentially the same—they just become more specific to the individual. The use of computer technology and modern management techniques that include employee input can overcome this obstacle.

Based on a clear understanding of the employee profile, an accurate and effective plan design can be developed by using the BBIC formula and the Fishbone diagram. Differing employee profiles make it necessary to understand the basics of behavioral psychology with the same degree of expertise that the basics of traditional compensation are understood. That is the topic of the next chapter.

Notes

1. Lawrence Holpp, "Achievement Motivation and Kaisen," *Training and Development Journal*, October 1989, pp. 53–60.
2. Mark Roman, "Beyond the Carrot and the Stick," *Success*, October 1986, p. 39.
3. Carla O'Dell and Jerry McAdams, *People, Performance, and Pay*, a report on the American Productivity Center/American Compensation Association national survey of nontraditional reward practices, American Productivity and Quality Center, 1987.
4. William Johnson and Arnold Packer, *Workforce 2000: Work and Workers for the 21st Century* (Indianapolis: Hudson Institute, 1987), pp. 75–103.
5. O'Dell and McAdams, *loc. cit.*

2

Intrinsic Incentive Compensation

As a manager, have you ever been involved in a situation where you were required to manage a diverse group of employees, ranging from the highly motivated, enthusiastic, and participative down to others who failed to get involved at all? What was the general outcome of the work effort? If your experience was like thousands of others that happen every day, you relied most often on the highly motivated employees to perform the tasks. By and large, motivated employees receive a greater share of the workload than do the undermotivated employees, if for no other reason than that they seek it out.

Does that make good business sense? Is it fair to all the employees? Is it the best utilization of resources from the standpoint of productivity and cost? Wouldn't it be better to address the issue of motivation and, in doing so, enhance the contribution of all employees?

But how to address the issue? How do you motivate someone? Is the ability to motivate a talent that only a few charismatic individuals such as Vince Lombardi or General George Patton are born with? Or is there a technique that, followed properly, can be successfully utilized by anyone?

Motivation is a tough subject to analyze. It's seated in human emotions and based on individual perceptions. It can be initiated by a wide variety of factors, depending on the individual and the circumstances. You would think those factors make it almost impossible to delineate. In order to grasp this concept we need a theory of what motivation is and a framework of application.

Motivation Is Needs Fulfillment

The current thinking among social scientists is that the ability to motivate people is not so much a gift as it is the application of theories derived from the study of human behavior. This study is called *behavioral science,* and its focus is to understand why people behave the way they do. The basic tenet that has been established by behavioral psychology is that people, all people, behave in a manner that results in their needs being fulfilled.

Lou Holtz, championship-winning football coach of the University of Notre Dame, understood this when he said, "You can get anything you want if you help enough people get what they want." The application of this concept was obviously effective for him, and it can be effective for you as well.

Behavioral psychology provides a theory of motivation that we will use to develop our Fishbone diagram from Chapter 1 into a Fishbone of Needs (see Figure 2-1, which shows the basic Fishbone, before any needs have been added to flesh out the structure). We first identify the key human needs that can be fulfilled in the workplace and then use the Fishbone structure to place these needs in a framework that will have direct application in the design of incentive compensation plans.

Once we have fully developed the Fishbone diagram, addressing the needs of both employees and the organization, it will be possible to integrate behavioral psychology into a compensation system. This is behavior-based incentive compensation, and will provide the employees with the opportunity to fulfill their needs through behavior that impacts specific, well-defined organizational needs.

Current thinking in the field of organizational development has generally defined motivating work as that which provides the satisfaction of doing something interesting or challenging, of performing work that has value. This value is not necessarily value to the organization but a "sense" of value that is provided to the employee. Employee surveys show that employees who understand how they fit into the organization have a significantly better attitude about their jobs than employees who do not have this understanding. From this knowledge springs the environment of employee involvement, quality circles, participative action teams, and similar motivational techniques and devices.

This understanding supports the three factors that encourage employee responsibility that we observed in Chapter 1. For the purpose of developing a technology that will enable us to apply motivation to incentive compensation systems, we will propose that these factors, empowerment, focus, and positive reinforcement, are critical to the concept of motivation.

These are the three key components on the intrinsic compensation side of the Fishbone because, in general, the intrinsic human needs that can be fulfilled in a business situation can be classified under one of these factors. As we progress, we will add the elements

Figure 2-1. BBIC Fishbone of needs.

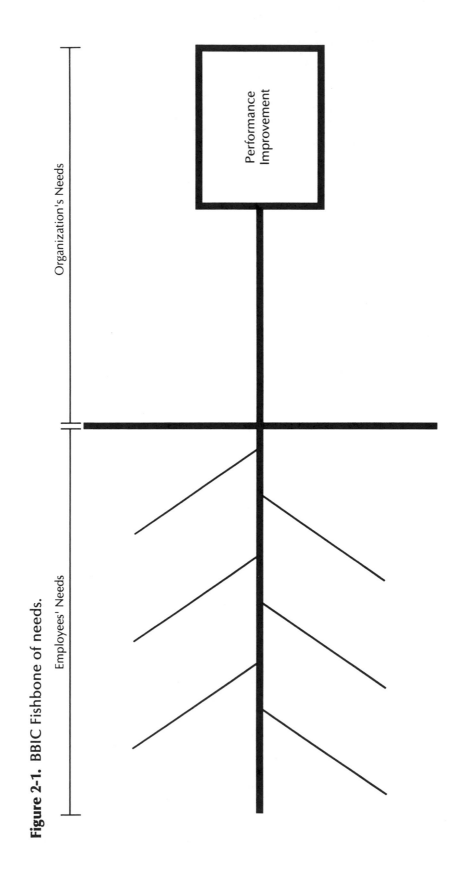

that define each factor. These elements will provide the basis for concrete actions that management can take on a daily basis to support the objectives of the incentive compensation package. For above all of its other attributes, behavior-based incentive compensation is a management tool.

Why These Three Factors?

Empowerment, focus, and positive reinforcement have been chosen because they best represent the spectrum of human needs that exists in all of us. The term *focus* indicates a sense of purpose and direction. It is closely associated with the basic human need for membership, belonging, and acceptance. The term *positive reinforcement* represents the basic human need for achievement and accomplishment and the reassurance those elements provide to personal esteem. The term *empowerment* has been chosen to convey the basic need of the individual somehow to feel in control of his or her environment, with some ability to make an impact. Empowerment has a strong relationship to the basic human need for self-fulfillment.

In support of this position, information gathered by the consulting firm of Hewitt and Associates and provided at a variable compensation seminar conducted in Boston in 1989 indicates that motivational elements in the workplace include such items as:

Involvement Identification }	Nonexempt Emphasis
Extrinsic Rewards Pressure/Accountability }	Exempt Emphasis

Observations and experience indicate that existing systems of employee performance management seem to emphasize involvement and identification on the nonexempt level and extrinsic reward and pressure/accountability on the exempt level. An extreme scenario would include quality improvement teams for the nonexempt and incentive-driven business objectives (e.g., MBOs) for the upper-level exempt. Behavior-based incentive compensation provides the methodology and financial reasoning to blur this distinction and apply all four elements to both exempt and nonexempt employees, with a special emphasis on extrinsic rewards being linked to specific, measurable performance results.

While much of this book addresses motivation from a micro standpoint, it is helpful to understand from a macro standpoint the very first thing that happens to the employees when the organization starts to take their needs into consideration in the workplace. For when the three key factors that make up the employees' intrinsic needs are satisfied or fulfilled, this reduces anxiety on the part of the employees. As this occurs, employee attitudes change from resistance and avoidance to proactive and opportunistic. Thus, the first big change is a change in attitudes. How significant is this?

Research by the Hay Group, a nationally recognized compensation consulting firm, indicates that employee attitudes are an indicator of motivation.[1] The research goes on to say that employee attitudes are formed as a result of how the employees perceive such workplace issues as

- Pay
- Respect
- Job challenge

If attitudes are a good indicator of motivation, then it is significant to note that in another Hay Group survey less than 60 percent of the responding middle managers rated their organizations favorably on the topic of job security. On the topic of advancement opportunity, less than 45 percent rated them favorably. Obviously, we are on to a good thing here in behavior-based incentive compensation, because any capability to have a positive impact on employee attitudes can be a very timely and useful tool.[2]

The professional consultants have stacks of data to support the position that involvement, identification, respect, job challenge, accountability, and pay/extrinsic rewards are the major motivational elements in the workplace. These are the elements that fulfill the basic human needs that we have identified. This fulfillment is a form of compensation because it is provided in the workplace by the employer in return for the employees' continued contribution.

This list of motivational elements fits very nicely into our Fishbone diagram. Pay is a financial contract between the employer and the employee and is part of extrinsic compensation, which will be discussed in Chapter 3. In this chapter, we will concentrate on the elements of intrinsic compensation—involvement, identification, respect, job challenge, accountability—which are all part of a psychological contract between employer and employee.

The BBIC Fishbone diagram in Figure 2-2 includes our basic human intrinsic needs for empowerment, positive reinforcement, and focus. Intuitively we can see that accountability and challenge are manifestations of the need for empowerment; respect, of the need for positive reinforcement; and identification and involvement, of the need for focus. An organization that provides these elements to its

Figure 2-2. Basic BBIC Fishbone diagram.

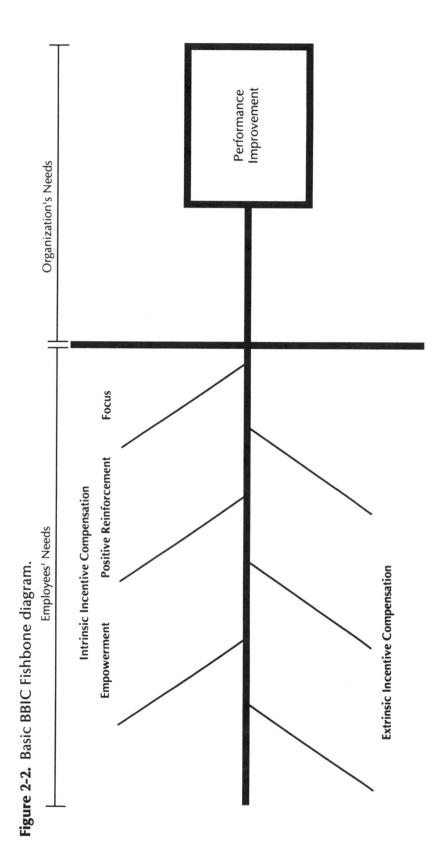

employees is fulfilling their intrinsic needs. That's why the surveys report that these elements have a strong association with employee motivation.

The Role of Behavioral Psychology

Changes in attitudes bring about changes in behavior, and changes in behavior can result in a change in performance. (Thus, you need to be careful how you change attitudes and behavior so that you get the desired results.) Based on all this, we can postulate a response to the question, What is motivation? The answer, for our purposes, is that *Motivation is the ability to change behavior.* The successful use of incentive compensation to change and channel behavior requires an understanding of why incentives work, why they provide motivation.

As with any discipline, in behavioral psychology there are breakthrough theories and figures. Three major contributors in this field are Frederick Herzberg, Abraham Maslow, and B. F. Skinner. We will briefly discuss each and identify the elements of their theories that can be utilized to transform incentive compensation into behavior-based incentive compensation.

Frederick Herzberg's Two Sets of Needs

As a professor of psychology at Case Western Reserve University in Cleveland and a leading behavioral scientist in the field of the human relationship to work, Frederick Herzberg's major goal was to achieve a fundamental understanding of the attitude of workers to their jobs.

One of the results of Herzberg's research was the Motivation-Hygiene Theory, which presents a definition of mankind's total needs. In simplified terms, this theory revolves around the duality of the human nature. Herzberg believes that we have two sets of needs: one for the positive satisfaction that psychological growth provides ("motivation") and the other to avoid physical deprivation and the physical and emotional discomfort that accompanies it ("hygiene"). According to his research, the factors associated with the need to avoid deprivation cause an individual to take action. Because of this, they can be labeled as motivating factors. However, based as they are on avoidance, these factors do not provide for positive satisfaction because they do not provide the individual with a sense of growth. Herzberg's extensive research identified the common element for positive job attitudes as being associated with a feeling of psychological growth.

Herzberg found that employees work for two reasons: for profit in order to avoid physical deprivation, and to enjoy the happiness and the meaning that achievement provides. Employees look to have their intrinsic needs fulfilled in the workplace. By adding behavioral technology to traditional incentive compensation, we can fulfill the human needs associated with psychological growth. A good compensation system provides the intrinsic growth opportunities that employees seek in addition to the extrinsic material rewards that they seek in order to avoid discomfort. By doing this, the proper compensation will tap the unlimited human potential associated with positive feelings.

Abraham Maslow's Hierarchy of Needs

The work of Abraham Maslow, a professor at Brandeis University, adds support to Herzberg's findings while at the same time providing another facet to our understanding of human behavior. In his research, Maslow also found the universal tendency in human nature to strive for growth and avoid discomfort. But he went beyond Herzberg, identifying a set of intrinsic human values that he arranged into a hierarchy of needs.

Maslow based this hierarchy on two conclusions. First, the universal human needs are either of an attraction/desire nature or of an avoidance nature. It is significant to note that this conclusion, which was made independent of Herzberg's work, is in complete support of and agreement with the Motivation-Hygiene Theory.

The second of Maslow's conclusions is that humans are wanting animals: Once they have satisfied one desire, another desire comes forth to take its place. He theorized that these wants, or needs, could be organized in a priority leading from the avoidance of discomfort to the acquisition of psychological states of growth that provide a positive feeling he termed "psychic reward." He identified five levels of needs as the cornerstones of motivational theory: physical comfort, security/safety, social acceptance/affection/belonging, self-esteem, and self-actualization/self-fulfillment. Figure 2-3 is the traditional depiction of these five levels of needs.

Intrinsic Compensation: Based on the Hierarchy of Needs

Traditionally, compensation plan designs have addressed the needs of the lower levels of the hierarchy, those of physical comfort and security. That is understandable because in the past the contract or agreement between the employee and the employer was, for the

Figure 2-3. Maslow's hierarchy of needs.

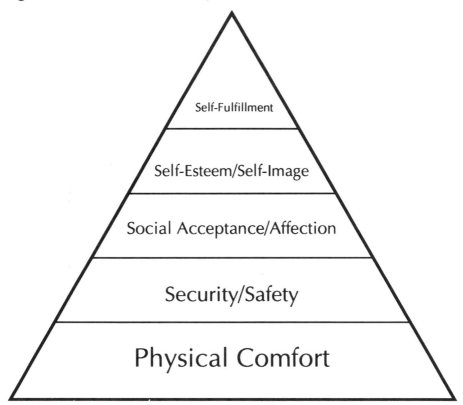

most part, a financial one. But many employees in the 1990s have shown themselves to focus less on the avoidance element that is associated with the lower levels of the hierarchy and more on the higher levels, which provide psychic rewards. For many, the lower-level needs have been fulfilled, and their needs are progressing up the scale, farther from the need for physical comfort and security and closer to self-realization. Thus, extrinsic compensation is not enough; organizations must now consider addressing the employees' higher-level needs with psychic or intrinsic compensation.

The relationship between behavior-based incentive compensation and Maslow's hierarchy of needs is illustrated in Figure 2-4. The needs at the lower levels of the pyramid—physical comfort and security—are addressed by extrinsic compensation, but the higher, personal needs of social acceptance, self-esteem, and self-fulfillment are addressed by intrinsic compensation.

One of the reasons that quality of work life has become as important as base compensation to today's employees is that it addresses their high-priority, intrinsic needs. How can we incorporate this approach into our compensation plan design? What are some good examples that fulfill intrinsic needs and how can they be used?

Figure 2-4. Relationship between Maslow's hierarchy of needs and the BBIC Fishbone.

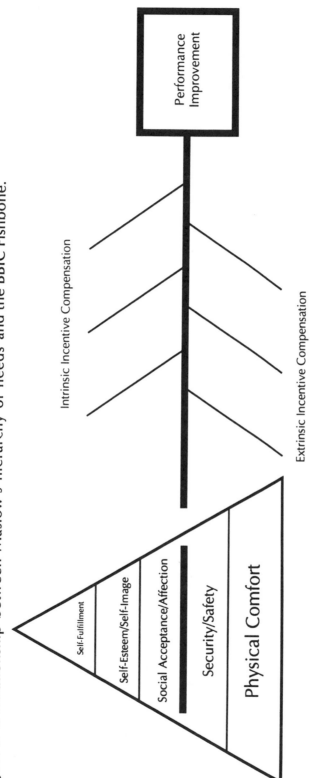

These questions can only be answered if we think of compensation as a motivational tool to be used in the larger context of an organization's management style. By thinking in this manner, we can include elements such as employee involvement techniques in our compensation plan design to fulfill the need for self-esteem and self-fulfillment. Specific, tactical management support activities will work to fulfill the need for social acceptance and can be easily included in the fabric of a compensation plan that measures performance and requires interaction. These are examples of elements of intrinsic compensation that fulfill the intrinsic needs of the employees with no increase to base compensation. Any effort on the part of an organization to provide this nonfinancial form of compensation to the employees has been shown to produce a receptive and responsive audience. The individual who can show us how to apply this concept is B. F. Skinner.

B. F. Skinner: The Application of Theory

Maslow postulates that people will do almost anything in their power to satisfy their needs. If he is correct, and the data indicate that he is, then behavior-based incentive compensation is truly the key to the source of human potential. It becomes our responsibility as managers to develop a process by which we can fulfill the employees' needs in a manner that is beneficial to the organization.

As managers, we can affect the physical, social, and psychological environment of the workplace. Our ability to do so makes B. F. Skinner's Behavior Theory the most functional concept available to us in terms of day-to-day application of motivation in the workplace.

Skinner was an eminent and highly controversial behavioral scientist. While Maslow is concerned with motivation theory, Skinner is concerned with behavior theory. The difference is that behavior theory takes into consideration both motivation *and* the environment. This is a significant development in the path toward application of theory.

The Law of Human Behavior

Skinner identified a basic law of human behavior that forms the foundation of an applied behavior technology. This technology can be used to motivate employees through specific actions that fulfill their needs. In applying this behavioral technology, it is possible to develop a win-win environment. Skinner's theory of human behavior provides a means for tapping the vast reserves of our employees' ability to make a difference in an organization's effectiveness and its economic value.

Dr. Skinner observed that on an individual level, a stimulus will initiate behavior that will, in turn, generate a result. To put it another way: Results are a consequence of behavior, and all behavior generates some type of result. If the consequences of the behavior are positive to the individual who created the behavior (that is to say if they are considered desirable because they fulfill some need), the relationship between the behavior and the consequences will have generated a situation that fulfills the individual's need for positive reinforcement.

Skinner also observed that if a certain behavior resulted in a positive consequence, then the individual would have a tendency to repeat that behavior. The consequences would modify the behavior and, in effect, act as an incentive.

These two observations are the source of the concept of positive reinforcement. Of all the concepts that we will discuss here, the ability of certain behavior/consequence relationships to fulfill the employee's need for positive reinforcement will prove to be the most important from the standpoint of practical application in the workplace.

The Behavioral Model

The use of Figure 2-5 will be helpful in developing a clear understanding of the implications, impact, and application of behavioral technology in the field of incentive compensation.

It is a graphic depiction of the relationships that Skinner observed. Those relationships combine to fulfill the need for positive reinforcement. An antecedent is anything that precedes behavior and acts as a stimulus to initiate it. Management is well educated and experienced in the disciplines of training, organization, and systematization. As a result, they tend to manage by the antecedent tools that

Figure 2-5. The behavior model.

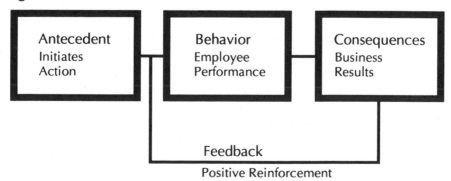

Positive Reinforcement

these disciplines provide, such as memos, training, policies and procedures, instructions, work assignments, and job descriptions.

Behavior, in the context that we are discussing it, is an employee's performance that takes place as the result of the antecedent stimulus. For example, "I need this document produced in finished form by three o'clock this afternoon" can be an antecedent that initiates employee performance.

There are two important points to be drawn from the behavior model. The first is that the quality of the results will be directly related to the quality and timeliness of the antecedent. The more specific the antecedent is and the closer in time it is to the behavior, the greater will be its effect on the behavior. It's a rare individual who has not experienced a situation where the delivered result of a work assignment did not live up to expectations. Upon analysis, the cause is generally found to be that the antecedent, the understanding of the intent of the assignment, was not specific.

The second point to derive from the behavior model is that consequences provide feedback to the individual. This feedback acts as an antecedent. In many cases, the feedback replaces the original antecedent and modifies the performance.

Employees are often placed into a position, given an overview of job activities and performance expectations, and then left to their own initiative. Everyone likes a self-starter who requires little managing, but as the model indicates, more face-to-face interactions bring performance closer to the level of expectations by providing feedback that will modify future performance.

A good example of this concept as it applies to incentive compensation is the back office operation of a credit card processing center in which the employees are responsible for processing credit card payments. Until they are processed, these payments represent receivables rather than revenue. There is an identifiable value to the company for timely processing of payments, and because of that there is a clear opportunity for a portion of each employee's cash compensation to be in the form of an incentive tied to performance.

In such a scenario, payment processing becomes an important consequence to the employees. As employees perceive the opportunity to increase personal income and thereby fulfill material desires, the quantity or volume each individual processes becomes important. Most employees will try to process more payments in order to receive more compensation. Thus, timely performance feedback in the form of daily or, better yet, hourly results will act as encouragement that will drive the employees' performance.

The behavior model is a very powerful tool that can be utilized to provide opportunities that will fulfill the employee's intrinsic needs. As such, it is a key element in the design of any behavior-based

incentive compensation plan. In the BBIC Fishbone diagram, it is one element of the intrinsic need for positive reinforcement.

What Is Rewarding?

Elements, actions, or situations that the employees will perceive as opportunities to fulfill their needs are also opportunities for management to provide rewards. In order to provide rewards that are contingent upon performance, it is necessary to understand what constitutes a reward. The concept of rewards is based on both performance and perception. By definition, a reward is something that is perceived as desirable by the recipient and is obtained as a result of some action. If it is not perceived as positive, then it isn't rewarding to the recipient. If it is not obtained as a result of some action, it is a gift or good fortune, not a reward.

In order to be perceived as positive, the reward must fulfill a need. Because each employee has different needs, no single reward will be perceived as positive by all employees. Of course, one could say that base compensation is a universally positive reward because it fulfills the basic needs of security and physical comfort. But what about people of independent means who work for other reasons? What constitutes a reward is a matter of perception on the part of the recipient, so we must continually be sensitive to each employee's perception of the situation. As we progress in our development of the Fishbone diagram, we will encounter situations and information that will enhance our sensitivity in this direction.

The choice of what elements to include in a behavior-based incentive compensation plan deserves serious consideration. For example, if an employee's basic need for security manifests itself in the need for good, reliable child care, then the company's ability to provide such care is perceived as rewarding and attractive. To other employees child care may have no significance at all. Different levels of employees have different intrinsic and extrinsic needs. The needs of executives are not likely to be the same as those of production workers. It is important to single out key needs in order to determine what elements of a compensation plan will incite employees to action and drive results. The Fishbone diagram and the other tools in this book will provide the capability to identify the elements that are perceived as positive by the employees and that will be compatible with the organization's business needs.

To provide some insight, let's take what we know about rewards and needs fulfillment and use it to examine the intrinsic and extrinsic needs of the average executive. According to Maslow, we would probably find that the intrinsic needs for recognition, self-respect, and self-realization are dominant over the extrinsic needs for security

and physical comfort. That's a safe assumption based on the size of most executives' extrinsic compensation packages. But the compensation package isn't the only factor in the formula. Most of these people are in their positions because they have a drive and desire that goes beyond basic compensation. It would be fair to generalize that their intrinsic needs outweigh their current extrinsic needs. Thus, if we want to design an incentive compensation plan that would be motivating for this level of employee, we would do well to incorporate a heavy measure of intrinsic compensation along with the traditional measure of extrinsic compensation.

Many companies recognize their executives' need for both intrinsic and extrinsic compensation and provide a number of executive perquisites. These perks serve a function, but as the behavior model shows us, their return on investment would be much greater if they were treated as rewards and made contingent upon performance.

What Modifies a Reward?

Anything that is received as the result of performance and is perceived as positive by the recipient can be considered a reward. Within these criteria are rewards of varying strength. Behavioral researchers have found that there are two modifying elements that determine the strength of a reward: timeliness and certainty.

Extensive experimentation has shown that the more immediate a reward is in relation to the performance with which it is associated, the more that performance will be positively affected or strengthened. That seems pretty obvious, but we tend to lose sight of this important fact when faced with the difficulties associated with administering an incentive compensation plan. One way to enhance the motivational effectiveness of such a plan is to pay closer attention to the impact that the timing of a reward can have on performance.

The second modifying element of a reward is certainty. Experiments and observation show that the surer an employee is of receiving a reward as a result of a specific set of actions, the greater the probability that he or she will take those actions initially and then repeat them with greater frequency. What this means in a business setting is that the employee's performance is almost guaranteed.

So we see that an ideal reward would be positive, immediate, and certain. In fact, in the world of behavioral psychology, this is often called the PIC criteria for a reward, and it works strongly in association with the behavior model. In the BBIC Fishbone diagram, the PIC criteria is an element of the intrinsic need for positive reinforcement.

The Importance of Delivery

We all know that the wrapping often affects how the value of a gift is perceived. That's why florists and jewelers don't use brown paper bags to wrap their product even though most other merchants do. Along those same lines, it's often the presentation or delivery of a reward that determines how it is perceived.

As an example of this phenomenon, let's take a situation where a company's employees have become disgruntled with their compensation. Yet, the pay practice is in line with the marketplace and the competition. What to do now? Looking deeper into the situation, management discovers that the employees are not really disgruntled with the amount of pay (although they may say that they are due to an inability to clearly define and articulate the issue). The problem is that the delivery system does not meet the employees' expectations; it does not fulfill their intrinsic needs for focus, positive reinforcement, or empowerment.

The reason is that the "immediate" and "certain" elements of the delivery are so removed and so weak that the employees have no sense of reward for effort. Thus, the paycheck has very little relationship to performance and is delivered too long after the fact. It may be mailed to the home or deposited directly into the bank or, at best, handed to the employee in an envelope with no discussion about performance or results. The positive reinforcement, the psychic income, the comfort level that is provided by being identified with the contribution is not provided by the process. As a result, morale and performance are affected.

The best way to address this issue would be to associate performance more closely with compensation in a manner that shows the employees that their contributions result in the company's ability to continue issuing paychecks. A good start would be the implementation of a process that kept all employees informed as to the organization's business plan and performance numbers. In this way, management would begin to utilize intrinsic compensation to fulfill employee needs and develop a focus on performance.

Perspective is important here, too, for the element of certainty depends on the employee's point of view. For an incentive compensation plan to be effective, the employees must perceive the reward as being certain, guaranteed by their act of delivering the performance. For them it is a contractual arrangement. From a management perspective, the concept of certainty can be termed a contingency, since managers perceive the reward as being contingent on specific performance. This dual perspective on the element of certainty adds some insight as to why properly run incentive programs are so effective. The perception of reward-as-certain/reward-as-contingent is a classic view of a win-win situation. The perspective is different, but the result is mutually agreed upon.

Another good observation that supports the relationship of rewards to the motivational criteria of positive, immediate, and certain is the volume of employee activity surrounding the performance evaluation process. Figure 2-6 illustrates a phenomenon that everyone who has ever managed employees has observed. It represents the increase in an employee's activity and/or performance during the period of time associated with his or her performance evaluation. Then, as the evaluation and the associated merit-increase recommendation recede into history and the future evaluation is not yet in sight, performance generally tapers off.

This same activity graph also applies to those employees who are eligible for incentive compensation. Only this time the vertical axis should indicate frequency of phone calls to the compensation administrator. Anyone who has ever had the responsibility of calculating management incentive payouts is well aware of the increase in calls as the payout becomes more immediate and certain. Money is a motivator, no doubt about it. How well it motivates, and what type of behavior it initiates, are functions of how the concepts of the behavior model and the positive, immediate, and certain motivational elements are applied.

Reward Elements in the Fishbone

The behavior model shows that rewards have both a material and a psychic nature. Financial compensation is probably the most common example of a material reward. It exists independent of the employee and, in our BBIC formula and Fishbone diagram, is labeled extrinsic compensation.

Social recognition in the form of a service award is a good example of the psychic nature of a reward. Normally of nominal financial value, such awards nevertheless provide employees with a sense of self-worth by acknowledging the contribution they have made. This element of sense of self-worth exists only within the employee and, for the purpose of developing our BBIC formula and Fishbone diagram as tools, can be considered part of intrinsic compensation.

Financial rewards, with their emphasis on the material, are normally distributed in a somewhat secretive manner. We tend to rely on the quantity of the reward to provide the satisfaction. Psychic rewards, on the other hand, require less financial cost and obtain much of their impact from the ceremony that is a key element in any award system.

Figure 2-6. Activity vs. the PIC criteria.

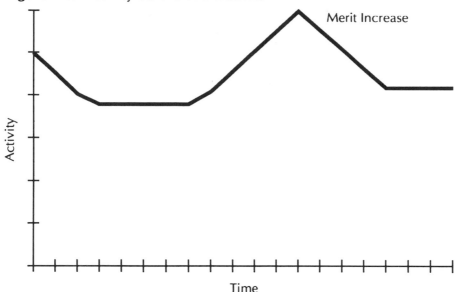

Ceremony fulfills several levels of the human needs Abraham Maslow identified—namely, security, self-esteem, and peer recognition. Ceremony fulfills these needs primarily by lending legitimacy and value to a situation in the perception (there's that word again) of the participants and observers. The marriage ceremony, religious services, and even the inauguration of heads of state recognize and incorporate this premise. Ceremony is, in effect, part of the validation of the recipient's self-worth by society. This powerful element should be incorporated into incentive compensation whenever possible. By doing so, the effectiveness of the reward can be improved dramatically at little cost.

The behavior model and the motivational elements positive, immediate, and certain are both key components to be used in the evaluation and design of any incentive compensation plan. Figure 2-7 shows the intrinsic compensation side of the Fishbone, incorporating the behavior model, the positive, immediate, and certain motivational criteria, and other elements that will be developed by the end of the chapter. As we develop the elements of the Fishbone, keep in mind that they are interrelated and that they will be placed in the position of their apparent primary relationship, where they make the greatest contribution.

More Bang for Your Buck Using Intrinsic Reward Elements

The point that the three motivational elements—positive, immediate, and certain—make so well is that it is not mandatory to increase the

Figure 2-7. Intrinsic elements of the BBIC Fishbone.

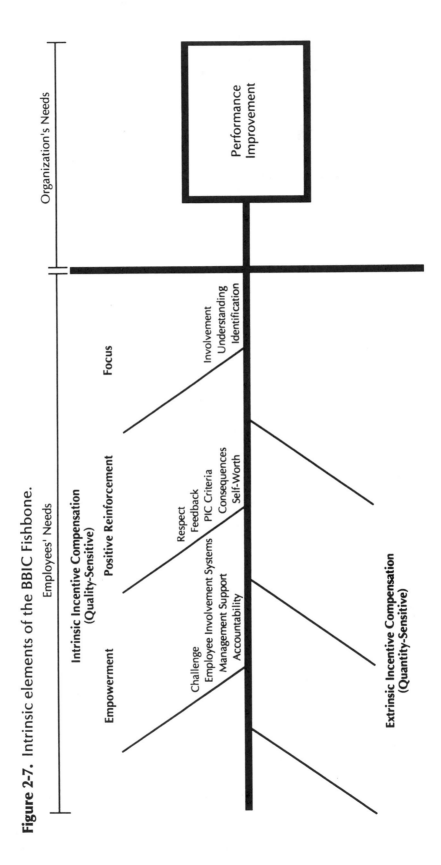

amount of compensation in order to increase its motivational effectiveness. Financial reward is only one component in a behavior-based compensation plan, whether it's incentive compensation or base compensation. In Chapter 4, we will examine a case history to see how nonfinancial, intrinsic compensation components can improve employee performance. We will also review a case history that proves that combining psychic rewards with incentive compensation will not only improve performance, it will *maximize* performance.

Today's employees have developed a cost-benefit relationship with their material and psychic needs. Many dual-income families have more money than time, and that situation affects their value systems. They tend to spend their energies in areas that provide the most reward to them. The BBIC tools can be used to understand this energy budgeting relationship and how to best fulfill it. If you fail to understand this relationship, you will be frustrated in the lack of response the employees will show toward your efforts to increase their participation.

Richard Bartlett, president of Mary Kay Cosmetics, understands this energy budgeting element of employee motivation. His company's productivity is very high in the cosmetics industry, and he relies heavily on the use of both intrinsic and extrinsic incentives. He states that what motivates people to perform at a higher level is not just compensation, it's self-esteem and self-fulfillment. While the employees who perform well at Mary Kay enjoy a fine standard of living, Bartlett doesn't try to overwhelm the motivation issue with money. Instead, he tailors his programs to utilize the full range of the nature of rewards. Business meetings with the company's representatives are celebrations of success where top performers are identified and their contributions recognized with great fanfare and peer approval. These individuals are provided with symbols of success that make them feel special.

Incentives vs. Recognition

No discussion on behavior and motivation would be complete without touching on the difference between incentives and recognition. All too often the confusion between these two methods of reward results in a program design that is ineffective.

Incentives and recognition are both methods of providing a reward. A good analogy is that of a personal computer. A PC will produce extraordinary results when the correct software is provided. However, try performing a spreadsheet analysis with a word processing application and the results will be disappointing. The same concept applies to the choice of reward method. If you apply the wrong approach, the employees will not respond in the way you had anticipated. You must use finesse in choosing the right application to obtain the desired result.

Incentives

An incentive drives performance. It is basically a contract established prior to the performance that promises a reward for specific action: "Do this, get that." An incentive can be of an intrinsic type, such as when employees fulfill their own need for positive reinforcement just from the fact of having performed well, but most incentives are of an extrinsic type. They fulfill the need for positive reinforcement with tangible rewards, such as cash, merchandise, or travel, or with such nontangible rewards as time off or free child care.

Incentives should be designed to reward results. They should also be self-funding so that if there are no results, there is no cost involved. When the program is designed properly, incentives are the most cost-effective, results-effective, and risk-free form of compensation that there is.

Recognition

Recognition is an after-the-fact display of appreciation for a contribution. In many cases, it is a surprise to the recipient who performed well for reasons other than the recognition.

It is generally a form of social reinforcement, where a ceremony involving management and peers provides strong intrinsic rewards by addressing the individual's need for self-esteem and belonging. Where incentives emphasize specific behavior that leads to results, recognition emphasizes the emotional feelings that are associated with the fulfillment of the need for positive reinforcement.

As previously noted, ceremony is more of a factor with recognition, and the visual element plays a key role. In most cases, the ceremony includes the presentation of a material object that symbolizes the cultural values held by management. The symbol should be congruent with the organization's culture and values; so should the purpose of the presentation. An example of a program where recognition is in conflict with culture is one in which organization talks the value of teamwork but recognizes, in a formal manner, only contributions by individuals.

Recognition has a strong effect on the rest of the organization. The material award, often minimal in extrinsic value, is an important symbol of management's sincerity and commitment to the corporate values. In this manner, recognition can have a significant impact on morale and, to a lesser degree, on performance. Everyone sees what the employees are capable of, and that raises the esteem of the whole organization.

A Master of Recognition: Stew Leonard

Stew Leonard, president of Stew Leonard's dairy store in Norwalk, Connecticut, is a master of the use of recognition to develop a company culture that impacts the bottom line. Stew Leonard's is not your ordinary dairy store. With 106,000 square feet of retail space it is the world's largest. Packed with over 100,000 shoppers a week, it is probably the most profitable.

Stew is successful, in part, as a result of lavishing attention on his customers and his employees. His SuperStar-of-the-Month award is an honor won by only one employee in each department. The award is presented with considerable fanfare. Costumed animal characters bring out the balloons, and fellow workers gather around as the plaque is presented right on the floor of the store. Customers add to the value of the occasion as they see the workers being honored. Who said ceremony has to be stuffy? Stew makes it fun—and an important occasion for his staff.

So Why Not Us?

There is no doubt that Stew's approach is highly effective. With his kinds of results, you might ask the question, "Why should I get involved with broad-based incentive compensation at all? Why not just use recognition to motivate the employees?"

The answer involves considerations of leadership and style. The Fishbone diagram shows that recognition weighs heavily on the behavioral psychology side, where it is a key element of the need for positive reinforcement. Recognition is almost pure intrinsic compensation, and Stew's approach is almost pure behavioral psychology. His approach is effective as a result of the strength of his personality. All other things being equal, the magnitude and intensity of the intrinsic compensation he provides is sufficient to impact performance.

Of course, Stew Leonard's approach is unique and would not fit everywhere. Ask yourself if your chief executive officer could stand next to a six-foot-tall duck and hand an employee a fistful of balloons. Is your organization of a size and makeup where this approach could be successfully implemented by all managers and supervisors? If you cannot answer yes, then a motivation program based on pure recognition is not for you.

But take heart. Behavior-based incentive compensation, a tactical combination of recognition and incentives, allows you to design a motivational plan around a structure rather than a personality. Such a plan has an advantage, too: It provides the opportunity for control and consistency. This is important because employees must know what the organization expects from them and what they can expect from the organization.

In Chapter 3, we use the Fishbone diagram to examine how the combination of intrinsic and extrinsic compensation result in a behavior-based incentive compensation plan. We also examine how a BBIC plan addresses both the company's needs and the employees' needs in a win-win situation.

Notes

1. *Linking New Employee Attitudes and Values to Improved Productivity, Cost, and Quality,* The Hay Group, 1990.
2. "Bringing Middle Managers Back: Repairing the Downsizing Damage," *Organization and Strategy Quarterly,* Winter 1989.

3

Extrinsic Incentive Compensation

The United Way Strategic Institute is responsible for charting the path into the future for all of the United Way's member organizations. The Institute sponsors research to help these organizations develop plans to provide social services that will meet the changing needs of American society.

Dr. George Wilkinson, president and senior fellow of the Institute, has summarized the research findings in a report, *What Lies Ahead: Countdown to the 21st Century*. One of the report's predictions is that the cost of health care will triple to a staggering $1.5 trillion by the year 2000 in part because of the increased compensation benefits that an aging workforce will require. This increase in costs will have a significant impact on a company's bottom line. Indeed, benefit costs are an issue already. For example, according to the United Way report, the 1989 cost of health benefits adds about $600 per car to the cost of an automobile that is made in Detroit compared to an automobile that is made in Japan.[1]

It is easy to see that an increase in the cost of benefits will put a squeeze on the dollars available for direct compensation. This is yet another reason why it is critical to maximize the return on compensation investment. Behavior-based incentive compensation is the most effective technique for obtaining full value for compensation dollars spent. For that reason, it is necessary to understand how performance and cash pay (extrinsic compensation) relate to each other.

Traditional Thinking

It is the employees, performing on a daily basis, who determine the real acceptance in the marketplace of an organization's product or service. Companies in the thick of competition are embracing this concept and developing a variety of employee involvement techniques designed to encourage workers to make a contribution. But if we look beyond employee relations and organizational development to the compensation function, we see a different situation.

In most companies, incentive compensation plans are provided only to the sales force and to the top 10 percent or so of the managers. According to traditional compensation thinking, these people are the only employees capable of making a significant contribution to the organization's profitability. Following this line of thinking, if a traditionally minded compensation department were to compose the organization's employment ads, they would most likely read like this: "Help Wanted: Mass-produced, voice-activated robots. Must be equipped with analog data processing capabilities." In real life, of course, most organizations emphasize features other than their traditional cost-focused compensation philosophy when soliciting human resources.

In today's social and economic realities, organizations can no longer afford to follow a compensation practice that is based solely on cost. The human element has become a critical consideration. Market-driven businesses require creativity and individual contribution as well as teamwork to be successful. Behavior-based incentive compensation will more than pay for itself by encouraging those very traits among all employees in a process that is financially controlled. Thus, the disciplines of compensation, employee relations, organizational development, and training must become a closely knit operating unit.

The Reality of Change

If an organization is to survive and prosper in a competitive and fast-paced marketplace, it must be flexible and be capable of changing traditional ways of doing things. But how can an established organization, especially a large one with well-entrenched policies, procedures, and methods, become flexible? The answer is to be found on the individual level.

Being the sum of its employees, an organization will only change to the degree that its employees change their way of doing things. For the average employee, personal change is difficult. It requires learning new ways of doing things and is full of uncertainty. Change carries with it a fear of the unknown and is uncomfortable for the majority of employees. Naturally, they tend to resist change. The easiest resistance is passive resistance, where there is acceptance of management's exhortations to change but little or no action to make the change take place. In these circumstances, an organization cannot simply mandate change and expect it to happen—it must actively encourage change. But how can this be done?

You Don't Always Get What You Want

Providing a more effective response to the needs of customers is a daunting task for any organization. The focus, interaction, and involvement that are required on the part of all employees have not generally been a part of American management style. With a few notable exceptions, such as Nordstrom, Inc., the retailer, it is an expectation far beyond anything that management has previously requested of the individual employee.

Does topnotch customer service exceed the bounds of currently perceived "terms of employment"? To answer that question, we must look at it from two different perspectives, that of management, on one side, and that of the employees.

Management's view of what constitutes terms of employment is based on the job description, preemployment discussions, and assignments the employee is given at the beginning of the job. The employee's perspective on terms of employment tends to be of a more immediate nature. It is based on the daily performance level that management has shown to be acceptable for wages paid.

The business reality is that the performance level that you as a manager are paying for is the performance level that you are receiving. In the current compensation practice, with little direct linkage between performance and pay, you don't get what you pay for, you pay for what you get. In the eyes of the employee, if this level of performance is not sufficient, then managers, in their role as stewards, would certainly take action to change it. This is a quandary, because all too often management is aware only of the disciplinary actions that can be taken, and those actions appear ineffective in stimulating participation or change.

If you, as a manager, want to stimulate participation or change by matching compensation to the quality or quantity of the employees' performance, there are three general approaches you can take.

1. *Reduce the level of compensation to match the current level of performance.* This assumes that the employees are not currently doing their full, fair share but that they will remain with the organization after the reduction in compensation. Some organizations have utilized a two-tier approach that applies the pay reduction to new hires. Experience has shown that employee morale tends to decline in this

type of environment. That fact, together with the current and future labor outlook, leads to the conclusion that this course of action is not a good first choice.

However, as we will see in the case of GTE examined in Chapter 4, where, in an environment where the base pay is well in excess of the 50th percentile, providing the opportunity for incentive compensation while placing a portion of base pay at risk can provide effective results in quality improvement and cost reduction.

2. *Maintain the current level of compensation and increase performance.* But how? Through force? The "that's what I pay 'em for" response generally doesn't work well today. But if that's the organization's position, it will be necessary for management to support it with disciplinary action and removal when the employees don't respond. This approach may be effective in a labor-rich market, but that's not the environment that exists in the 1990s.

3. *Migrate to a system that makes compensation contingent on performance.* To do this effectively, managers must change their perspective and view the issue of motivation and compensation from the standpoint of those being asked to do the work. By offering employees the opportunity to share in the gains of improvement, management provides them with a reason to participate and to increase the level of their contribution.

Point of View Determines What You Do

One key to developing a successful and motivationally effective compensation plan is to view the problem from the employees' perspective. Business issues aside, from this perspective options 1 and 2 appear heavily weighted toward the organization's financial needs, with very little opportunity for the employees. From their perspective, option 3 appears more attractive.

Incentive compensation provides all participants with a vested interest in the success of the effort. Rather than performing as robots, with no ownership or involvement, each individual is provided with a reason to develop the most effective means of reaching the organization's objectives and fulfilling the organization's needs. The employees begin to act as owners of the company because they have an opportunity to fulfill their extrinsic needs through the process of successfully fulfilling the organization's needs.

To clarify this concept, let's take a scenario where you no longer consider the current level of employee performance acceptable. You wish to change it, and you accept the validity of behavior-based incentive compensation as the most cost- and effort-effective approach. You realize that you will need to address both the intrinsic and extrinsic needs of the employees. To address the intrinsic needs, one of the first things you consider is providing them with some rationale for the need to change. This will help to reduce anxiety and promote acceptance of the change. This rationale, while primarily a financial-based decision, can be supported and nurtured through the aid of the human resources community. The application is basically a communications and training awareness campaign.

From an extrinsic standpoint, some opportunity for the employees to improve their standard of living through an increase in financial compensation must be provided. This opportunity will give the employees a reason to modify their performance. But the extrinsic element is a budget issue, and senior management will want to be provided with some financial rationale as to the issues and why this approach will be effective.

The Economic Rationale

Data from the U.S. Bureau of Labor Statistics and the U.S. Bureau of Economic Analysis show that from 1981 through 1990 the Employment Cost Index for wages and salaries increased at an average annual rate of 4.7 percent for civilian workers. (The Employment Cost Index is a fixed employment-weighted index that tracks the quarterly change in labor costs.) During the same period, the annualized growth of the Consumer Price Index for urban consumers (one indicator of inflation) was 4.4 percent. One conclusion we can draw from this is that wage rate increases in these industries were driven by inflation and not by performance.

These data also indicate that labor costs grow faster than output. The average compound rate of growth for the Gross National Product during the period 1981 through 1990 was 6.7 percent. With wage rate growth at 4.7 percent and annualized growth in total employment at 1.8 percent, the difference between output growth and labor cost growth is 0.2 percent:

$$6.7\% - (4.7\% + 1.8\%)$$

But this 0.2 percent is *before* we consider benefits costs, which have increased by over 6 percent annually since 1981. In 1990, these costs were 30.8 percent of the total compensation cost in goods-producing industries and 26.0 percent of the total compensation cost in the service-producing industries. And these costs continue to increase.

From the employees' perspective, this means that their real standard of living has been declining, not increasing. Any opportunity to increase their standard of living, even one that is contingent upon performance, should be well received.

A Logical Conclusion

From a business perspective, the current cost/output relationship provides only two solutions that make good sense: Reduce compensation and benefits costs, or increase output.

We have already seen that in the labor market of the 1990s reduction of compensation and benefits is not a first-choice course of action. The other alternative, to increase output, can be implemented by tying pay to performance so that output growth is accelerated to an acceptable level. This approach changes the application of compensation from a cost of doing business to a functional tool in support of a company's business plan. Compensation then becomes a financial investment applied in a manner designed to maximize its return. Incentive compensation makes sense because, by definition, it is contingent upon performance and is therefore self-funding.

The PepsiCo Plan

Many Fortune 500 companies are exploring a wide variety of methods of utilizing compensation to improve their profitability. The concept of compensation is expanding beyond the paycheck into a realm where rewards in various forms are tied to results. Because of the newness of this approach, the applications are as varied as the organizations that use them and the individuals who design them.

Equity-interest plans, a general form of incentive compensation, have a long history of application on the executive level. By the same token, profit-sharing plans have long been applied on all levels of the organization. An innovative plan that combines elements of both equity-interest and profit-sharing plans has been instituted by PepsiCo as a keystone of its employee-motivation program.

PepsiCo has added to its long history of leadership in developing aggressive compensation programs by implementing a broad-based stock option program called Share Power. More than 100,000 employees were granted options to buy shares equal to 10 percent of their prior year's compensation. With no out-of-pocket expense, the employees will benefit from the appreciation on about $200 million worth of stock each year. This is certainly a strong incentive for employees to take an active interest in the performance of the organization. PepsiCo management has thus demonstrated its commitment to the concept that each individual can make a difference by providing each individual a reason to do so.

Charles Rogers, PepsiCo's vice-president of compensation and benefits, says that the impact of the program cannot be overstated.

"I don't think there is a single initiative that we've taken in our corporation in the area of human resources that's had as much impact." Being shareholders themselves, everyone in the organization is now focused on ways to increase the shareholders' value.

The Fishbone Fills Out

We are now at the point where we can fully develop the employee's side of the BBIC Fishbone diagram. In Figure 3-1, the left half of the diagram contains the two general categories of employee needs, intrinsic and extrinsic. Extrinsic compensation encompasses the elements that fulfill material needs. There are three key factors to extrinsic compensation: "why-pay," "what-pay," and "how-pay." These are familiar factors to anyone who has worked with compensation, but for the purpose of using these factors in the Fishbone diagram, it will be necessary to clarify their definition.

Why-Pay

Why-pay is the results-oriented factor of extrinsic compensation. It establishes the rules to which both the employee and the organization must conform in order to benefit. From the employees' perspective, the factor of why-pay defines the criteria by which they can earn incremental compensation. It provides indicators from which the individual employee, based on job knowledge, can extrapolate the types of behavior and performance that are necessary in order to realize the opportunity that is being presented.

From the organization's standpoint, why-pay defines what performance improvement is. It identifies the business objectives that need to be met in order to generate improved results. It identifies the method of measuring performance improvement. It establishes the performance baselines, targets, goals, and increments of improvement for which the organization is willing to provide extrinsic incentive compensation.

What-Pay

What-pay is the financially oriented factor of extrinsic incentive compensation. It establishes the relationship between the why-pay criteria and actual performance. From the employees' perspective, it defines the size of the incentive opportunity that is available and, in conjunction with the why-pay criteria, allows each individual to develop an informal cost-benefit tradeoff analysis. The results of this

Figure 3-1. Behavior-based incentive compensation sensitivities.

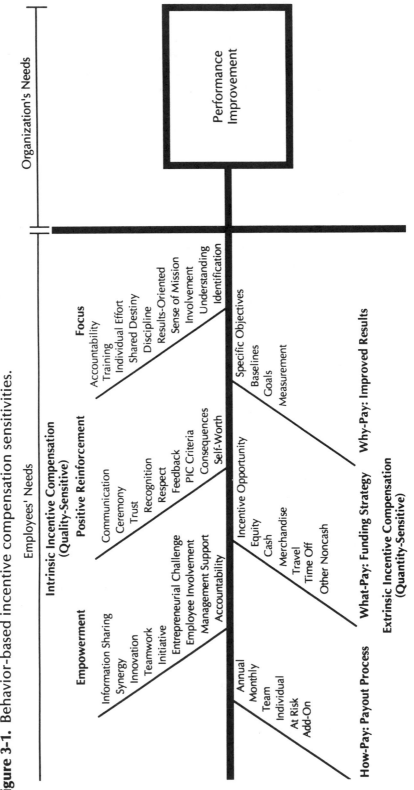

analysis are what determine whether or not the employee will view the opportunity as sufficiently attractive to be worth pursuing.

From the organization's perspective, what-pay defines the business case. It establishes the financial rationale for creating this contract. It is the organization's position on what constitutes an acceptable return on investment for a variable compensation plan. It defines the extrinsic incentive compensation opportunity that is available to the employees as a result of increased returns to the organization. What-pay is a volume, or quantity-sensitive factor and derives a high degree of its incentive ability from the quantity of material appeal that it provides.

What-pay is most familiar as the cost-containment factor in a traditional compensation plan. This presents a problem. Designing an incentive program with too much focus on cost containment (what-pay) and not enough focus on performance improvement (why-pay) will result in a program that the employees will fail to respond to. Thus, a conscious effort must be made to redefine the criteria and view this factor through the eyes of the participant.

How-Pay

How-pay is the modifying factor of extrinsic compensation. It is the factor that turns the concept into reality, the mechanism by which the compensation is delivered to the participant. From the employees' perspective, the elements of how-pay provide the fulfillment to extrinsic and intrinsic needs by delivering on the contract that is defined in the why-pay and what-pay criteria.

From the organization's perspective, the criteria of how-pay define the way to deliver the rewards that are necessary to fulfill the incentive compensation contract. Caution should be exercised not to overlook the powerful modifying impact that this factor has. It contains elements of why-pay and what-pay and has a meaning to the organization that is almost diametrically opposed to the meaning that it has to the employee. The organization may perceive it as purely an administrative function, while the employees will perceive it as the source of fulfillment. How-pay is the factor in a behavior-based incentive compensation plan that provides management with the means to interact with the employees through the delivery of rewards based on performance.

Balancing the Factors

You can benefit from consideration of these factors when you develop the extrinsic compensation portion of an incentive compensation plan. They have the capacity to impact and modify the intrinsic factors. The interaction of all six factors—focus, positive reinforcement, empowerment, why-pay, what-pay, and how-pay—plays a significant part in the design of a behavior-based incentive compensation program. You can address the complete spectrum of employee needs through the use of both intrinsic and extrinsic incentive compensation. By balancing the mix of the quality and quantity of the compensation, you will be able to maximize the results while minimizing expenditures of both effort and cash.

The Fishbone as an Analytical Tool: PepsiCo's Plan

Let's use these newly developed tools to analyze PepsiCo's Share Power incentive plan design from a behavioral point of view. We now can see how the plan provides opportunities to the employees to fulfill both their extrinsic and intrinsic needs.

The PepsiCo plan is a strong one because it has more than one extrinsic compensation factor. Consider the factor of why-pay, which defines the business needs of the organization. From the beginning, PepsiCo management wanted to encourage an increased sense of focus, so they decided to utilize a broad performance objective like stock value. At first glance, this may sound a bit contradictory, but it makes good sense if we view the term "focus" from a broader perspective. This company-wide sharing of ownership helps to develop a sense of mission and a feeling of unity among all employees. Viewed from the BBIC Fishbone, stock options appear as a strategic element of the why-pay factor.

The extrinsic factor what-pay represents the business case for the organization and defines the magnitude of the employees' opportunity for fulfillment. As previously noted, the design challenge is to balance these perspectives so that both the organization and the employees perceive what is being offered as equitable. In PepsiCo's case, utilizing stock options as the extrinsic incentive gives each employee the opportunity to share in the gains of the improvement that he or she generates. Having the opportunity to control to some degree the amount of this gain provides fulfillment to the employees' need for empowerment. They perceive the message that it's all right to exercise initiative and be entrepreneurial in spirit.

Because it contains the funding strategy, the factor of what-pay is very sensitive to the concept of quantity. This is important, because the employees' perception of the equity of the distribution (is the company providing me a fair share for my increased contribution?) is critical to the success of the plan. If the employees don't perceive the plan as equitable, they will refuse to participate.

At PepsiCo, rather than designing a plan that would require some form of control over the quantity of the payout, management placed the quantity control in the hands of the employees. They realize their day-to-day performance as individuals and as members of a team will have a cumulative impact on the organization's effectiveness and economic value. All other things being equal, this will impact the value of the stock and subsequently their earnings.

Hats off to the designers. They recognized the true essence of incentive compensation and placed it at the heart of the plan's design. From the employees' perspective, the upside potential is unlimited and, therefore, well worth their effort to become involved and participate.

Looking at the elements that make up the factor of how-pay in the Fishbone diagram, we see that the incentive opportunity is an add-on to base compensation. PepsiCo's stock options are in addition to base pay and represent a real opportunity for the employees to increase their standard of living. While the payout is by no means immediate or certain, stock quotations and financial statements concerning the organization's economic health help to provide timely feedback to the employees and act to reinforce their involvement and participation.

This test of the Fishbone as a tool has shown how incentive compensation plan elements can be identified and combined to address specific employee needs.

Perspective and Control

In the design of an incentive compensation plan, the strong financial nature of the extrinsic reward element often results in overemphasis on the economic needs of the organization, with minimal consideration for the needs of the individual. Historically, the factors of how-pay, why-pay, and what-pay have been viewed from the perspective of the organization as a need to control costs. It is important to reiterate that the challenge in structuring a motivationally powered incentive compensation plan is to view these factors from the employee's perspective as opportunities to be rewarded for improved performance. The Fishbone diagram has shown how PepsiCo did that when they developed their "fair share" program.

On the other hand, is PepsiCo overresponsive to the needs of the employee in the design of their program, thus failing to be fiscally responsible? Charles Rogers says the dilution in shares attributable to the plan in 1991 will be less than a penny a share. This is because the program designers included a funding strategy for repurchasing market shares to minimize dilution. Thus, the PepsiCo program addresses the needs of both employee and organization in a design that is beneficial to both. In Chapter 4, we examine in much greater detail the relationships that exist between the employees' needs and the organization's needs. Achieving balance in this relationship is what powers a successful incentive compensation plan.

Return on Investment

Behavior-based incentive compensation is effective in terms of both compensation dollars spent and performance improvement results. In 1990, the consulting group Towers, Perrin, Forster & Crosby completed a survey of 177 cash-based group incentive plans in 144 companies. Their findings indicate that these plans yielded significant quantifiable improvements and greater employee involvement. Beyond that, the survey respondents reported that the degree of employee participation hinged on the plan design.[2] Why is that not surprising?

The plan design that we are developing is a blend of base compensation, incentive compensation, and psychic compensation. This balanced equation is the basis of behavior-based incentive compensation. It provides the best return on investment because each dollar of extrinsic compensation works with elements of intrinsic compensation to provide maximum motivation to the employees.

Evolving Systems

Compensation systems are continually evolving in order to address various important needs. The current systems have been developed to address five needs:

- To achieve equity with and among employees
- To assure legal protection for the organization
- To comply with regulations
- To administer large numbers of employees in an orderly and cost-effective manner
- To provide management with accurate, organized data concerning a significant operating cost.

It is of course necessary to incorporate all these functions in the new generation of incentive compensation plans. But, because the design of incentive compensation must take into consideration the perspective of the employee, it is necessary to define these five needs from that point of view. Failure to do so will result in a plan that favors the organization at the expense of the employees and at the expense of unrealized performance improvement.

As an example, let's look at what we mean by equity. It has been common practice to represent an organization's position on equity through the use of a payline. A relatively linear payline would represent a relatively even relationship between total cash compensation and the grades or job positions within the organization.

Figure 3-2 is an example of a payline that appears to represent equity in total target cash compensation. Thus, high-level employees are paid more because of their wide responsibilities and their ability to impact the organization. But wait! This payline, while accurate, is easily misunderstood from the standpoint of equity. The total target cash relationship is not linear throughout the organization. At some point in the exempt ranks, incentive compensation becomes part of the total target cash package, and on a graph that keeps the axis measurements fixed, the payline develops a stairstep.

Figure 3-3 is a more definitive representation of equity because it shows a significant difference between employees with incentive compensation and those without. If a company wants a payline that is relatively linear, this depiction makes it easy to see that providing all employees with an incentive opportunity will accomplish that. Providing incentive compensation opportunities to all employees makes good sense from an equity standpoint. It provides the oppor-

Figure 3-2. Total target cash compensation payline #1.

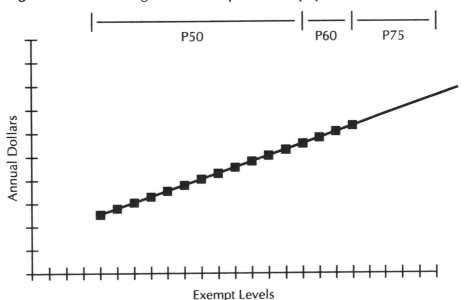

Figure 3-3. Total target cash compensation payline #2.

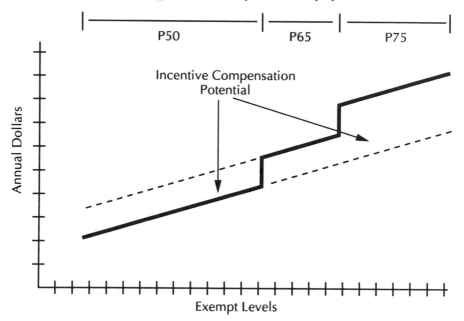

tunity for pay parity based on performance, and it goes a long way toward promoting cultural unity.

Darryl Hartley-Leonard, president of Hyatt Hotels, believes that cultural unity and a sense of equity are powerful elements that fulfill the psychic needs of his employees. He works hard to instill this feeling in his organization through a variety of employee reward and recognition programs. His goal is for all guests to experience the impact of this effort when they check into a Hyatt Hotel. The point he makes is one of simple reciprocity: "If you behave generously toward employees, they are more likely to respond in kind." This is another way of saying that the most effective way to understand a performance situation is to look at it from the perspective of the individual who is doing the job. This is a mindset that you will find critical when you are developing the payout structure of your BBIC plans. Be generous. Why not? Your control is in the fact that the payout is contingent upon the gains in performance.

In most companies, the underlying philosophy of the compensation program is to pay for performance at a level that is both fair and competitive. To support this philosophy, there are normally three elements to the compensation program: position, performance, and pay. Together these p's determine the compensation an employee receives.

In the past, program design emphasized the elements of position and pay. In fact, an entire service industry developed to support the assessment of job value and competitive pay levels. The element of performance was considered on an annual basis, often in a subjective manner. Unfortunately, these plans did not demonstrate much of a relationship between wage increases and company performance.

In today's business environment, organizations have seen the need to add emphasis to the performance element in determining the level of compensation. From a traditional compensation standpoint, the best reason to utilize an incentive compensation plan is to align pay with results. A quick review of where we have been will help us see where we need to go.

Brief Review of the Basics

As we have seen, traditional base compensation programs are generally viewed by employees as terms of employment. They are budgeted programs, often shrouded in secrecy. Any increase to base pay is tied to an annual review that has very little to do with performance toward specific objectives. This traditional approach is a zero-sum process that lacks motivational dynamics. We can use the Fishbone diagram to help review the basics and pinpoint how to build on the old structure.

Traditional compensation systems classify the value of a job to the organization either by assigning it points or by placing it into a specific grade. Each of these classifications has a range of pay associated with it. Employees are slotted into the pay structure, their performance is evaluated on an annual basis, and, based on their rating, they are awarded a merit increase, a raise. Putting these elements into the Fishbone, it is clear that employee needs are nowhere in sight. There is no intrinsic compensation to address psychic needs here, and the extrinsic factors of why-pay, what-pay, and how-pay are addressed to the organization's needs. There is not much partnering here.

Is the merit increase process an issue in the current business environment? A survey of 1,600 companies, conducted in 1987 by the American Productivity and Quality Center and the American Compensation Association, indicates that routine increases are losing favor. Among respondents, 35 percent reported reducing across-the-board increases, and over 25 percent reduced the use of cost of living adjustment.[3] These companies have realized that when compensation is divorced from performance, it does not provide an effective return on investment.

Traditional pay ranges have a minimum, a midpoint, and a maximum. The minimum pay level is normally for entry-level employees who do not yet possess the skills or knowledge to perform at a fully satisfactory level. The maximum is the salary cap for the position; generally, it cannot be exceeded without executive approval. The midpoint is usually competitive with the marketplace rate for the position and takes into consideration the competitive profile the company chooses to maintain, cost issues, and the availability of labor.

What the employee is paid in relation to the job's midpoint is called the comparatio. If the pay is less than the job's midpoint, the comparatio is less than 100 percent. If the pay is more than the midpoint, the comparatio is greater than 100 percent. Comparatios are important for two reasons. First, they provide management with some understanding as to how the organization's compensation strategy compares to the marketplace. Second, they determine the size of the employee's merit increase in dollars and therefore act as a factor that can control costs.

In order to strike a balance between costs and compensation, a traditional compensation strategy reduces the percent of the merit increase in proportion to the comparatio. Figure 3-4 illustrates the example of a long-time employee who is consistently rated as an above-average performer. This employee has been in the same grade classification for a number of years, and his salary is now above midpoint, with a comparatio of 110 percent. As a result, his merit increase is held down in order to slow his rate of compensation growth.

The traditional rationale for this employee's situation is that he is receiving a base wage that is greater than employees in the same grade who have less experience and/or a lower level of performance. For the employee, the downside of this type of thinking is that annual merit increases are less in terms of percentage than the increases awarded to employees with an equal performance rating and a lower comparatio. Employee equity begins to dissolve when two people with the same performance rating receive different merit increases.

It is easy to understand why traditional compensation systems must hold tight the reins of control. Without controls, it is possible to escalate an employee's salary beyond the limits of what the company, and the market, is willing to pay for the job. The comparatio must be applied because real, measurable performance is not linked to the compensation process. In focusing on this issue of control, traditional systems pay scant attention to the need to reward the top achievers. Failure to reward these achievers can lead to their departure, especially in a tight labor market.

The disassociation of compensation from results has a tendency to build on itself. Because there is no relationship of compensation to performance, compensation is perceived and treated by management as a budgeted expense. As such, compensation is basically a

Figure 3-4. Merit matrix.

Comparatio

	Less Than 80%	80%–88%	88.1%–96%	96.1%–104%	104.1%–112%	112.1%–120%
1 Excellent	0 to 12%	0 to 11%	0 to 10%	0 to 9%	0 to 8%	0 to 7%
2 Above Expectations	0 to 9%	0 to 8%	0 to 7%	0 to 6%	0 to 5%	0 to 4%
3 Fully Satisfactory	0 to 6%	0 to 5%	0 to 4%	0 to 3%	0 to 2%	0 to 1%
4 Marginal	0 to 2%	0 to 1%	0%	0%	0%	0%
5 Unsatisfactory	0%	0%	0%	0%	0%	0%

Performance Rating

closed loop, a zero-sum game with no opportunities for self-improvement.

The Zero-Sum Game

The zero-sum concept provides a fine insight into the basic difficulties that traditional base compensation is experiencing in today's business environment. We start with a decision, normally made by the board of directors before the start of the fiscal year, as to the amount of money that will be made available to the organization for merit increases in the coming year. This decision is based principally on what the competition is paying, what profitability goals the organization has set, how the job market and inflation have moved the pay ranges, and what the organization's pay philosophy is. The result is that some percentage increase to the payroll budget will be allocated to wage and salary increases.

If, for example, the board decides to authorize a salary increase budget equal to 6 percent of the current payroll budget, that increase may consist of a 2-percent upward movement of the range to adjust for inflation and 4 percent in merit increases. This equates to a 6-percent raise that is available to all employees.

The obvious drawbacks to this method of compensation, aside from its lack of relationship to performance, is that it encourages information hoarding and discourages teamwork. If some employees are to receive increases above the average allocation, they must do so at the expense of fellow employees. There is no way for the employees to win as a team in this scenario.

The BBIC Fishbone shows how teamwork and information sharing can augment the effectiveness of a compensation system by providing a form of intrinsic compensation. A sense of teamwork fulfills the employees' needs for focus and empowerment by encouraging all employees to work together. Information sharing fulfills the need for positive reinforcement through performance feedback and the sense of being in the know.

We have seen that the traditional zero-sum approach to compensation provides very little extrinsic incentive because it is not contingent upon performance. We now see that it actually removes intrinsic compensation and, in doing so, acts as a disincentive. All of this is the result of viewing compensation as simply a cost of doing business. If we change our perspective and view compensation as an investment with an expected payback, then we are free to develop pay practices that are capable of paying people according to what they are worth.

Edward Lawler III, a renowned professor in the University of Southern California Business School, thinks that a job-evaluation approach tends to depersonalize employees by equating them with a set of job functions. It tends to deemphasize paying them for their skills, performance, and participation. Yet it is precisely these qualities that are in demand today. This tells us that we are on the right track when we include intrinsic incentives in our pay practice.

Position, performance, and pay are three necessary elements for the successful administration of a compensation system. In order to change the perspective of compensation from that of an administrative task to that of an investment, we can include behavioral psychology as the fourth element in this p-sequence: position, performance, pay, and psychology.

Classic Incentive Compensation: Lincoln Electric

The extreme opposite of a zero-sum payroll is a system where compensation is almost totally contingent upon results. The ideal compensation plan here would be 100-percent contingent upon performance. This design would provide the best correlation of salary budget to corporate profit. Companies coming close to this approach are generally very successful. A good example is Lincoln Electric of Cleveland, a classic example of the benefits of contingent compensation about which much has been written. Almost 100 years old, Lincoln is a manufacturer of industrial electrical motors and welding equipment. In an age where manufacturing and assembly jobs are going to countries where labor costs are substantially cheaper, Lincoln is thriving.

The secret of Lincoln's success lies in its multiple compensation plans, which are heavily weighted toward extrinsic reward. Employees receive no base salary or wage. Regular earnings are made up of compensation on a piecework basis. For every acceptable piece produced, the employee receives a specific dollar amount. Bonus payments are made to employees based on both company and individual performance. The year-end profit-sharing bonus is close to 100 percent of regular earnings and is based on such criteria as output, quality, dependability, and suggestions.

The work environment is intense at Lincoln, and peer pressure to perform is significant. Heaven help anyone who causes a slow-down or a quality problem! It is obvious that these folks are in it for the money, for the extrinsic compensation. But if we use the Fishbone and look at the situation more closely, we will observe that a very powerful form of intrinsic compensation exists, too. There is a strong sense of empowerment provided by the employee-involvement systems that encourage and act on employee suggestions. Improvements that come about because of employee input result in an increase to the compensation the employees receive.

Empowerment is activated and supported by employees having the ability to directly influence their standard of living. At this point in the evolution of this organization, management's support no longer acts to nurture this sense of empowerment. The employees are now so empowered that they demand that management fulfill the role of facilitator, helping them to accomplish their goals. As a result, the performance associated with employee empowerment pervades the environment. Teamwork, sense of mission, performance feedback, respect for contribution—all these elements and more exist and provide intrinsic compensation in support of the needs for focus, positive reinforcement, and empowerment. There is a unique sense of teamwork, of membership in an elite group, the fulfillment of the need for acceptance, that is generated by this incentive-saturated environment.

Lincoln Electric's plan emphasizes extrinsic rewards and has attracted employees who want material rewards and who can comply with the stringent performance requirements that such a plan design requires. Because of the linkage between intrinsic and extrinsic rewards, however, the intrinsic rewards are also great. The employees at Lincoln Electric essentially control the quantity of extrinsic compensation that they can receive. Thus, they fulfill their intrinsic need for empowerment and, as a result, provide a channel for the overwhelming flow of human potential that is focused on results.

Obviously, the Lincoln environment is not for everyone, nor could the majority of today's organizations successfully administer and manage this extreme of a behavior-based incentive compensation plan. Lincoln's plan is the result of a long evolutionary process. Organizations that are just entering the field of incentive compensation need to find some middle ground between a Lincoln-style system and a traditional compensation system—and to find a plan that fits their management style and their marketplace.

A Period of Transition: Alternative Compensation Plans

Compensation, as a discipline, is experiencing a period of transition and exploration. Economic and social evolution have created a business environment where traditional, well-established approaches to compensation are no longer adequate. The consulting firm of Hewitt and Associates has gathered compensation data showing that the use of incentive opportunity for nonsales, nonexecutive salaried employees is on the rise.

In their search for plans that fit their individual environments, organizations are creating many alternative compensation strategies that contain varying degrees of both intrinsic and extrinsic compensation. While the combination of incentives varies from program to program, they are all focused on taking greater advantage of the potential that is within each employee. They are less interested in issues of cost than in providing the opportunity for all employees to improve their performance.

These compensation plans, with pay contingent upon results, are strong alternatives to conventional systems of base pay increases. In 1988, the Hay Group and *Business Week* magazine conducted a survey of 425 companies with alternative compensation plans.[4] Many of these companies had more than one plan in place. In the following pages, we will review the top seven types of plans in the order of their prevalence:

1. Individual incentives
2. Key-contributor programs
3. Profit sharing
4. Long-term incentives
5. Lump-sum payments
6. Group incentives
7. Gainsharing

We will utilize the Fishbone diagram to analyze each plan's reward structure as it relates to intrinsic and extrinsic needs. This will provide us not only with experience in using the Fishbone as an analytical tool, but also with some general insight as to the various combinations of intrinsic and extrinsic compensation that are effective.

Individual Incentives

Over 45 percent of the survey respondents said they had individual incentives in place. These programs were designed to provide incentive reward based on individual output against standards set by management. The survey did not distinguish between plans for executives only and plans designed for the general employee population. For our purposes here, we will use the Fishbone to examine the broad-based individual incentive compensation plans.

Lincoln Electric's strong position in the marketplace, driven as it is by incentive compensation, indicates that individual incentives can be highly effective. But they have limitations as well. Using the Fishbone as a tool to examine the Lincoln plan in regard to the six major compensation factors, we see no drawbacks related to four factors—what-pay, how-pay, empowerment, and positive reinforcement. (The employees at Lincoln are empowered to manage the process and are reinforced for doing so by the incentive compensation they receive as the result of performance gains.) However, in this type of environment, the factors of focus and why-pay may be constrained and limited.

The focus of the employees—that is, the performance objectives for which they are being rewarded—can become so important to the employees that they may focus on only one set of performance criteria at the expense of others. One potential situation would be the reluctance of employees to participate in the variety of indirect activities, such as housekeeping, ancillary record keeping, and cooperation with staff support, that are necessary for an organization to function successfully as a whole. This may be a detriment to the overall health of the organization, depending on its culture and objectives.

In addition, any future need on the part of the organization to change the standards or refocus the employees' efforts could be perceived by them as a giveback or takeaway. An environment where the focus is on individual contribution may not necessarily be the most beneficial to an organization that requires teamwork and cooperation.

Key-Contributor Programs

Over 40 percent of the respondents in the Hay Group survey reported having programs that rewarded individuals or groups *after* they had made a significant contribution. Usually, these programs are limited to a maximum of 10 percent of the population annually and are in place as part of the corporate human resources policy. The employees are nominated by their supervisors based on the impact of their efforts on the company. These nominations may be for performance throughout the year or during a special project. A senior evaluation committee generally makes the final decisions.

These after-the-fact bonus payments are most often used by management to show their appreciation. As such, key-contributor programs fit the criteria of a recognition program more closely than those of an incentive compensation plan. Using the Fishbone to examine the extrinsic compensation design of key-contributor programs, we see that the factor of why-pay usually is not well defined; indeed, there are generally no specifically defined objectives that drive performance.

We have seen that the factor of why-pay is a key determinant in the effectiveness of incentive compensation because it defines the criteria on which the performance must be focused to improve results. When this factor is supported mainly by discretionary elements, it has a weak motivational impact.

Using the Fishbone to examine the intrinsic compensation design of key-contributor programs, we see that the employee's need for positive reinforcement is fulfilled, at least to a degree, by the elements of recognition and respect that are received in conjunction with the reward. But the need is weakly addressed. The major motivational elements positive, immediate, and certain (PIC), are not present, and therefore the design fails to drive peak performance. Thus, as a compensation strategy, key-contributor programs are not the most effective in achieving results. They are, however, effective in retaining employees, especially if the recognition reward is in some restricted form that requires vesting over a period of years.

Profit Sharing

Close to 30 percent of the companies that participated in the Hay survey had some form of profit sharing. These plans share a portion of the annual profits with all employees based on a formula. The payout may be cash that is distributed at year-end, or payment may be put into a qualified retirement program. Of the estimated 450,000 profit-sharing plans in existence as of 1990, approximately 30 percent offered a choice between immediate distribution and deferred option.

There are a tremendous amount of variations on the profit-sharing theme. One variation that was widely written about in the business journals was a plan developed by the DuPont Company's fibers division. It was an innovative approach that was introduced in 1988 and withdrawn in 1990 due to payout complications. The plan essentially tied profit sharing to base compensation and included all of the division's 20,000 employees. The program, called achievement sharing, was developed by a task force with the aid of a compensation consultant. Participating employees were required to put some of their compensation at risk in return for the opportunity to share a portion of the profits.

The plan put 6 percent of each employee's future increases at risk and was to be phased in over three to five years. At the end of the phase-in period, the employees would receive a 3 percent payout if the unit's performance was at 80 percent of the profit goal for the year, a 6 percent payout if the annual profit goal was met, and an 18 percent payout if profits exceeded the annual goal by 150 percent. In the latter case, their compensation would be 12 percentage points higher than that of their peers throughout the DuPont Company. The downside was that if profits fell below 80 percent of target, no bonus would be paid. In effect, the employees were in an incentive compensation plan where they would "break even" if the organization met its profit plan.

Not surprisingly, the extrinsic reward factors in DuPont's plan were well thought out and strongly functional from the perspective of compensation mechanics. However, if we look for intrinsic reward in the design, we can see where stress could occur and reduce the plan's effectiveness. One limitation is the result of the type of delivery mechanics in the factor of how-pay. Since payouts were basically tied to a year-end bonus, the motivation that is associated with more immediate reward delivery is missing.

Another limitation is the choice of division-wide profit as the sole payout indicator. Because this is such a remote measurement, there is significant risk in considering it as a primary performance measurement for employees at the department level. The linkage of performance objective to individual or group performance is weak. As a result, neither the behavior model nor the motivational criteria of positive, immediate, and certain are in motivational support as strongly as they could be. Of course, this could be offset by an increased application of other types of intrinsic compensation. Timely performance feedback and extensive information sharing in regard to how profit is determined could go a long way toward overcoming this problem.

When profit is used as a performance indicator, significant additional communications as to what each individual employee can do to influence the bottom line is a necessity. In addition, the employees would need to be educated as to how the economy, world events, and other outside influences can affect the profitability of an organization. In effect, they must buy into the concept of oneness, of shared fate with the organization. Moreover, the fibers division had about 7,000 union employees, and even in a nonunion environment the concept is difficult to sell.

The flip side of these difficulties is that the design has elements that can fulfill the employees' need for focus through the sense of mission that such a sharing program generates. The question is, Which way will the employees perceive the opportunity?

The employees' need for empowerment is bounded by two elements. On the one hand, the entrepreneurial importance of having a stake in the profits provides significant perception of opportunity; on the other hand, profits are difficult for an individual to control, and so the actual receipt of the extrinsic compensation is uncertain. Using some of the elements of the Fishbone diagram in our analysis, we can see that this plan could be perceived by the employees as perhaps positive, not immediate, and not certain. Will such a plan be successful in motivating employees to the extent that they will boost profitability, or is the design better suited as a recognition program that works toward increasing a sense of community, esprit de corps, and a shared destiny? Is the primary impact of such a design performance oriented, or is it an agent for changing the organization's culture?

The DuPont Company withdrew the plan in 1990, when poor profit results precluded any incentive compensation payout. In retrospect, the choice of profit as the criterion for the why-pay factor proved to contain too many elements that were beyond the employees' control. Much to its credit as an innovative organization, DuPont realized the inequity of asking the employees to put their compensation at risk in such a situation.

Profit-sharing plans have proven themselves to have a certain degree of effectiveness in impacting employee morale during periods of economic stability. Even so, they require a significant investment of attention and effort in the area of administration, training, communication, and promotion. This awareness process can be used to provide the intrinsic compensation required to offset the extrinsic shortcomings that are the result of slow reward delivery and lack of direct control.

Long-Term Incentives

As with profit sharing, almost 30 percent of the companies in the Hay Survey reported having long-term incentive plans. Typically, these programs offer some form of stock or appreciation value and run anywhere from three to five years. They are most commonly used for senior management because the payout design primarily encourages employee retention. They have also been used effectively in retaining specific skilled engineering and technical talent. In general, however, this type of plan has a relatively narrow scope of application outside of the executive ranks. While it does encourage teamwork to a certain degree, the intrinsic reward elements are weak. There is so little application of the behavioral model or of the PIC—positive, immediate, certain—motivational criteria that the plan has little impact on the average employee's performance.

In examining the next design, we enter the area where usage of incentive compensation plans is less widespread. The next three plans—lump-sum payment, gainsharing, and group incentives—have a transitional relationship to each other in that one plan may set the stage for progression into the next plan. (An awareness of this relationship could prove useful to you as your organization's compensation philosophy evolves into behavior-based incentive compensation.)

Lump-Sum Payments

Lump-sum payments are generally given in lieu of increases to base compensation. For the most part, these plans are used to control costs. They are able to do this because the lump-sum payments do not add to the growth of fixed payroll costs or of benefit costs.

A Fishbone analysis shows that this type of a program is not the best solution to the need for organizational effectiveness and economic growth because the structure fails to address the employees' intrinsic needs of focus and positive reinforcement. A lump-sum payment provides no timely direction or sense of accountability. It is a kind of merit increase that is paid all at one time, and the relationship of performance to results is remote and uncertain.

There are times when lump-sum plans can be used quite effectively, however, especially in transitions from a fixed-salary plan to an incentive compensation plan. The payout structure can be designed to freeze salary levels until they stabilize at a selected percent of midpoint. From a budgetary standpoint, if these salary levels are designed to stabilize below market value or below the organization's total compensation budget, then an excess of funds will accrue. Those funds can then be used to initiate a group incentive or gainsharing plan as the employee's "at risk" portion.

Group Incentives

Only 18 percent of the organizations in the survey reported using group incentives. This is an interesting statistic because group incentives are a highly effective means of providing motivation and impacting results. An educated guess as to the reason for this low level of utilization is that a group-incentive plan requires a high level of detailed design and administration, a relatively sophisticated and receptive environment, and a much greater understanding of the relationships between intrinsic and extrinsic compensation. These issues are not so difficult when tools such as the Fishbone diagram are available, but it is understandable why an organization would initiate its entry into the arena of broad-based incentive compensation with a program that is less complex.

Group incentives require that groups or teams be defined within the workplace. These teams can be functional work groups, such as all employees who perform the same general function, or they can be cross-functional, such as a team that is defined by product line. Each group must have performance objectives that are in direct and identifiable support of the organization's business plan. A formula can then be established that will share with the employees a portion of any improvement in results that they bring about. For group incentives to work, the value of an increment of improvement must be defined and the team's contribution to that improvement must be evident.

The team element in the how-pay factor is significant because it makes this approach both complex to set up and very effective in generating results. Group incentives are rich in both intrinsic and extrinsic compensation. Using the Fishbone diagram, it is easy to see the high degree of intrinsic reward that is generated as a result of the delivery mechanism that defines the plan. For example, because payout is based on group performance, these programs strongly encourage and support teamwork, which in turn provides fulfillment to the employee's needs for focus and empowerment. There are many other intrinsic elements that are created as by-products of the group payout design. These elements are viewed as desirable because they provide to the employees an opportunity to fulfill psychic needs. These intrinsic compensation elements can be utilized to enhance the attractiveness of the total compensation package beyond that of just offering an additional opportunity to gain cash.

The factor of why-pay defines a set of specific objectives that the individuals of the team can impact. These, in turn, will create intrinsic reward elements such as accountability for results, a sense of shared destiny, and a drive toward sustained performance. All these elements in some manner provide fulfillment to the employees' need for focus.

Management can easily augment these intrinsic elements that are generated by the extrinsic design. This is most often accomplished by adding human resources systems that provide opportunities for employee involvement and contribution and thus fulfill the employees' need for empowerment. These systems have a natural relationship to plans based on group designs, where there is strength in numbers. They allow the group to initiate improvements that will affect the quantity of their extrinsic reward. It is this kind of empowerment that provides the greatest potential for integrating employee-involvement programs with an incentive compensation plan.

Rewarding group performance encourages teamwork and information sharing because the emphasis is on increasing overall performance. This creates a more cooperative environment where individuals feel less vulnerable and more supported. Employees working together fulfill the organization's need for improved organizational effectiveness.

Through this kind of analysis, we begin to see how the design of the extrinsic reward—the factors of how-pay, why-pay, and what-pay—does much more than just track costs and issue checks. Each design contains inherent elements of intrinsic compensation that can be utilized to fulfill employee needs. The choice of extrinsic design determines the type and quality of the intrinsic rewards that will be available for use.

Gainsharing

At 10 percent, gainsharing showed the lowest utilization of the major programs mentioned in the survey. The Scanlon, Rucker, and Improshare plans that are normally identified with gainsharing are all a unique form of group incentives that encourage broad employee support and involvement through a focus on productivity improvement. Typically, a formula that calculates the gains as a function of cost reduction or productivity improvement is used to determine the payout to the employees.

Where gainsharing plans differ from group-incentive plans is in the factors of why-pay (the definition of performance objectives) and how-pay (the distribution mechanics). Also, the teams in gainsharing tend to be company-wide in size, and the performance measures tend to be broad in scope. The net effect of these differences is that gainsharing tends to be less effective than a group incentive design in fulfilling the employees' intrinsic needs of focus and positive reinforcement.

In an organization that has little or no experience with incentive compensation, a transition strategy that proceeds from lump-sum payment to gainsharing to group incentives offers a continuity of design that would allow the employees to understand and accept the change. The strongpoint of such a strategy is that it would provide the employees an opportunity to earn both intrinsic and extrinsic compensation with each step and it would provide the organization with performance improvement at each step.

Benefits of a Balanced Formula

The Hay Group/*Business Week* survey ranked the top four plans in terms of their reported ability to generate results. In order of effectiveness, they were: group incentives, long-term programs, gainsharing, and individual incentives.[5] That's not surprising based on what we have seen in our evaluation of their design elements. If we put aside the long-term incentives as being utilized primarily at the executive level, the remaining three programs are the programs whose structures exhibit the most balanced BBIC formula. These plans incorporate a balanced amount of intrinsic and extrinsic rewards in a mechanism that links the rewards to results:

Behavioral psychology + incentive compensation = improved results

General or Transactional Measurement

We have reviewed incentive plan designs that tend to emphasize one of three things: the mechanics of the payout, the extrinsic reward itself, or the organization's needs. Stock options and profit sharing have a performance-measurement element that is general in scope. These plans tend to use a blanket approach, hoping all employees will do the right thing on their way to the extrinsic reward. They rely on the high profile of the payout mechanism to drive the process.

Plan designs that utilize group incentives emphasize the performance-improvement requirements (the why-pay factor) that are part of the incentive contract. They have a measurement element that is transactional; it is a well-focused measurement that simply says, "Do this, get that." These plans are supported with an equally strong factor of how-pay that includes a high degree of conformity to the behavior model and to PIC, the positive, immediate, and certain motivational criteria. As a result, these programs strongly fulfill the employees' need for positive reinforcement. They make better use of intrinsic rewards to drive performance and results, they go deeper into the organization, and they are more controllable and contingent.

In Chapter 4, we discuss the organization's needs as they relate to the employees' ability to impact them. In doing so, we will complete the right-hand side of the Fishbone diagram and use it to identify the proper balance of intrinsic and extrinsic rewards to maximize the motivational impact of incentive compensation on performance improvement.

Notes

1. *What Lies Ahead: Countdown to the 21st Century,* United Way of America, 1989.
2. *Achieving Results Through Sharing: Group Incentive Program Survey Report,* Towers Perrin, April 1990.
3. Carla O'Dell and Jerry McAdams, *People, Performance, and Pay,* a report on the American Productivity Center/American Compensation Association national survey of nontraditional reward practices, American Productivity and Quality Center, 1987.
4. *Worklife,* 8:1 (July 1988), p. 4. (Newsletter of the American Productivity and Quality Center, Houston.)
5. Ibid.

4

A Balanced Formula: Behavior-Based Incentive Compensation

In this day and age, all organizations are striving for "excellence"—a competitive edge that is the result of an organization's effectiveness and the economic value it is capable of generating. Tom Peters, in his book *In Search of Excellence*, analyzes the workings of companies that exhibited superiority in their arenas of competition. Other researchers have also focused on excellence, to the point where a great deal has been observed and documented about this concept. One of the results of all this analysis has been the identification of certain elements that are always present in an environment of excellence. Those elements can be described in terms of aim, effort, and self-expectation/pride/commitment.

That we find these elements present is not surprising. Each organization that exhibits excellence will focus on its business objectives. It will concentrate the energies of its employees in that direction and will set aggressive and specific goals that challenge its employees. As a result, companies that contain the elements of excellence within their corporate culture will be top performers, constantly and consistently striving to improve results.

Behavior-based incentive compensation can be useful in improving business results. If results are a function of excellence and if incentive compensation drives results, there should be some relationship between the elements of behavior-based incentive compensation and the elements of excellence.

Using the Fishbone diagram, we can see a direct relationship between behavior-based incentive compensation and excellence. The elements of excellence either exist within, or are a product of, BBIC.

Thus, the element of *aim* is really the employee's intrinsic need for focus, expressed in an action form. We have seen that extrinsic compensation is the primary force driving behavior-based incentive compensation systems and the source of many intrinsic rewards. In reexamining the Fishbone diagram's extrinsic factor of why-pay, we can see that any organization that utilizes incentive compensation to motivate its employees will have the elements of objective identification and performance measurement available to provide fulfillment opportunities for the employees' intrinsic needs of focus and positive reinforcement.

Objective identification can be used to fulfill the employees' intrinsic need for focus by providing the structure with which to target performance and the benchmarks from which to evaluate progress. Performance measurement can be used to fulfill the employees' intrinsic need for positive reinforcement by providing information on progress. In doing so, it encourages *effort* and reinforces *self-expectations* and *pride*. The extrinsic factor of what-pay supports the employees' *effort* and *commitment* by answering the question, "What's in it for me?" Thus, behavior-based incentive compensation is a tool that will support and reinforce the elements that define "business excellence." That's an excellent reason to utilize this type of compensation . . . in theory.

Do They Respond?

The theory on which the BBIC Fishbone is based states that behavior-based incentive compensation will support excellence within an organization. But we need to do a reality check to see if employees actually respond to it and if, in doing so, they improve results.

We can check effectiveness by referring back to the Hay Group/ *Business Week* report (see Figure 4-1) that studied the broad-based incentive compensation plans of 425 major business organizations.[1] Almost 50 percent of the study participants utilized individual incentive plans. Of this group, 77 percent reported favorable reaction by the employees to this type of reward program, and 50 percent reported more favorable business results since the installation of the plan.

Close to 20 percent of the respondents reported using group-incentive plans. Of this group, 81 percent reported favorable reaction by the employees to this type of reward program. This tells us that incentive compensation is effective because, by addressing the employees' needs, it makes them "feel good."

Interestingly, 67 percent reported that results had improved after the installation of a group-incentive plan. While other broad-based

Figure 4-1. Employee reactions/performance results.

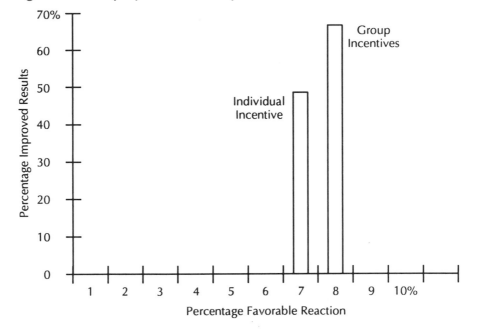

incentive compensation plans such as gainsharing and profit sharing scored slightly higher in the category of favorable employee reaction, no other plan that was reported scored higher in the category of improved results. The data show that from a results standpoint the most effective plans closely tie the potential for each employee to obtain fulfillment for his or her needs to performance improvement. This fits nicely with the behavioral psychology data showing that when positive consequences are attached to performance, the performance improves.

Perspective

The focus of this book is the study of broad-based employee incentive compensation from a micro level to understand why it works and to learn how to design BBIC plans and implement them in the most effective manner. To do this, it will be helpful to consider the macro level as well. From this point of view, the wave of the future is a growing service economy supported by the advent of ever more powerful personal computers. Thus, employees are more and more likely to be part of a team producing a common output rather than individual contributors. They will be handling a much greater amount of information. Accessibility to large amounts of data about the marketplace will accelerate change in the workplace. In order to keep up with these changes, employees will have to be increasingly flexible.

This dynamic environment and the desirable jobs within it will require mental skills, active involvement, and participation. These are three things that you cannot make people do. Involvement, participation, and mental attention are intrinsic, voluntary contributions that can be coaxed from employees but never demanded. Offering sufficient compensation in a form that addresses the priority needs of these employees is a proven, effective way of coaxing these contributions. It's simply the age-old use of the carrot rather than the stick.

The essential perspective to have when designing a successful compensation plan is to think like the recipients, the employees who are going to participate in the plan. Ask yourself the question, "If I were in their situation, what would my needs be?" If you get no value from this book other than the internal realization of the importance of this perspective, then your time and money will still have been well spent.

The Three Design Challenge Factors

There are three factors to take into consideration when designing innovative compensation plans to motivate employees and provide them with the proper incentive to contribute "discretionary" time, energy, and creativity to their work. These factors are perspective, paradigms of thought, and matters of balance/proportion. We have already discussed the importance and value of perspective, so let's move on to the next two factors.

A paradigm is often used in reference to a model or pattern of excellence. This model consists of elements whose relationships are such that they can be combined in a variety of ways and still produce the same consistent results. For example, a "paradigm of compensation" is a compensation plan that relies on job point evaluation or grading. These plans have been very successful and, as a result, have become the compensation patterns of excellence. The modifications to compensation planning that exist today are the result of the combination and interchange of the elements of this paradigm.

The challenge for the 1990s is to use compensation to manage the rapid change that is taking place in the human resources environment. In order to design the next generation of compensation plans, we must step outside the boundaries of traditional thought, outside the paradigms that have developed in compensation.

Figure 4-2 offers a good example of paradigmatic thinking. The current approach to compensation thinking is represented by the nine elements arranged in the configuration of a square. The white

Figure 4-2. Compensation paradigm of economic value.

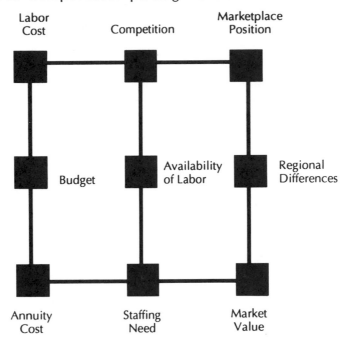

background of the page represents the business environment in which this paradigm exists. This environment is stable, and compensation is viewed as an operating cost. All of the nine key elements in this concept of compensation are connected by five straight lines that represent their interrelationship.

Now let's envision that the business environment has changed and that the requirements of compensation have changed with it. The new environment is highly competitive, both for market share and for human resources. The overall effectiveness of the organization in these areas will determine its success or failure in a competitive marketplace. The response to this change requires that the key elements of the compensation paradigm be connected by only four lines instead of five. Can you do it?

Figure 4-3 shows that it is necessary to go outside established boundaries in order to be successful. In this example, we must change from thinking about compensation as a cost to thinking about compensation as a tool to achieve organizational effectiveness through improved use of human potential. The Fishbone diagram has shown that human potential can be realized by addressing the employees' needs for focus, positive reinforcement, and empowerment. By adding these elements, we have developed a new compensation paradigm that will enable us to accomplish our mission.

Figure 4-3. Compensation paradigm of organizational effectiveness.

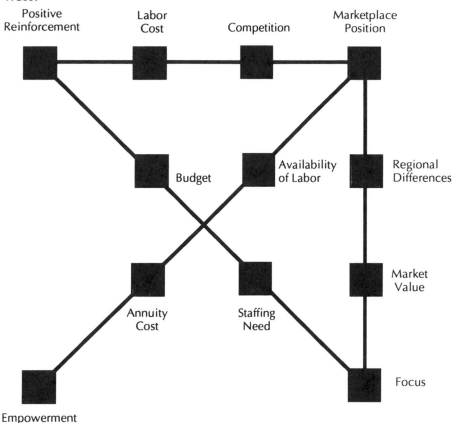

The Final Formula

The BBIC formula and Fishbone diagram can be used to help expand and change the paradigm of compensation. These representational tools help us to see the relationships that exist between the organization's needs and the employees' needs. The left-hand side of both the formula and the diagram represents the needs of the employees, and the right-hand side represents the needs of the organization. In the Fishbone diagram, the organization's needs are represented by two key factors—organizational effectiveness and economic value. These two key factors are the major benefits that accrue to organizations that utilize a combination of behavioral psychology and incentive compensation to motivate their employees.

Organizational effectiveness and economic value are each composed of a unique set of factors. In Figure 4-4, the list of factors is an example of this concept. In developing a BBIC Fishbone for your organization, you will find a unique set of factors that defines

Figure 4-4. The developing BBIC Fishbone.

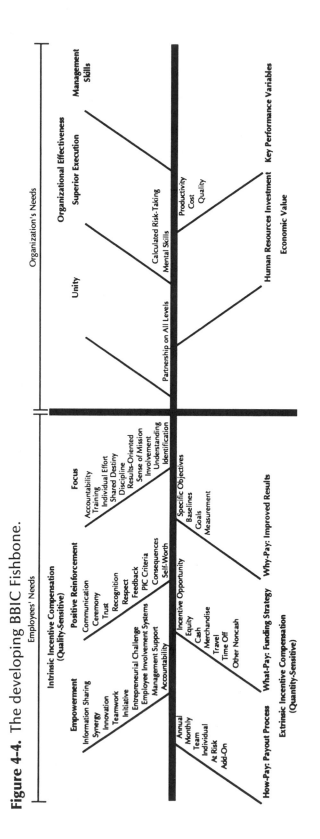

the meaning of organizational effectiveness and economic value to your organization.

It is easy to see that the factors that define the two key organizational needs have a direct relationship to the elements that define, support, and fulfill the six key compensation needs of the employees. They could be considered mirror images of each other in the sense that the elements that support and fulfill the employees' needs can also fulfill the organization's needs. The BBIC Fishbone is a graphic display of the concept of reciprocity: If you address the employees' needs, you will also be addressing the organization's needs.

Maintaining Perspective with the Fishbone

There are no hard and fast rules that govern the relationships between the employees' needs and the organization's needs. However, there is an underlying affinity between certain classifications. For example, the employees' needs in the general category of intrinsic compensation relate primarily to the organization's needs for organizational effectiveness. Thus, a compensation plan that provides the employees with the opportunity to fulfill their needs for focus, positive reinforcement, and empowerment is likely to bring about an improvement in the organization's overall effectiveness.

The employee's needs in the general category of extrinsic compensation tend to relate primarily to the organization's needs for economic value. As a result, if we design a plan with an incentive payout ratio of 5:1, we can expect to net $5 for every $1 we pay out. A wise businessman would conduct this type of exchange all day.

The exact elements that fulfill needs will of course differ from situation to situation. So, too, will the relationships between the employees' needs and the organization's needs. For example, let's look at a plan where the intrinsic factor of empowerment has been designed to impact organizational effectiveness. In such a plan, the employees' need for empowerment is addressed by providing the opportunity to join problem-solving teams. In addition, the plan calls for specific, demonstrable management support and the mechanism through which employees can implement their ideas. These elements of empowerment provide the platform for the active involvement, participation, and information sharing on the part of the employees. The result? From the standpoint of organizational effectiveness, the results manifest themselves through improvement in such areas as risk-taking mentality, partnership on all levels, and enhanced application of mental skills.

In a slightly different design, the intrinsic factor of empowerment could impact the organization's need for economic value.

Empowering the employees to identify and resolve cost and quality problems by letting them share in the gains of improvement would have a specific impact on the factor of economic value.

The relationship between the employee's needs and the organization's needs is determined by the organization's culture and the types of elements that are utilized to fulfill employees' needs. In keeping with the observation that the designer's point of view has an impact on the effectiveness of a plan, we should take a moment to review our perspective. When we talk of "elements" that support employee needs, we are referring to the results of specific financial payouts and environmental actions, such as establishing employee action teams, that are formal parts of a written compensation plan. It is important to keep in mind that what a designer views as the legal, financial, or administrative components of a plan will appear to the employees as opportunities. A good question to keep in mind during the design stage is, Will the result of this design element be viewed as an opportunity by the employees?

A Matter of Balance and Linkage

The design of an effective behavior-based incentive compensation plan is a matter of balance. And the way to achieve this balance is to work backward through the BBIC formula. The right-hand side of the formula, performance improvement, deals with the organization's specific, functional needs; the left-hand side deals with the employees' psychic and material needs.

Maslow and Skinner have shown us that the human drive to fulfill specific needs will produce specific behavior. We have also seen that specific behavior will produce specific results. By identifying the desired results in specific terms, we can work backward and identify the behavior that will generate those results. Next we must identify the employees' intrinsic and extrinsic needs that are within the organization's power to fulfill. By providing the opportunity to fulfill those needs, and by making such opportunity contingent upon the specific performance that has been identified, it is possible to link the needs of the employees and of the organization. The first step in this process is to identify the results we want.

Different organizations have different goals. For example, a company's position in the business life cycle will be a significant determinant of the type of behavior that it wants to elicit from its employees. A young company concerned with the need for rapid growth in a dynamic, competitive environment would probably be more concerned with issues such as cycle-time analysis and calculated

risk taking. On the other hand, an organization focusing on profitability in a mature, regulated environment would most likely have specific functional needs such as controlling costs, enhancing quality, and improving the people skills of the managers.

Once the organization's specific functional needs have been identified, the next step is to use the BBIC Fishbone to identify the psychic and material needs of the employees that relate to and will impact them. By providing the opportunity for fulfillment of both the intrinsic and extrinsic needs of the employees, management will encourage employees to focus on delivering specific, targeted behavior that will provide specific, targeted results.

Figure 4-5 provides a good illustration of the concept of a balanced formula. The quality and quantity of opportunities for intrinsic and extrinsic compensation that are provided to the employees will determine the degree of their involvement and participation, which will, in turn, determine the amount of improvement that an organization will experience. The more opportunities provided to the employees, the more potential there is for performance improvement.

How Much of What Is Enough?

One of the challenges in designing an effective behavior-based incentive compensation plan is to balance the formula so that the organization receives the maximum performance return for both the financial investment and management effort. Most compensation plans leave a significant amount of performance "on the table." They don't consider the maximum performance return on dollar spent because, as we have seen, the dollar spent is not closely associated

Figure 4-5. Balance beam.

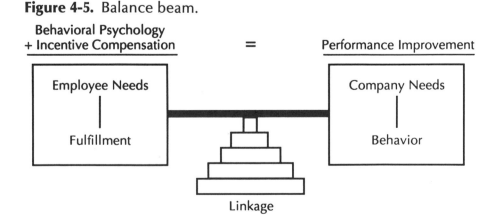

with, or contingent upon, the performance. One of the reasons that these plans don't provide the maximum return is that the whole compensation process is disengaged from the daily work effort. As a result, management and supervision are involved only from the standpoint of administration and distribution. This is the extent of their effort to apply the process as a tool. Because these compensation plans are viewed as costs, management efforts are designed to be kept to a minimum.

Adding intrinsic incentives to a compensation plan results in a behavior-based incentive compensation plan that requires a high degree of effort to apply the process as a tool on the part of management. BBIC plans provide the opportunity for a substantial level of interaction with and among the employees. Later in this chapter, we will use the Fishbone diagram to review the case history of a plant where management added intrinsic compensation to traditional base pay. The analysis should show us that in a traditional environment the amount of effort that management focuses on the intrinsic compensation contributes to the impact of the base compensation plan and results in greater employee participation and a higher return on investment. It is important to note that intrinsic incentives require management to take an active role in the compensation process. Behavior-based incentive compensation plans do not do well in a corporate environment where management rules by authoritarian directive. This type of environment leaves very little opportunity for the application of intrinsic incentives.

How can we determine the proper balance that will provide both the employee and the organization with the greatest return on investment? To answer this question, it is helpful to view the intrinsic and extrinsic elements of the BBIC formula in a more subjective form. Critical to determining the proper mix of elements in the formula are the concepts of quantity and quality.

Quantity

Naturally, the quantity of incentive opportunities will have an impact on overall results. Looking back at Figure 4-5, we can see that the more compensation opportunities that are placed on the left side, the more results that can be anticipated for the right side. There is a natural homeostasis here, a tendency toward a state of equilibrium between the different but interdependent elements. Intuitively we can see that the more contingent incentives that are provided to the employees, the more results will be generated (up to the point where the employees' needs that are being addressed have been fulfilled).

In an organization that has not experienced this type of compensation, almost any combination of intrinsic and extrinsic opportunities

will improve results at first. The concept of quality circles is a good example of management providing intrinsic compensation in the form of opportunities for employee involvement and recognition. Based on Maslow's observations concerning the human hierarchy of needs, however, we assume that at some point we will reach the point of diminishing returns for a specific combination of incentive opportunities. (This became evident in the case of quality circles.) At this point of saturation, a different combination of incentive opportunities would generate greater results. Enter the additional element of quality, which will help keep us from wasting either our effort or our compensation budget.

Quality

As it pertains to the design of a behavior-based incentive compensation plan, quality is the result of the proper combination of intrinsic and extrinsic compensation factors based on their priority, weight, and linkage. The concept of priority can be defined as the stack ranking of key compensation factors that identifies those factors that precede others in the development and implementation process of a compensation philosophy. This ranking of factors will allow us to concentrate on first things first.

Weighting of the key compensation factors provides an indication of the relative impact on results that each factor has in a stand-alone situation. Weighting assists us in configuring the most effective plan for a specific environment.

The concept of linkage can be defined as the relationship that exists between the various need factors. Understanding how needs relate to each other will allow us to design incentive opportunities that will fulfill multiple needs using the same elements. It will also allow us to identify the employee needs that have the most direct linkage to the specific functional needs of the organization. Management by wandering around is a useful technique that can be applied when developing linkage. Managers who spend time in the workplace talking with the employees tend to develop an understanding of the needs of their employees.

Applied Evolution of Incentive Plan Design

Figure 4-6 illustrates a model to help develop an understanding of the relationships that exist between the intrinsic and extrinsic factors of employees' needs. The purpose of this model is to aid in predicting trends in incentive program design that correspond to observed program results. The six factors in the model are derived from the

Figure 4-6. Priority, weight, and linkage model.

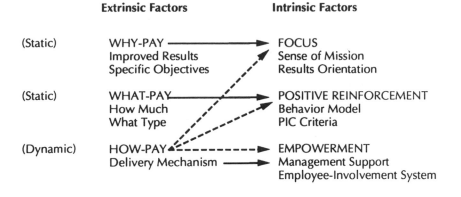

BBIC Fishbone diagram and have been assigned positions based on their priority in the design and implementation process. The solid arrow lines indicate their primary linkage to each other; the dotted arrow lines indicate a strong secondary linkage.

By observing the effects that these factors have on performance results, we are able to assign a numeric relationship that gives a weight or value to each factor. Figure 4-7 shows the numeric relationships that can be used to represent a basic incentive compensation plan design. By establishing a number of points that represent this basic design—in this case, twelve—the ranking model can be used to identify the amount of divergence or convergence that other plan designs have in relation to the basic plan design. Ultimately, an understanding of the priority, weight, and linkage of the factors that are incorporated into a plan design will allow us to balance those relationships to achieve maximum motivational impact.

Keep in mind that these models have been developed to provide insight into the design relationships of an incentive compensation plan. The weighting values are assigned somewhat arbitrarily, as opposed to being scaled to the actual levels of human response. Nonetheless, it is still possible to glean an intuitive understanding of particular relationships. As such, the rating model forms an important bridge between compensation and psychology. It provides a means of communicating between two disciplines that often see the world from widely divergent perspectives.

Extrinsic Compensation: Priority, Weight, and Linkage

In examining this model, we will use two general criteria: first, the tendency on the part of the recipient to perceive a factor as compensation, and second, the ability of the factor to impact results (keeping

Figure 4-7. Total effectiveness rating for basic incentive compensation.

Extrinsic Factors			Intrinsic Factors		
Factor	Weight	Weight	Factor		Rating
Why-Pay	1	+ 1	Focus	=	2
What-Pay	2	+ 2	Positive Reinforcement	=	4
How-Pay	3	+ 3	Empowerment	=	6
				Total Points	12

in mind that employees generate the results). In addition, we will work under the premise that employees contribute their energies to an organization primarily as a means of obtaining financial support. We will examine the Fishbone category of extrinsic compensation first, because it provides the employees with the opportunity to obtain financial support and thus to adjust their standard of living.

Why-Pay

The extrinsic factor of why-pay can be assigned the first position in the stack ranking of priorities because it defines the criteria by which employees can earn additional compensation. It defines specific objectives and results and provides the necessary information as to where employees can focus their energies and direct their mental attention. It sets the stage for action. These are the traits that link the factor of why-pay to the employees' intrinsic need for focus.

The extrinsic factor of why-pay is assigned a basic weighted value of one point because it is a static factor. Its presence is necessary to initiate the process, but once established, it remains fixed as part of the structure. Employees will respond to the direction provided by management and, except in extreme cases where it would be to the obvious detriment of the company or themselves, they will pursue the direction that is established for them. To some degree, employees have the opportunity to determine their own objectives. For the most part, however, management is responsible for establishing not only the strategic direction but also the tactical objectives for the organization. At this stage in the development of behavior-based incentive compensation plans, employees have a degree of detachment from the dynamics of the why-pay factor that results in it being assigned a low motivation weighting. In a future world where employees set their own objectives, the factor of why-pay will have a greater ongoing impact and receive a higher weighting.

What-Pay

The factor of what-pay can be assigned the second position in the stack ranking of priorities because it comes after, and builds on, the why-pay factor. It defines the quantity of incentive opportunity that is made available to the employee. Together, the factors of why-pay and what-pay provide the employee with a clear understanding of the degree of effort required to realize the opportunity.

From the organization's standpoint, the factor of what-pay provides the financial justification for incentive compensation based on the value of an increment of improvement. From the employee's perspective, what-pay provides the opportunity to make a cost/benefit tradeoff decision. If the employees perceive their portion of the gain as being too small for the additional effort required to obtain it, they will most likely not consider this as an opportunity and elect not to participate. The factor of what-pay contains elements that mainly deal with "how much" and "what type." These traits act as a source of positive consequences and link the factor of what-pay to the intrinsic need for positive reinforcement.

The type of incentive that is offered will also have an effect on how the employees perceive the opportunity. Cash can be utilized to fulfill material desire and has a strong impact because of its ability to provide immediate gratification. Shares of stock or nontraditional compensation such as time off or college tuition offer deferred gratification, which may affect the degree and intensity of additional energies that an employee will contribute. (Because of their ability to impact the employee's perception of value, and thus ultimately impact results, nontraditional rewards can be an important part of incentive compensation programs; they are described in detail in Chapter 9.)

The factor of what-pay is a static factor. As is the case with why-pay, its presence is necessary to initiate the process, but once established, it remains fixed as part of the structure. It is assigned a basic weighted value of two points because it has significant motivational power. In the most basic sense, it acts as an on-off switch to an employee's decision to participate. The quantity and type of incentive is either perceived as an opportunity or it is not. The rest is a matter of degree.

How-Pay

The factor of how-pay is assigned the third position in the stack ranking of priorities because it is dependent upon the factors of why-pay and what-pay being in place. In essence, how-pay is a modifier of the preceding two factors. It can act to enhance or detract from the perceived value of either or both of them. This ability is the reason why the factor of how-pay plays such a powerful role in the design of behavior-based incentive compensation.

As an example of this, let's develop an incentive compensation plan that shares the gains that are generated in the areas of productivity and quality. For this example, we don't need to specify how those objectives are defined or measured. Let's simply assume that the workforce is stable and experienced and that performance has been steady for a considerable period of time. A 10 percent improvement in these areas would not be considered unreasonable. In our example, each 1 percent increment of improvement in either objective is worth $20,000 to the organization in profit, and 20 percent of that improvement will be shared with the employees in the form of cash. The plan has a high perceived value to the employees because the share ratio is such that, at a 10 percent increase in productivity and quality, each employee will earn 20 percent of their base compensation. The factor of why-pay is strong, the factor of what-pay is strong, and the employees are excited about the opportunity to raise their standard of living.

We will now add the how-pay criteria and observe what happens to the effectiveness of the other two factors. In our how-pay criteria, we will stipulate that the employees must put 10 percent of their base compensation at risk, that the entire organization will be considered as a single team, and that the payout will be issued at the end of each fiscal year. The Fishbone diagram shows that the result of this one-time, company-wide reward would be to diminish the sense of opportunity perceived by the employee. The reward is not only remote, it is also removed from the immediate control of each employee. Thus, the plan's ability to stimulate individual performance has been diminished, and overall results will be less than they could have been.

The factor of how-pay is assigned a basic weighted value of three points because of its strength. It is a dynamic, ongoing factor that maintains continuing impact on employee motivation. As Figure 4-6 shows, how-pay, unlike the other factors, has a strong linkage with all three intrinsic reward factors. Its primary linkage is with the intrinsic factor of empowerment because it is a delivery mechanism.

How-pay is the factor that enables management to increase their application effort. Indeed, the act of delivering the incentive compensation to the employees has the potential to fulfill needs in the areas of focus, positive reinforcement, and empowerment. It emphasizes to the employees that they are clearly focused; it has strong secondary linkages to the other intrinsic factors; it provides positive consequences for current performance; and it provides the real measure of management's commitment. Delivery is an ongoing process, and each time it occurs it provides an opportunity to fulfill intrinsic needs and reinforce improvement. It is easy to deduce that a design plan that emphasizes frequent reward delivery will be a strong motivational design. As we apply the rating model to the analysis of incentive compensation plans, we will see just how much impact the factor of how-pay has on the total effectiveness rating.

One of the challenges in the design of a behavior-based incentive compensation plan is to offer fulfillment to the maximum number of needs. For example, which reward factors should be emphasized to reach an acceptable ratio of clear definition of responsibility (focus) to identification of contribution (positive reinforcement) while at the same time developing a good integration of the individual into the team. Dr. Alyce Dickenson of Western Michigan University has conducted extensive research into reward systems. Among her results, she has found that the most motivationally effective incentive designs are those that combine both individual and group elements. These are elements of the factor of how-pay. Her observations tend to support the position of how-pay as a factor that can affect the strength of other program design elements. The net effect of this observation is that we can use how-pay to provide intrinsic compensation in the same way and with the same impact that we use what-pay to provide extrinsic compensation.

The tremendous power of the factor of how-pay is based on the employees' perception of such issues as the timing of reward delivery, whether or not the reward is earned as the result of individual or group performance, and whether compensation is at risk or the incentive is an add-on. These are subjective issues to the employee and can be effective as motivators only insofar as they are positioned to be perceived as enhancements to the original incentive opportunity as defined by the factors of why-pay and what-pay.

Intrinsic Compensation: Priority, Weight, and Linkage

Figure 4-6 shows how the compensation factors that can be utilized to fulfill the needs of the employees tend to progress from an objective state to a subjective state. They span a range from the concrete reality of cash in hand to issues that are more a matter of perception. The factors involved in extrinsic compensation are primarily objective. As an example, the factor of why-pay, first in priority, is essentially objective because it consists of such elements as specific measurements and well-defined performance objectives. Next in priority ranking, the factor of what-pay is objective but has subjective traits as well. Cash, merchandise, and stocks are all concrete, but time off and travel are more subjective, and their value is based more on perception.

When we reach the intrinsic factors of focus, positive reinforcement, and empowerment, the effectiveness of the intrinsic compensation elements that satisfy these needs is determined almost entirely by employee perception. They have their greatest effectiveness when used in a support role to enhance the perception of the incentive opportunity.

Focus

The factor of focus can be assigned first priority because of its linkage to the extrinsic factor of why-pay. Focus is the internalization of why-pay and is based heavily on a sense of mission. It is a powerful modifying factor because it is closely associated with human emotions. As a result, these elements that support progress toward the mission's goals, such as training and discipline, will be perceived as opportunities and could be utilized as elements in an incentive plan design. The factor of focus is assigned a basic weighted value of one point because its strength is related to perception more than to action.

Positive Reinforcement

The need for positive reinforcement can be assigned the second position because of its relationship to the extrinsic factor of what-pay. Elements such as the behavior model and the motivational criteria of positive, immediate, and certain have a strong impact on the factor of positive reinforcement because they require a positive perception of the opportunity on the part of the participant. Positive reinforcement is assigned a basic weighted value of two points because it is action oriented; its strength is in its ability to stimulate performance. We often refer to incentive designs that "drive" performance. This is a manner of expression that is not quite on the mark, because the most effective incentive will not drive performance, it will have performance chase after it.

Empowerment

The factor of empowerment is assigned the third position because in order for it to be effective the other needs must be addressed first. The abstract concepts of initiative and entrepreneurial spirit are most effective in an environment that provides focus and an incentive to act. The factor of empowerment is assigned a basic weighted value of three points because, like the extrinsic factor of how-pay, to which it is linked, it is action oriented. It also provides the opportunity for management to interact with the employees.

The employees' need for empowerment gives management the opportunity to add elements that are not inherent in the incentive process but that can fulfill intrinsic and extrinsic needs by enhancing the employees' ability to participate. Systems like action teams or suggestion programs allow employees to become involved and maximize their incentive opportunity. In such an environment, management support is a critical modifier that, at the very least, tells the employees that they have approval to participate. At the most, managers become facilitators for the employees as they pursue the business objectives laid out for them in the why-pay criteria.

David Engelman, director of incentive compensation of GTE, has been involved with a pilot incentive compensation plan that includes 4,000 management employees in a West Coast operation. Later in this chapter we will analyze this plan, but at this point it is important to note a change in their compensation philosophy described by Engelman: "What we are doing is not about a compensation plan. Compensation is used to support the process of putting teams to work on problems, issues, productivity, and quality." Indeed, GTE's experience has demonstrated to management the tremendous capability that an incentive delivery mechanism has to fulfill the employees' needs for focus, positive reinforcement, and empowerment.

Rating Incentive Compensation Plans

Figure 4-7 shows how the model we have developed can be used to measure the motivational effectiveness of an incentive plan design. A numerical value can be calculated by adding the assigned weights of the key factors across their primary linkage. In this way, we can achieve a weighted value for that relationship. The higher the number, the more motivational impact the plan will have. In an incentive compensation plan without any special behavioral emphasis, one that is designed mainly to improve some area such as productivity or cost reduction, each factor and need would assume the normal weighted value we have established. Figure 4-7 shows that a basic design would receive an effectiveness rating of twelve points. This, then, becomes the standard of measurement against which other designs can be compared.

In an incentive compensation plan that incorporates behavioral psychology, the factor of how-pay is a powerful modifying element. Because how-pay is dynamic and has a wide-ranging impact on all of the intrinsic needs, its basic weighted value (three points) can be applied not only to the intrinsic factor of empowerment, to which it is primarily linked, but also to the other intrinsic needs, to which it has strong secondary linkage (see Figure 4-6). The resulting numerical relationship is exhibited in Figure 4-8, where the model displays an effectiveness rating of twenty-one points for a behavior-based incentive compensation plan design. This, then, becomes the peak rating against which other designs can be compared.

The peak rating value was computed using the following process. The basic weighted value for the extrinsic factor of why-pay (one point) is added to the basic weighted value for the intrinsic factor of focus for a subtotal of two points. In a behavior-based incentive compensation plan, the extrinsic factor of how-pay is strongly emphasized and has a direct impact on the intrinsic factor of focus. The basic weighted value for how-pay (three points) is added to the subtotal of two points for a total of five points for this reward factor category. In the ideal behavior-based incentive compensation design, the factor of how-pay has the same modifying effect on the intrinsic factors of positive reinforcement and empowerment. This effect is visualized by the addition of the how-pay basic weighted value (three points) to the rating subtotal of the other reward factors.

A Performance Culture

In an organizational culture that emphasizes results, the norms and attitudes within the organization all relate to performance. In order for a reward system to be effective, it must match this culture in its design. The ideal behavior-based incentive compensation plan would place just as much emphasis on the application of behavioral technology as on the compensation payout design matrix. This would require the addition of such elements as the training of management in the specific skills of applied behavior management. Is such a magnitude of effort worthwhile? Figure 4-8 shows the motivational im-

Figure 4-8. Total effectiveness rating for behavior-based incentive compensation.

Extrinsic Factors		Intrinsic Factors		Subtotal Rating	How-Pay Modifier	Total Rating
Factor	Weight	Weight	Factor			
Why-Pay	1	+ 1	Focus	= 2	+ 3	= 5
What-Pay	2	+ 2	Positive Reinforcement	= 4	+ 3	= 7
(strong) How-Pay	3	+ 3	Empowerment	= 6	+ 3	= 9
					Total Points	21

pact that the ideal behavior-based incentive compensation plan can have. According to the rating, the application of behavioral psychology in conjunction with extrinsic compensation will almost double the effectiveness of an incentive compensation plan.

Keep in mind that the total effectiveness rating model evaluates the motivational impact that plan design factors have on employee performance, not on the importance the factors have to the organization. The model is intended to rank the design factors based on their ability to impact the perception of the employees.

Those elements that modify how the reward is provided have a significant impact on the employees' intrinsic needs. The behavior model and the motivational criteria of positive, immediate, and certain have shown us that the timing of an award determines the intensity of the positive reinforcement that it provides. Team or individual earning opportunities will determine the degree of empowerment that an employee feels. The issue of team and/or individual also determines how specific the objectives and measurement can be. The clarity and detail of the performance objectives, in turn, impact the degree of focus an employee feels.

The numeric relationships of the effectiveness rating models demonstrate how an incentive compensation plan that incorporates elements of behavioral technology will influence employee perceptions and provide the wherewithall to address their intrinsic needs. Such a plan will have the greatest motivational impact on employee performance.

At this point, let's take what we have learned and analyze a few case histories. We will look at the broad-based nonexecutive incentive compensation plans that have been developed by GTE and Frito Lay. Once we have identified the key factors in each plan, we can apply the process of priority, weighting, and linkage (PWL) that we have developed to gain a clear understanding of the emphasis and potential to impact results of each plan's design.

Frito Lay's Incentive Compensation Plan

As far back as 1985, Frito Lay's management accepted the fact that improvements in the technology of their business would bring only a limited degree of incremental improvement. David Halleck, manager of compensation at Frito Lay, tells us, "To meet our corporate goals of providing quality products to the consumer while keeping manufacturing costs flat, employees, the single most important variable, had to be leveraged as a resource. Executive management commissioned a task force of manufacturing, employee relations, management development, and compensation managers to study the opportunity. The task force assignment was to develop a program that supported the business strategy through the coordination of management practices, employee participation, and shared rewards. The result of the assignment was a productivity incentive plan based on cost, quality, and productivity volume. Employee participation and feedback systems were designed and installed to support the process. In addition, incentive plan success criteria were designed and incorporated into the review cycle."

Because of normal management transitioning, it took almost two years to develop a program that would address Frito Lay's specific needs. Senior management was kept apprised of the progress, and eventually a plan was developed that would include the supervisors, the clerical nonexempt employees, and all hourly production workers. As a result of the ongoing communication during the developmental process, there were no surprises to anyone on any level when it came time for the implementation. In order to enhance the acceptance of the program, it was rolled out not as a new compensation program from corporate but as an employee relations initiative and manufacturing incentive plan.

Frito Lay has a cultural history of utilizing the test process to explore different alternatives. Like many organizations, they use testing as a method of gaining company-specific information and data for assessment. Two plants were selected to participate in the test of incentive compensation. One plant was to be the test plant, the other plant was to be the control. The plants were selected based on a list of criteria that included comparable plant size and age, similar workforce demographics and experience, similar styles of management, and commonality of products (this would remove any variance based on seasonality).

The test plan consisted of three major elements: education, involvement systems, and rewards. Looking at the Fishbone diagram, we can see that these three plan elements would work to address the intrinsic needs of focus, positive reinforcement, and empowerment. The performance-improvement objectives were to reduce cost and improve quality. According to David Halleck, "Productivity measurements are part of a common business language within our plants. Employees and managers are provided with training which assists them in understanding how the results are obtained and how to correct any deficiency. The difference that occurred with the installation of the incentive compensation program was a shift from the stick method to the carrot method of improving performance. The change in direction helped us facilitate the cultural shift in aligning employees with the business."

The first step was the implementation of an education campaign. Operations managers were given orientation as to the compensation plan design and mechanics and were coached on how to adapt to their new roles. Their old style was simply to assign tasks; the new system called for them to work with the hourly employees in order to draw out their contributions and tap their potential.

Next, business training was provided to the nonexempt employees. Cost accounting was explained so that they could understand such issues as the impact of waste on profitability. The level of detail here included not only the cost of the product lost but also the other expenses involved, including cleanup and removal. "It provided them with an understanding of how their actions impacted the business. It gave them a sense of accountability," says David Halleck. Testing validated the training. At least 80 percent of the employees were required to achieve 80 percent or better on the test before the process could continue.

Upon successful completion of the training, the next step was the installation of systems that would allow employee participation. Prior to the pilot program, neither plant had employee-involvement systems. The nonexempt workers were generally older people who came to work, put in their eight hours, and went home. The participative system that was installed consisted of periodic meetings at which managers and workers would review cost and quality figures together and discuss the reasons for increases or decreases. The employees were encouraged to ask questions, examine the data, and, as a group, develop responses to trends and issues.

According to David, "Based on the results of an employee attitude survey, the workforce felt more aligned with the business, a result of increased participation in the identification and resolution of cost and quality issues. The alignment has also caused a role change in management from task supervisor to manufacturing consultant." The employees responded positively to the opportunity to fulfill their need for focus and empowerment. Down the road, as the employees grow, there are plans for more sophisticated data analysis and statistical process control.

These initiatives to provide intrinsic fulfillment to the employees' needs for focus and empowerment were present at both plants. The same opportunities for education and for employee involvement were also provided. The employees at both plants responded well, as indicated by the test results and the participation rates. At this point, the test plant separated from the control plant.

At the test plant, extrinsic compensation was added as an element of the plan. The employees were provided the opportunity to receive incentive compensation for the improvements that could be generated. Thus, at both plants Frito Lay management could observe the specific impact that the addition of extrinsic incentives had on results.

Based on the results at the test plant, they could evaluate the added impact that these incentives contributed to the process.

The Incentive Compensation Design

The test plan was designed around two elements, group participation and individual payout. Thus, management followed through on the observations of Dr. Alyce Dickenson that the most effective incentive designs are those that combine both individual and group elements. A decision was made not to complicate the process by adding the emotional issue of adjusting base pay in this pilot program, so the payout was an add-on to base pay. As such, the employees perceived the plan as a nonthreatening opportunity put forth in good faith.

As stated, the performance objectives were to reduce cost and improve quality. Cost reduction was measured against the standard run rate of the prior year. The previous year's standard cost of production was compared against the ongoing cost of production. Cost savings served as a source of funding for the employees' incentive compensation.

Performance in the area of quality was measured by a composite consisting of such indicators as customer complaints, deviation from the standard color, texture, and density of the product, and the AIB inspection score, which is based on an industry inspection for cleanliness. This composite became the standard against which the performance in quality was compared. According to David, "There was nothing new about these measurements. All production employees were aware of them, but they had never been rewarded for them."

The employees received their share of the gains of improvement on a monthly basis. There was a lag time of one month because of the administrative constraints of data capture and payroll processing. But once the program was up and running, the employees received extrinsic incentive reinforcement on a monthly basis. The compensation was funded from the measurable dollar gain resulting from cost reduction and the more abstract dollar gain resulting from the improvement in quality. The positive dollar variance resulting from a reduction in cost was divided in half, 50 percent to the company and 50 percent to the employees. Each month product quality was measured against the established standard, and the percentage of improvement was determined. That percentage was then multiplied by the month's positive dollar cost variance obtained from the cost improvement. The resulting value was added to the dollar variance to obtain the total incentive compensation for the month. The formula looked like this:

$$\$\text{ cost (employees' share of the gain)} = \frac{\text{positive dollar variance for cost}}{2}$$

$$\$\text{ quality} = \$\text{ cost} \times \%\text{ quality}$$

$$\%\text{ quality} = \frac{\text{quality standard}}{\text{quality performance}}$$

$$\text{incentive compensation} = \$\text{ cost} + \$\text{ quality}$$

In order to assure that there was the proper balance between quality and cost, both performance indicators had to be positive for there to be a payout. This assured the organization that it would pay only for results, and it intuitively told the employees that they were empowered to make balanced decisions that would maximize results for the organization.

Each month, 25 percent of the employees' pool was placed in a reserve account. Because the employees were now partners with the company, this account was to offset the employees' portion of any negative results. At the end of the year, however, any funds in the account were distributed to the employees. Thus, 75 percent of the employees' pool was paid out monthly based on hours worked. The total hours for that period were divided into the employee pool to arrive at a share per hour. Each employee's total hours were multiplied by the share per hour to calculate the incentive compensation earned for the period. Viewing this calculation from a purely financial perspective, the use of total hours worked to determine payout could be seen as rewarding overtime. Frito Lay's management, in the best spirit of behavior-based incentive compensation, chose to view hours worked as a measurement of contribution and reward it. In fact, part of the reason for the one-month lag between performance and payout was the time it took the payroll department to compute overtime. For overtime calculations, the incentive payout was considered as compensation and added to the base pay.

The Results

What were the results of this effort? Was it worth the risk? The answer for the first year was a definite yes, as cost and quality performance exceeded management's expectations. At the test plant, cost and quality performance each improved by more than 10 percent. At the control plant, an increase in volume affected the cost indicators and an increase in new employees to handle the volume affected the quality measurements. Even so, the results were positive. Cost performance improved by 3 percent, and quality performance improved by 4 percent. (Management feels that if these changes had not taken place, performance in both categories would have improved greater than 10 percent.) To add perspective to the performance improvement, it is significant to note that the average Frito Lay plant had an annual improvement rate of 5 percent in both quality and cost during this year. Employee ideas increased by 30 percent in the test plant, by 20 percent in the control plant, and by 10 percent in the average plant in the system.

As part of the evaluation, Frito Lay's management conducted preplan and postplan opinion surveys. The results and variations in the survey responses are as follows:

	Percentage Increase, Control Plant	Percentage Increase, Test Plant
Feedback	4%	10%
Communications	5	10
Working Conditions	4	9
Employee/Management Relations	6	10

Employees at both facilities reported feeling that their job security had improved. They saw the program as an indicator of management commitment and viewed that as a positive addition to the environment.

What a difference in performance results! There is almost a two-to-one difference between the test plant and the control plant. Both plants provided the same intrinsic incentive to improve performance, and the control plant indicates that, by itself, intrinsic incentives had a positive effect on results. Both plants had the same training, performance feedback systems, and employee participation processes. The difference was that one facility provided extrinsic incentives that powered the process.

Total Effectiveness Rating Analysis: Frito Lay

Armed with an understanding of the environment, culture, and compensation plan design, we can use the total effectiveness rating model to analyze the designs. We will first look at the numeric relationship at the control plant. Figure 4-9 shows that classic employee involvement used by itself to fulfill the intrinsic needs of the employees generated a rating of six points. This type of process incorporates only intrinsic compensation and therefore only the intrinsic weights for the factors of focus, positive reinforcement, and empowerment are calculated in the rating.

Next we will look at the numeric relationship at the test plant. Figure 4-10 shows that this pilot facility scored three times higher than

Figure 4-9. Total effectiveness rating for Frito Lay control plant.

Extrinsic Factors			Intrinsic Factors			
Factor	Weight		Weight	Factor		Rating
Why-Pay	0	+	1	Focus	=	1
What-Pay	0	+	2	Positive Reinforcement	=	2
How-Pay	0	+	3	Empowerment	=	3
					Total Points	6

did the control facility. This was the result of combining extrinsic incentive compensation with the employee-involvement systems that provide intrinsic compensation. Adding extrinsic incentive compensation provided the additional source of motivational power in the relationship between the factors of why-pay and focus. The ranking model reflects this relationship by adding their weight values together for a subtotal of two points.

The factor of what-pay was present in sufficient degree to add its basic weighted value (two points) to positive reinforcement, for a normal score of four points. Could this part of the design be enhanced for even greater motivational impact? Perhaps. If, for example, the what-pay opportunity had been 50 percent of base compensation, it certainly would have had a much greater incentive appeal to the participants. As such, we would have assigned it a weight value double its normal weight (from two points to four points, for a subtotal rating of six points).

We can see that the modifying factor of how-pay added considerable weight to the overall total score as a result of its motivational impact. Utilizing a design that included three elements—timely payout, individual payout, and add-on payout—we can see that the factor of how-pay added a triple source of fulfillment to the three intrinsic factors. This modifying influence is reflected in the how-pay modifier points that were added to these factors. The strong secondary motivational impact that how-pay has on the factors of both focus and empowerment can be visualized by the addition of half its basic weighted value (one and one-half points) to each in the modifier column. The greatest impact, however, was on the need for positive reinforcement, which can be visualized by the addition of the full basic weighted value of three points to the modifier column. The three payout elements fit the motivational criteria of positive, immediate, and certain. They powered the behavior models, which relies on positive consequences to drive behavior.

Figure 4-10. Total effectiveness rating for Frito Lay test plant.

Extrinsic Factors		**Intrinsic Factors**		Subtotal Rating	How-Pay Modifier	Total Rating
Factor	Weight	Weight	Factor			
Why-Pay	1	1	Focus	= 2	+ 1.5	= 3.5
What-Pay	2	2	Positive Reinforcement	= 4	+ 3	= 7
(strong) How-Pay	3	3	Empowerment	= 6	+ 1.5	= 7.5
					Total Points	18

Could the design of the plan have been enhanced to increase the motivational effectiveness? From the standpoint of a perfect program, the answer is yes. The factors of focus and empowerment could have been increased by using smaller teams with more specific objectives over which the employees had more control. The performance measurements were general in nature and were applied to all employees as a single team. While the single-team concept most likely promoted unity, the general nature of the performance measurement provided very little in the way of individual accountability.

The performance results of both plants support the analysis of the effectiveness ranking model. Both the effectiveness rating and the performance results demonstrate the impact of behavior-based incentive compensation. The test plant is now considered one of the premier plants in the Frito Lay organization.

GTE's Incentive Compensation Plan

In order to understand the real capability and usefulness of the total effectiveness rating model, we will next use it to analyze an incentive compensation plan that was designed with an emphasis on reducing costs and improving competitive position.

Prior to 1987, performance in the areas of cost and quality in GTE's California telephone operations was not as competitive as senior management wanted it to be. The environment for many years had been one of a regulated utility. The workforce in the telco operations was mostly mature, long-term, and in the upper range of the pay scale. A survey of the salaried employees indicated that they were aware they were paid well, but they had a problem perceiving the link between pay and performance. Instead, they felt that the company paid for seniority. The statistics verified this when the data failed to show any significant variation in performance between the top-ranked employees and the bottom-ranked employees. The linkage between the extrinsic compensation factor of why-pay and the intrinsic factor of focus was weak. The factor of why-pay was failing to fulfill the employees' need for focus, and as a result, performance was lacking.

Dave Engelman, CCP, director of incentive compensation for GTE is enthusiastic about the concept of incentive compensation for the general employee population. According to Dave, "The challenge was to get the employees to feel that what they did meant something in their paychecks." So the compensation department was assigned the task of developing an incentive compensation system that would address the issue. In order to close the performance gap quickly, a consulting firm was called upon to assist them. A study was conducted in October 1987, and the program was launched in January of 1988.

A Volunteer

California thus became the pilot location to test the applicability of utilizing incentive compensation in GTE's telephone operations. While GTE management recognized the impact on performance, quality, and cost that the hourly employees make, it was decided to include only salaried employees in the pilot program.

There was some consideration, but little concern, about the perceptions that might arise on the part of the Public Utilities Commission and consumer watchdog groups over the use of incentive rewards in a rate-regulated environment. Incentives were tied to improvement in business results and were paid in a lump sum, thus not increasing base pay. This would effectively keep salaries down and reduce benefit and annuity costs, benefiting the ratepayers. While these issues are not overly complex, their nuances could be lost on a zealous consumer group to the detriment of the company. However, this was not an issue that the management group would allow to hold them back. Perhaps part of their confidence came from the fact that the competitive telephone companies have been using bonus plans for several years.

Employee focus groups were formed to determine how the employees would feel about an incentive compensation plan that would provide an annual payout in lieu of merit increases. Being middle-aged, the employee population expressed an interest in the effect this would have on benefits and retirement annuities. Any concern in this area was displaced by the potential for payments that would be larger than the merit increases as a result of being tied to performance. Dave Engleman says, "This program is part of a process that will take many years to get in place and have people use. The employees understand and accept it intellectually, and we are working to address the emotional response through their perception. We want them to understand that 'as the company goes, so goes your future and fortune'."

Teams

As part of its organizational development program, GTE Telephone Operations conducts process management training for all managers. This is a transactional analysis approach to the telco operations. The training shows managers how the work flow is organized, breaking the process down to the smallest function and providing insight into how to manage it.

Utilizing this process-management approach, employee-involvement groups were utilized to help identify the teams. Some teams were obvious combinations, and some required the combination of a cross section of disciplines. In order to avoid creating an artificial organization, teams were made up of functional work groups whenever possible. The team leader was the manager of the functional group. In those situations where it was necessary to create a cross-functional group, the manager with the most employees in the group was designated the team leader.

Management established and communicated the objectives of customer focus, quality, and cost. The latter two objectives, quality and cost, are elements of the organization's need for economic value. This is congruent with management's concern for the competitive position of the organization and provides the proper focus to the employees. Once the objectives were established, it was the responsibility of the teams to develop their own criteria for improvement within the context of the overall objectives.

Because the incentive plan was to be team-based, a program was developed to provide team leader training. This training consisted of a history of the evolutionary process that resulted in the current compensation planning, a thorough review of the mechanics of the incentive compensation plan design, and basic leadership skills. A module on compensation was provided to all participating employees, along with training on how to work within a team.

The team leaders were considered to be the first source of information for the team. It was up to them to communicate the program and its impact on the organization to the team. Other forms of communication consisted of quarterly employee meetings, where performance was reviewed, and the employee newspaper. The meetings provided feedback to the team as to their performance and the performance of the organization as a whole.

After the plan had been designed, the next step was to enlist the active involvement of the senior executives. That was not difficult because management was enthusiastic about closing the performance gap between the California operations and their competition. The president was active in the program roll-out and the quarterly performance review meetings.

The Compensation Mechanics

The overall concept of using compensation as a tool to manage performance consisted of two elements. The first element was the traditional focus on control of compensation costs. The organization's goal was a pay practice where the total cash compensation would be at midpoint of the marketplace. The second element involved the use of incentive compensation. The salaried employees' total targeted cash compensation was to be 90 percent of base pay with 10 percent variable incentive pay tied to specific performance indicators.

The first step in the implementation was to put in place a process that would result in establishing the average base compensation at 90 percent of market midpoint. This would be achieved over a three-year period by freezing the range movement and splitting the annual pay-increase budget in half with 50 percent to be used in merit increases for employees identified as exceptional performers. This concept of rewarding individual performance was called "pockets of excellence." No more than 75 percent of the employees could receive this increase in one year. By freezing range movement and reducing merit increases, salary growth would be slowed. When the employees' base compensation reached 90 percent of market value, the merit increase process would maintain it at that level.

Figure 4-11 shows the three-year plan to reach the desired payline. Relying on projections of inflation and market demand to control the range movement, reductions in merit increases were used to put 10 percent of the employees' compensation at risk. That 10 percent was utilized to fund the variable portion of the compensation plan. With this approach, management was assured either a reduction in compensation costs or an improvement in performance for the same costs.

The merit increase budget was allocated in the following manner.

50% variable lump sum:	50% company objectives
	50% team objectives
50% merit increase to base:	75% of population eligible

Half of the merit increase budget was allocated for the incentive compensation plan. Half of the incentive budget (25 percent of the merit increase budget) would be paid to the employees for performance against their team-defined objectives and the other half would be paid out for performance against the company-defined objectives. According to Dave Engelman, "The purpose of having two levels,

Figure 4-11. 90-10 split.

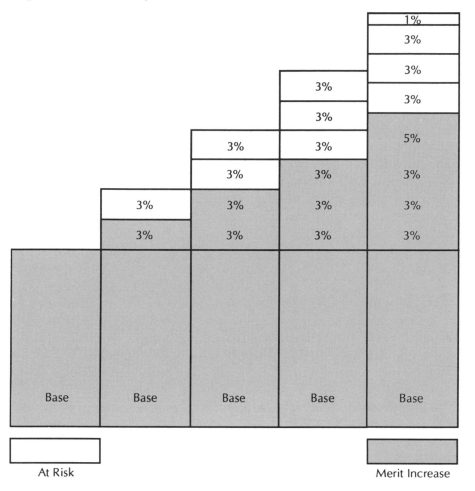

team and company, was to get the employees focused on the company's needs as well as their team's needs. There was a time when the employees didn't know what these company needs were. We had to get them to be more outside focused. We wanted them to become aware of the need to satisfy their customer, internal or external, and to meet the financial needs of the organization. We used compensation to reinforce how important these indicators are to the company." The plan was designed to utilize the extrinsic incentive factor of why-pay to fulfill the employees' intrinsic need for focus and to use the extrinsic incentive factor of what-pay to fulfill their intrinsic need for positive reinforcement.

The performance objectives were set aggressively because of the competitive position that the organization was in. During the month of April, the employees would receive their incentive compensation for the year. If performance was at 100 percent of plan, the employees would receive 100 percent of the compensation that had been put at risk. If performance improved beyond plan, the employees would receive incremental compensation beyond 100 percent. This lump-sum payment was not considered base compensation and did not affect benefits or retirement calculations.

There was no specific attempt to attach a dollar value to an increment of improvement in the targeted categories. Due to the at-risk factor in the pilot plan design, management agreed to assume that, for the quality indicator, performance above 100 percent of plan would automatically generate savings sufficient to pay for the additional incentive compensation.

Improvement in performance over the baseline was calculated as a percentile. A multiplier of 10 percent would bring total targeted cash compensation to the midpoint of the new salary range. This was a control element that assured improvement in the organization's overall performance. An additional 10 percent was available based on overachievement. From a motivational design standpoint, this was the real incentive opportunity available to the employees. Management had some concern over the mechanics of the payout matrix because the quality measurement numbers were based on perception and were therefore subjective. As a result, the company decided on a payout cap of 20 percent as protection against overpayment.

The payout percentile was the same for each member of a team and was applied to their individual midpoints as a multiplier. The use of midpoint as the base from which the incentive compensation was calculated ensured that each employee was paid on an equitable basis. The issues of seniority and low penetration into the range did not become items of concern to the employees. In an environment where most of the employees were above midpoint, using midpoint as a basis for payout calculation rather than actual salary had a favorable impact on cost reduction and supported management's business objective. In addition, in order to be eligible for the team payout, an employee had to have been a member of the team for at least one year.

One of the difficulties with this design was the fact that salaries weren't slowing down quick enough. A stable economy with a relatively low rate of inflation kept the pressure off salary increases, but it also acted to slow the reduction process. Dave Engelman states that, "We were coming from a culture where everyone got something every year, and so we were conservative in our design. We wanted the transition time to be three years, but it looks like it will take four years, maybe longer at our first pilot site. We are learning from our pilot, and in the plans going forward we will utilize a 30/70 split—30 percent of the merit budget will be used as merit increases for our 'pockets of excellence,' with a maximum of 50 percent of the employee population being eligible. We intend to make the transition period as short as possible."

More important was a motivational issue that arose from the extrinsic compensation factor of how-pay. The California region is a large operation with over 4,000 salaried employees. Because the teams were defined by organizational and functional unit, some teams had as many as 400 employees in them. Feedback from employees told management that this design was not fulfilling their need for empowerment in the most effective way. They indicated a desire for smaller teams with more specific measurements that they could impact directly.

Dave relates that, "They felt that if the objectives were driven lower into the organization, they would have more control of things. They also told us they would like to have a higher proportion of their incentive tied to objectives that they could control. We listen to our employees, and while we are going to let the pilot run through the transition period, we are incorporating their suggestions into our telephone operations model. The design for the southern region includes small teams. The average team size will be twenty employees, and none will have more than fifty members. We are now incorporating a 30/70 split to the merit increase budget element, with 70 percent tied to performance. Of that 70 percent, 30 percent is based on company performance indicators and 40 percent is based on team performance indicators."

Results

Was the pilot plan effective? Did it have an impact on the bottom line and the competitive position of the telco operations? Did it encourage greater employee participation and performance? According to Engelman, "The rate of improvement is greater in our companies where it exists than in those where it doesn't." One indicator of effectiveness was that the business customer opinion survey conducted after the first year rated the California operation a full six points above the target. The average telco in the system rated two points above the target.

The overall concept was to use compensation as an element in a team-based process that would void the seniority issue and work on business objectives. The intent was to have compensation assume the function of a management tool that could be utilized in the human resources area. Other initiatives, such as operational adjustments and changes in the sales organization, were introduced in conjunction with the incentive compensation plan and affected performance results. Dave Engelman concludes that "Incentive compensation shouldn't be looked at as just a human resources program, it should be viewed as a dynamic tool that needs to be part of a dynamic management process."

The Total Effectiveness Rating Analysis: GTE

Armed with the background data that we have, we can use the total effectiveness rating model to analyze the design for motivational effectiveness. The numeric relationship displayed by the model shows the difference in motivational impact that a plan can have when the extrinsic factor of how-pay is emphasized. In Figure 4-12, how-pay did not act as a significant modifier, and therefore its basic weighted value was applied only to the intrinsic factor of empowerment. Large teams, requiring general performance indicators, do not provide the most focus, reinforcement, or sense of empowerment to the employees.

In addition, payout on an annual basis does not conform to the motivational criteria of positive, immediate, and certain. In the rating model, this is reflected in the relationship between the factor of how-pay and its influence on positive reinforcement. It is so insignificant as to have no relative impact, providing very little in the way of emphasis to energize the behavior model and reinforce performance. The design of GTE's pilot program appears to have been focused primarily on the compensation factors of cost and mechanics. The factor of what-pay is assigned a value of one point, 50 percent less than its basic weighted value (two points) due to the relatively low incentive opportunity. Owing to three factors—a relatively low incentive opportunity (what-pay), a relatively weak linkage of individual performance to reward, and a long time frame between performance to payout—the pilot plan rates eleven points.

This is not to say that the California plan was unsuccessful. Indeed, the data show that it was successful from the standpoint of performance improvement. It was also successful as a pilot plan

Figure 4-12. Total effectiveness rating for GTE California.

Extrinsic Factors		**Intrinsic Factors**			Subtotal Rating	How-Pay Modifier	Total Rating
Factor	Weight	Weight	Factor				
Why-Pay	1	1	Focus	=	2	+ 0	= 2
(weak)							
What-Pay	1	2	Positive Reinforcement	=	3	+ 0	= 3
(weak)							
How-Pay	3	3	Empowerment	=	6	+ 0	= 6
						Total Points	11

because it did all the things it was supposed to do. Pilot plans are essentially test approaches to help determine what works and what needs adjustment. GTE's management did exactly that.

The design for GTE's southern region shows a significant increase to the numeric relationships in the rating model. This design enhanced the extrinsic factor of how-pay and, in doing so, enabled it to influence and enhance the intrinsic factors of focus, positive reinforcement, and empowerment. Changing the design to accommodate small teams made it possible to measure the objectives and performance much more specifically, thus enhancing the employees' sense of focus. Combined with the change in the size of the incentive opportunity and how the incentive compensation was allocated, the small teams provided an opportunity for the employees to control a larger degree of their payout and significantly increased their sense of empowerment. Figure 4-13 shows a seven-point increase in the effectiveness rating indicator.

Could GTE further enhance the motivational impact of their southern region plan? From the standpoint of a perfect program, the answer is yes. Providing the payout on a more timely basis would increase the frequency of positive consequences to the employees and thus tighten the relationship between the factors of how-pay and positive reinforcement. The rating model would reflect this increase in motivational impact by adding weight value points to the factor of positive reinforcement in the how-pay modifier column. This would result in an increase in the overall effectiveness rating of the program design.

Observations

It's interesting to note that both the Frito Lay pilot and the GTE pilot initially started with large teams. While multiple small teams require

Figure 4-13. Total effectiveness rating for GTE southern region.

Extrinsic Factors		Intrinsic Factors		Subtotal Rating	How-Pay Modifier	Total Rating
Factor	Weight	Weight	Factor			
Why-Pay	1	+ 1	Focus	= 2	+ 3	= 5
What-Pay	2	+ 2	Positive Reinforcement	= 4	+ 0	= 4
(strong) How-Pay	3	+ 3	Empowerment	= 6	+ 3	= 9
					Total Points	18

a significantly greater investment in administrative effort, the behavior-based incentive compensation concept suggests that the returns could well warrant this effort. The real potential of incentive compensation lies in the fact that it allows employees to determine their own standard of living based on how much of a contribution they want to make. They need to perceive that they have the opportunity to make an impact.

On the one hand, we have seen that individual incentives will drive individual performance but may not be compatible with employee personalities or organizational business objectives and management styles. After all, much of business requires an army of good, steady performers who work in a cooperative environment. On the other hand, we have seen that large, amorphous teams provide the employees with little sense of control or contribution. Thus, one of the first questions to ask when developing a performance-based incentive compensation plan is "How will we group the participants to maximize the plan's motivational effectiveness?" It is important not to let administrative burdens determine the plan design.

Peter F. Drucker has been quoted as saying. "Performance becomes a job for which someone is responsible." The employees feel that way too. At GTE, they expressed a desire for smaller teams that would permit performance objectives to be more closely aligned with their ability to impact them. This requires two things: (1) development of performance-measurement systems for all aspects of the organization, and (2) management's willingness to make these data available to the employees. Not a bad idea really, and certainly one that most management theories espouse. The reality of the business world is that performance measurement and data management are extremely difficult administrative tasks. In the daily effort to get the product or service delivered to the client, this administrative function usually takes place to a degree sufficient only to satisfy minimum needs.

Take heart. The evolution of electronic data processing technology and the advent of the current total quality management movement have helped foster an acceptance of the fact that all performance can be measured. That's good, because the most effective behavior-based incentive compensation plans require an organization to address this issue in a formal manner. The development of systems to capture, manage, and report data more precisely than ever before will be much to the organization's benefit.

Note

1. *Worklife*, 8:1 (July 1988), p. 4. (Newsletter of the American Productivity and Quality Center, Houston.)

5

The Why-Pay Factor: Linking Organizational Needs to Employee Needs

In Chapter 4, we developed a ranking model that would allow us to tailor the outcome of an incentive plan by balancing the components. To maximize the effectiveness of this application, it is necessary to define in specific terms the business needs of the organization. To that end, we will apply the Fishbone diagram to the organization's side of the behavior-based incentive compensation formula:

$$\frac{\text{Behavioral}}{\text{psychology}} + \frac{\text{incentive}}{\text{compensation}} = \frac{\text{performance}}{\text{improvement}}$$

and use it to determine the critical success factors that are associated with an organization's performance improvement.

Figure 5-1 shows what the organization's side of the behavior-based incentive compensation Fishbone looks like. Any organization that is focused on performance improvement will be concerned with either or both of two major classifications: organizational effectiveness and economic value. Some of the critical success factors of organizational effectiveness are unity, superior execution, and management skills. Some of the critical success factors of economic value are human resources investment and key performance indicators. Like the important factors on the employees' side of the Fishbone diagram (to which they are linked), each of the organization's critical success factors is made up of multiple elements. These elements, which can be called specific functional needs, are the underlying needs that an organization must fulfill in order to maximize its potential. The closer an organization comes to fulfilling all aspects of these needs, the closer it will be to operating at peak effectiveness.

Figure 5-1. Organization's specific functional needs.

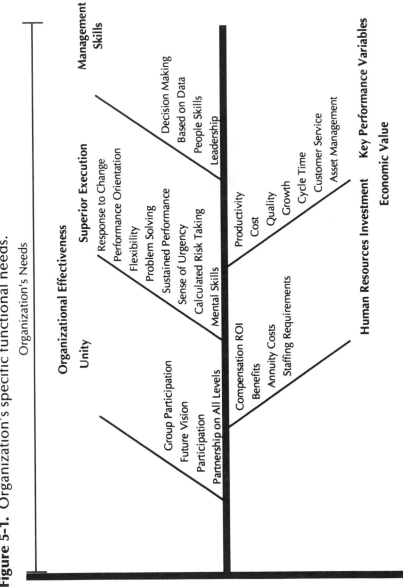

Organization's Needs

Organizational Effectiveness

Unity

Superior Execution

Management Skills

Group Participation
Future Vision
Participation
Partnership on All Levels

Response to Change
Performance Orientation
Flexibility
Problem Solving
Sustained Performance
Sense of Urgency
Calculated Risk Taking
Mental Skills

Decision Making
Based on Data
People Skills
Leadership

Compensation ROI
Benefits
Annuity Costs
Staffing Requirements

Productivity
Cost
Quality
Growth
Cycle Time
Customer Service
Asset Management

Human Resources Investment

Key Performance Variables

Economic Value

Organizational Effectiveness

Organizational effectiveness can broadly be defined as how well an organization's culture and environment support the business objectives. The classification of organizational effectiveness, located on the upper half of the Fishbone, encompasses the intrinsic needs of the organization. Like the employees' intrinsic needs, these organizational needs are "quality sensitive." They are directly linked to the human resources element of the organization and, for that reason, are issues of motivation.

In assessing the effectiveness of an organization's human resources, we can see that quality-sensitive elements fall under three categories: unity, superior execution, and management skills. Unity requires that all employees share the same vision of the organization's future and work together to realize that vision. Without unity, the employees will work at odds with themselves and the organization, thus diluting the effectiveness of their contribution. Unity is especially difficult in large organizations, where leadership is centralized and communications as to the organization's status are infrequent and diffuse.

Figure 5-2 illustrates the congruent relationships that exist between the specific functional needs of an organization and the intrinsic and extrinsic needs of the employees. It shows that the critical success factor of unity within an organization relates to the intrinsic factor of focus on the part of the employees. An organization that achieves unity will do so as a result of having provided all employees with opportunities to fulfill their intrinsic need for focus. In effect, organizational unity is a by-product of employee focus.

The specific functional needs that make up the organization's critical success factor of superior execution are elements of the need for all employees to perform, on a continual and ongoing basis, in a manner that achieves the organization's intended objectives. This requires that all employees assume ownership of the organization's objectives and of the results of their actions as they relate to the achievement of those objectives.

Figure 5-2 shows that superior execution relates primarily to the employees' intrinsic needs for positive reinforcement and empowerment. Employees who have a vested interest in the outcome, who are involved, committed, and provided with the opportunity to make a difference, will perform in a manner that will result in the organization realizing superior execution.

The third critical success factor of organizational effectiveness is management skills. These skills, possessed in varying degrees by all employees, determine the quality of interaction between and among all of the human resources. In the workplace, this interaction is

Figure 5-2. The congruent BBIC Fishbone.

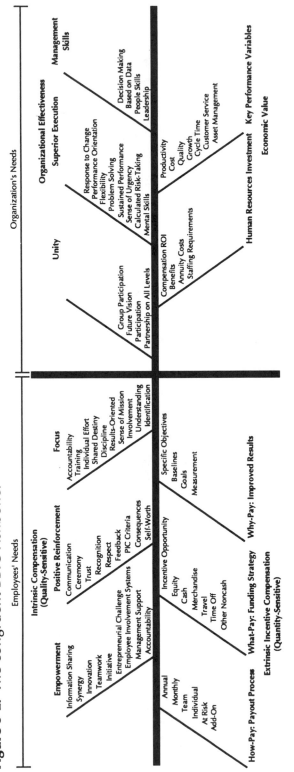

usually directive in nature and requires the specification of some outcome. Even though we call them "management" skills, in the day-to-day reality of the workplace these skills are required of all employees. They are the skills of interpersonal relations, of data analysis and decision making, and of leadership. The more these skills are utilized by the general employee population, the greater will be the organization's effectiveness.

Figure 5-2 shows that the specific functional needs that are the elements of management skills have multiple linkage to the employees' intrinsic needs of focus, positive reinforcement, and empowerment. This observation is in keeping with the definition of management skills as being skills of interaction. As was the case with unity and superior execution, an organization strong in management skills will have successfully addressed the employees' needs for focus, positive reinforcement, and empowerment. This multiple linkage shows in graphic form what we already knew intuitively: that management skills have a wide-ranging impact on the success of any incentive compensation program. The Fishbone diagram shows us that while incentive compensation programs may exist by reason of a compensation matrix, the degree of their effectiveness is a direct result of human dynamics.

Economic Value

In the Fishbone diagram, the classification of economic value deals with the financial implications of a behavior-based incentive compensation plan. We see in Figure 5-2 that the classification of economic value is located on the lower half of the Fishbone. It is assigned this position opposite the extrinsic needs of the employees' side of the Fishbone because economic value is an extrinsic need of the organization. From the standpoint of behavior-based incentive compensation, the classification of economic value refers to a favorable return on the financial investment that has been made in the human resources. Two critical success factors are normally associated with economic value—human resources investment and key performance variables. Human resources investment is in turn made up of specific functional needs that are associated with the underlying economics of labor cost, labor leverage on profitability, and other such issues. Key performance variables include specific functional needs that are associated with the performance-improvement opportunities that the employees can impact positively.

The critical success factors that make up an organization's economic value criteria are "quantity sensitive" in nature. The specific functional needs that are part of these factors normally have measurable values that reflect performance results. As such, they relate directly to the extrinsic compensation factors on the employees' side of the Fishbone diagram. This linkage completes the BBIC Fishbone and closes the loop of relationships between the needs of the employees and the needs of the organization. In the design of a behavior-based incentive compensation plan, this closed loop assures that if the employees are provided with the opportunities to fulfill intrinsic and extrinsic needs, the organization will, as a result, fulfill specific functional needs. These needs will be a function of the types of personal needs that the employees are given the opportunity to address.

The first consideration most managements have in developing a behavior-based incentive compensation plan is almost automatically one of cost control. We have seen that this is not necessarily the most effective approach to addressing the specific functional needs associated with organizational effectiveness and economic value. These needs can best be addressed by viewing the compensation budget as an investment in human resources in order to improve performance.

In a properly designed compensation plan based on the BBIC Fishbone, the organization's specific functional need for value in the human resources investment will relate directly to the funding strategy element in the employee's extrinsic compensation factor of what-pay and the improved performance results element in the employee's extrinsic compensation factor of why-pay. Put another way, the very nature of a properly designed behavior-based incentive compensation plan will ensure the greatest return on investment in the area of human resources by tying staffing and compensation costs to the key performance variables that provide economic value. The concept of compensation is no longer that of a financial cost but, at this point, has evolved into the concept of an operational tool for performance improvement.

Figure 5-2 is the complete, congruent behavior-based incentive compensation Fishbone diagram. The completion of this diagram provides us with a full picture of the concepts behind the BBIC formula. We now understand that performance improvement is the fulfillment of the organization's specific functional needs, both in the effectiveness of its operations and in the economic return on its investment in human resources. While other business models may emphasize strategic planning, the economic environment, or technological changes, in this formula employees are the key element. This operational formula deals with the excellence of execution.

Using the formula—which is, by definition, static in design—we can see that the amount of organizational effectiveness and economic value that will accrue to the organization will be directly related to the degree that behavioral psychology and incentive compensation are incorporated in the plan design. (See Figure 4-5.) We also know that the Fishbone diagram and total effectiveness ranking model can help determine the most effective combination of these elements.

Linkage: Economic Value and Extrinsic Compensation

Having established the foundation of BBIC and the tools by which to design and evaluate the proper balance of a motivationally effective program, we can use these tools to determine which compensation criteria will deliver increased economic value to the organization. The rest of this chapter will be devoted to the identification and discussion of these criteria. Moving from the conceptual to the specific, our discussion will parallel the approach you might take if given the assignment to develop an incentive compensation plan for the general employee population.

There are three key elements that should be held as the cornerstones of any behavior-based incentive compensation plan. The plan must be strategically sound, motivationally sound, and financially sound.

Strategically Sound

To be strategically sound, any plan must consider a company's organizational effectiveness and economic value. The employees' extrinsic compensation portion of the design should be based on the organization's business objectives. Using the Fishbone diagram, we see the specific performance objectives that the employees are focused on and that are determined by the extrinsic compensation factor of why-pay should be directly related to the organization's key performance variables.

This is obvious enough on the surface, but when we consider all of the factors that go into organizational effectiveness and economic value, they sometimes become difficult to prioritize. Strategically sound performance objectives are usually customer-oriented and help to position the company for the future. Many times the objectives are vaguely defined on the strategic level and become increasingly difficult to associate with the farther down into the organization they cascade. How, then, to tie them to performance?

The Fishbone and the BBIC formula can help establish and maintain our focus in this process. However, the best test for strategic soundness in the design of a BBIC plan is to see if you can deduce the organization's needs based on the why-pay design of the plan. When designing a behavior-based incentive compensation plan, it is necessary to understand the strategic factors that drive the success of the organization within its industry. These factors include the needs to be the low-cost producer, to be the highest quality provider, to be the most responsive and flexible to the market, or to be at the forefront in research. Time for the compensation professional to don the hat of the strategic planner.

Once the strategic factors have been identified, it is then necessary to understand how the local objectives pyramid upward into the organization's strategic objectives. If the organization's strategic objective is growth, do the local objectives relate to the need for fast-paced production capabilities? If the organization's strategic objective is dominance, do the local objectives relate to the need for partnering with the customer, the need for total organizational performance, or both? If the organization's strategic objective is profit, do the local objectives relate to the need for individual product emphasis and cost control? Will the improvement that you are paying for result in the operational improvement that you want? Does this operational improvement translate into financial improvement? Is the design such that the additional contribution of human potential will improve the company's position? Time for the compensation professional to don the hat of the chief financial officer and operations analyst.

Motivationally Sound

To be motivationally sound, any compensation plan must take into consideration the fact that employees have needs that are both intrinsic and extrinsic. We have seen that extrinsic compensation elements can be used to address the employees' intrinsic needs. The linkage between employee needs, organizational needs, and compensation becomes evident when we use the Fishbone to identify the specific functional needs of organizational effectiveness and the associated intrinsic compensation needs of the employees. These needs for organizational effectiveness can also be evaluated and linked to the organization's key performance variables. The result will be an extrinsic compensation package that utilizes the factors of why-pay, what-pay, and how-pay in a balanced manner.

The most effective plan design should be able to address the more esoteric performance issues such as "intent." Balanced properly, the plan elements should develop within each employee a sense of accountability for results and an attitude of total customer focus and then relate these attitudes to the fulfillment of personal needs.

By using the Fishbone as a tool to develop the plan, it is possible to address the specifics of employee performance that will fulfill the organization's needs. The Fishbone can answer the employees' question, "What can I do?" Generalities in the areas of performance objectives or measurement tend to dilute the impact of any incentive plan. Looking at it from the point of view of the employee, there is a big difference between a design structure that says "Improve profitability and share" and one that says "Improve your department's contribution as defined and measured by this specific set of criteria, and earn according to the following schedule of incremental improvement." The latter structure is positive, immediate, and certain.

The case histories that we have examined and will examine show that there is a direct correlation between specific objectives and measurement and the effectiveness of a plan. And the more the objectives are within the participant's control, the greater will be both the participation and the improvement. An exception to this rule is the objective of "quality." Often an end-user customer satisfaction index is used in conjunction with more immediate measurements to build a culture of quality awareness and performance. This exception is due to the difficulty of defining quality as it applies to the day-to-day performance of each employee. Because there is an esoteric element to its definition, employees accept the concept of quality with the understanding that "quality is what the customer says it is."

In order not to have a plan design that is overly protective to the organization from a financial standpoint and thus undermotivational to the employees, it is necessary to test the motivational soundness of the design. A good test for this is made up of the following questions:

- Does the plan focus the employees' energies on activities or results?
- Can the participants impact the objectives established by the factor of why-pay and thus earn the incentive?
- Is the reward substantial and attractive enough to stimulate participation?
- Is there a realistic opportunity to earn the reward?
- Will it work?

In general terms, if you place yourself in the position of the employee who will be participating in the plan and ask "What's in it for me?" and "How can I make an impact?" candid answers will indicate how motivationally sound the plan is. The other elements of motivation, such as the organization's environment and culture, communications, and training issues that fit in the psychic income factor of the formula, will be covered in Chapters 8 and 9 which discuss support structures and application tools.

Financially Sound

Addressing the needs of both employees and the organization is the way to achieve performance improvement. But it is all for naught unless it makes sense from a value standpoint. Can the organization's need for economic value and the employees' need for extrinsic compensation be satisfied in a mutually beneficial manner? The financial design of a plan should address the company's interests. The performance objectives, established as the result of a balanced relationship between an organization's key performance variables and the extrinsic compensation factor of why-pay, should be focused both internally and externally.

The elements that are focused internally should emphasize, encourage, and reward the involvement and commitment that results in good planning. These indicators are normally associated with budget issues. The elements that are focused externally should emphasize, encourage, and reward the participation and contribution that results in good performance. These indicators are normally associated with competitive issues.

A good test for financial soundness is to ask the following questions:

- Do we have the right pay philosophy?
- Does the total cash compensation remain within the company's pay philosophy?
- Is the financial well-being of the participant in jeopardy?
- Is the plan self-funding?
- Does the plan provide an acceptable return on investment?
- Is it worth it?

Interestingly enough, financial objectives that are driven to the department level will generate the sense of meaningful work that is sought by employees. The three cornerstones of an effective behavior-based incentive compensation plan—strategic soundness, motivational soundness, and financial soundness—are synergistic in their content, acting in concert to strengthen the plan's impact on employee performance.

In Support of Financial Soundness

All performance objectives, whether or not they are part of a behavior-based incentive compensation plan, have as a primary attribute a direct relationship to the factor of financial soundness. In turn, a company's financial soundness is generally indicated by its performance in four categories:

1. Strategic performance
2. External performance
3. Internal (within the organization) performance
4. Personal performance

Strategic performance can be defined for the purpose of behavior-based incentive compensation in terms of macro indicators such as the percentage of market share the organization holds, and the organization's reputation for quality in the marketplace. External performance is often measured by indicators such as how well the organization performs against the competition and financial indicators such as profit and return on investment. Internal performance is often measured by such indicators as conformance to budget, productivity, cost, and some nonfinancial indicators. Personal performance, in today's environment, is most often measured by such indicators as performance appraisals and Management By Objective-type techniques.

If we look at the organization's side of the BBIC Fishbone diagram—the side that indicates the organization's specific functional needs—we can see that most of these needs are associated with the personal and internal performance objectives and are measured by the indicators we have discussed. This observation helps narrow our focus in establishing the objectives for an incentive compensation plan. These personal and internal performance objectives can logically be listed on the employees' needs side of the BBIC Fishbone diagram, under the factor of why-pay.

The point here is that in a large and complex organization it is difficult to find aggregate results, be they financial (such as profit) or nonfinancial (such as productivity), that have a universal meaning to all participants. The strategic and external objectives are established by senior management. To be effective in a behavior-based incentive compensation plan, the specific functional needs of the organization should address and impact these objectives on an internal and personal level. This means that the deeper into the organization we go with incentive compensation, the more we will have to rely on local, perhaps nonfinancial measurements that are specific and controllable by the employee.

Incentive Objectives and the Nature of Work

In the design of behavior-based incentive compensation plans, the transfer from financial-based plan objectives to nonfinancial-based plan objectives seems to occur somewhere in the middle ranks of management. The reason for this appears to be that at this level the nature of work changes. Below this level, there is less opportunity for creative thinking, and greater emphasis is placed on information gathering and processing and also task execution. It is important to understand that the local objectives will change as the nature of the work changes. The objectives will be less strategic and external in nature and more internal and personal in nature. As such, the performance objectives that we choose for an incentive compensation plan will be most effective if they are relevant to the participants and address the meaningful aspects of their work. Naturally, these objectives should relate to the strategic objectives through some upward path.

It is at this transition level in the middle ranks that the structure of a behavior-based incentive compensation plan assumes a dual purpose. Here, focusing downward, a behavior-based incentive compensation plan functions to (1) provide strong direction to activities and (2) define levels of performance. We can see this by referring to the Fishbone diagram. On the employee needs side, we see that the intrinsic factor of focus contains the elements that direct activities, while the compensation factor of why-pay contains the elements that define levels of results. This is one more observation of how the factors interlink to support the effectiveness of the plan and why it is so important to be aware of these linkages as we design the plans.

It is important to note that the more the nature of work changes, then, the more the objectives will change, the more the type of incentive elements will change, and the more the communication needs will change. Long-term incentives on the executive level are designed for a specific nature of work that is more global in nature, whereas short-term incentives have proven to be more effective with a general employee population level because of the more specific nature of the work and the socioeconomic level of the participants.

The organization's objectives are established by senior management, and the employees' objectives should be elements that fulfill the organization's needs. Those elements can be found in the factor of why-pay, and it is to this factor that we now direct our attention.

Information Technology

While there is no doubt that specific, local, "personalized" measures can be hard to identify and difficult to administer, it's not an impossible job. First, the identification of these measures can be facilitated through the use of a tool appropriately called the objective-identification process (OIP) and through the use of employee focus groups. Second, although there is no getting around the fact that behavior-based incentive compensation plans will increase the organization's administrative burden, up-to-date information technology is increasingly easing the burden of these tasks.

In their vision of the not-so-distant future, Linda Applegate, James Cash, and D. Quinn Mills, all professors at Harvard Business

School, see a business environment where workers are better trained and more transient, where the work environment is more engaging and stimulating, where job descriptions that are tied to a set of narrowly defined tasks are no longer functional, and where compensation is tied more directly to contribution. In a *Harvard Business Review* article on the impact of information technology in the workplace, they conclude that employees will require the workplace to be rewarding and the compensation to be appropriate to their contribution.[1]

Applegate, Cash, and Mills also foresee an ability to track and report on each individual's contribution and degree of participation. This technology will provide the opportunity to pay each individual based on individual performance, resolving many of the administrative and equity issues that currently face those who desire to implement a broad-based incentive compensation plan. Thus, for the compensation professionals and the staff responsible for program administration, there is hope.

Performance Objectives

Although the objective identification process tends to focus on specific, immediate goals, long-term objectives also have a place in the design of incentive plans. There is no reason why a strategic objective, such as market share, could not be tied to a capital-accumulation incentive for the general employee population just as it is applied in the executive ranks. In fact, we have seen this approach taken by PepsiCo in their all-employee stock option plan. Quality is another objective that can benefit from either a long-term or short-term incentive possibility. It seems to be one of the few aggregate nonfinancial objectives that employees respond to enthusiastically. Perhaps this is because they realize that quality is an attribute of every action they take and, therefore, they can impact it.

A Big Picture Starts the Design

After considering all the macro issues that we have discussed, the first step in the process of identifying objectives and measures in a plan for nonsales, nonexecutive employees is to view the situation from the standpoint of its financial implications. In keeping with tradition, these financial implications are of a cost-focused nature. But this time the cost is seen not as part of the compensation budget; here it is cost of an operating nature.

In looking at opportunities, objectives, and the ability to make an impact on revenues, we will work under the premise that the sales function has the primary role. Looking at profitability, we see that senior management has the primary impact. Using this logic, we see that the primary opportunity in the operations function, a function that has structured policies and procedures and exists to serve the sales and executive functions, will be in the area of operating costs.

In developing the criteria for an incentive plan in the operations area, it will be helpful to look initially at how these operating costs relate to each other. In doing so, we can identify the cost category that will serve as an appropriate incentive compensation objective. For example, if we look at operating costs in relation to total revenues, we can develop an understanding of where the greatest opportunity for improvement exists. In a labor-intensive industry such as health care or banking, the relationship of costs to revenues could look something like this:

| Materials and capital: | 33% of total revenues |
| Labor costs: | 66% of total revenues |

Should the overall plan objectives focus on the cost of materials and capital or on the labor cost? If the area of greatest opportunity appears to be in the area of labor cost, then the next step in our consideration should be to include its impact on the economic environment. For example, we would then want to decide whether to manage labor costs in the manner similar to the GTE California operation we reviewed in Chapter 4, or to focus on raising productivity while maintaining costs at a constant level.

In another example, an organization has the following cost-to-cost relationships:

| Material costs: | 65% of total costs |
| Labor costs: | 15% of total costs |

In this scenario, should the incentive plan's objectives be to manage labor costs or to make the best use of the materials, perhaps by focusing on scrap and rework? Obviously, the plan's overall objectives here should focus on the elements of materials costs, the area of greatest opportunity.

A big-picture look at the relationship of costs to each other and to revenues can often provide insight as to what would be appropriate objectives and measures for an incentive plan design. But the real direction needs to come from senior management, and it is the job of the compensation professional to provide assistance, support, and professional guidance in this process. One very effective approach to identifying the organization's general objectives, especially when they are not obvious, is called the objective-identification process.

The Objective-Identification Process

OIP is essentially an executive group pinpointing process, a method of identifying and prioritizing those objectives that senior management considers to be of fundamental importance to the organization. OIP is normally conducted in a highly participative manner.

There are three stages to the objective-identification process. The first stage is to interview key senior managers and to generate a list of their twenty-five (or some other square number) key objectives. (This process requires the use of a square number for the calculation of priorities.) The second stage is to have each executive place a relative importance on each objective. This process will allow you to document individual priorities and group priorities. It will also provide data that will show levels of agreement between individuals and groups. The third stage is a facilitation process, where the data are discussed with the executive team. At this point, the disparate issues are identified and discussed, and a final list of prioritized objectives is established.

OIP is really an organizational-development technique and is yet another example of how the compensation process is expanding into other human resources disciplines. Effectively conducted, this process will arrive at the core organizational objectives from which all objectives for the incentive compensation plan will eventually be derived. The full explanation of this technique, with all the nuances that ensure success, is outside the scope of this book. However, when you are ready to apply the objective-identification process, support can be found from the organizational development group within your human resources organization. From a purely mechanical process, the procedure is as follows:

1. Determine the individuals who will participate in the process. Normally this would be the president and the executives who report directly to the president.
2. Obtain support from the executives.
3. Conduct a meeting where the president sets the expectations of the process. All participants in the meeting should be asked to prepare a list of the objectives that, from their functional perspective, they think the organization should focus on.
4. Interview the participants individually to develop a clear list that is formatted consistently.
5. Identify the top twenty-five statements and code them by assigning a letter of the alphabet to each one, to assist in prioritizing the list.

6. Ask all participants to sort your list of twenty-five objectives in the order that they perceive to be the priority *to the organization overall,* according to a normal bell curve pattern of distribution (see Figure 5-3). Placement within a column has no significance. However, the choice of columns should indicate the participant's opinion of relative importance. For example, the five objectives in column "0" are more important than the four objectives in column "–1" and are less important than the four objectives in column "1."

7. The analysis of the data can be accomplished with the use of a spreadsheet. With one axis representing the numeric values and the other axis representing the alphabetical coding, it will be possible to plot how each participant rated the objective.

8. An average value for each objective can be obtained by adding all the values for that objective and dividing the sum by the number of participants. This data can then be utilized to stack rank the objectives from highest priority to lowest priority.

A big-picture perspective on what the executive team perceives the organization's objectives to be can be developed by reviewing the objective statements themselves. At this point, try to group the statements into categories that relate to the organization's specific functional needs as displayed in the BBIC Fishbone, identifying which of the five major factors they most closely align with: human resources investment, key performance variables, unity, superior execution, or management skills.

Figure 5-3. Bell curve pattern of normal distribution.

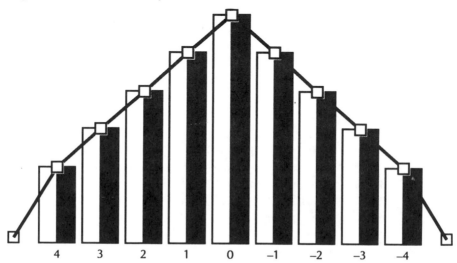

If you then go back to the numbers assigned to each objective, you will be able to see (1) if similar objectives were closely ranked together and (2) where they placed in the ranking. The final step is a process of executive alignment, resolution, and consensus. This process can be facilitated by a cross-functional team made up of professionals in the field of compensation and organizational development. The resulting information will provide the foundation for the identification of performance objectives. This information will place your focus on the organization's specific functional needs and will enable you to proceed to the next step, where you will define the specific elements that the employees must address in order to improve performance in the desired area.

In a downward-cascading approach, this same objective-identification process can be used with the nonexecutive employees in a focus group environment. On this level, the process should be aimed at identifying and prioritizing those objectives that the employees consider to be fundamental to their success. The end result of utilizing the process on this level will be a collection of statements that can be grouped into categories that relate to the employees' intrinsic and extrinsic needs as displayed in the BBIC Fishbone diagram. You can then identify which of the six major factors they most closely align with: focus, positive reinforcement, empowerment, why-pay, what-pay, and how-pay. This information will firmly place your focus on specific areas of the BBIC Fishbone diagram, enabling you to proceed to the next step, that of defining the specific elements of the employees' needs that must be addressed.

The objective-identification process is a valuable tool to use in identifying both organizational and employee needs and linking them to each other. This process provides the vehicle for each employee to see his or her job as a link in a chain of other jobs that make up the structure of the organization. The opportunity to communicate this linkage should be used to the utmost.

Once you have used the OIP to identify the organization's objectives and the employees' objectives, you can use the Fishbone as a relational reference tool. The diagram's graphic design will assist you in understanding which key factors of the employees' needs will relate to which key factors of the organization's needs. In one typical example, the organization's first priority might be the need for superior execution and the employees' first priority might be the need for empowerment. This relationship would tell you that the possibilities for improving performance in the area of execution would be in linking specific elements of superior execution (to be identified by a matrix process) to an opportunity for the employees to fulfill their need for empowerment. In a situation where the organizational needs and the needs of the employees cannot logically be matched, it will be necessary once again to enlist the aid of your organizational development colleagues to facilitate the process of conflict resolution. This type of situation is one where more fundamental issues must be resolved prior to developing compensation as a motivational tool.

Objectives Provide the Intrinsic Budget

Applying the objective-identification process on the executive level will pinpoint categories where performance improvement will result in financial improvement of one type or another. This is the start of the development of the extrinsic, or financial, budget.

On the nonexecutive level, OIP will identify categories that relate to the employees' needs. By utilizing a matrix process to carry this approach to a more detailed level, we can identify the specific elements that will provide opportunities for the employees to "earn" intrinsic compensation. This is the process by which an intrinsic budget is developed. Just as we match employee needs to organizational needs, it is necessary to match the opportunity to obtain intrinsic compensation with the opportunity to obtain extrinsic compensation.

The value of developing an intrinsic budget is supported in an article in *Quality Progress* magazine by Rosabeth Moss Kanter, author of *Change Masters* and professor at the Harvard Business School. Dr. Kanter states that the "new wisdom" is that employees perform better when they have a more comprehensive understanding of the goals and objectives of the organization and how their contribution fits in. Her research has found that employees in teams with well-defined and controllable objectives will manage their portion of the business as if they owned it.[2] Now, *that* is tapping the true potential of the individual, which is what behavior-based incentive compensation is designed to accomplish.

Reviewing the behavioral psychology discussed in Chapter 2, we can extrapolate several elements in the workplace that provide a level of comfort to the average employee. (For our purpose, comfort is defined as identification with the contribution that an individual is making.) Figure 5-4 shows five comfort elements and the BBIC Fishbone factors under which they fall. Three of the five elements relate to intrinsic compensation; the other two relate to extrinsic compensation.

Anatomy of an Employee-Performance Objective

What constitutes good employee performance objectives in the design of incentive plans? In a *Harvard Business Review* article,

Figure 5-4. Elements of comfort.

Comfort Elements	Fishbone Factors
1. Mission Statement	1. Focus
2. Specific Objectives	2. Why-Pay
3. Performance Measures	3. Why-Pay
4. Feedback	4. Positive Reinforcement
5. Being in the Know	5. Positive Reinforcement

behavioral scientists Steven Doyle and Benson Shapiro point out that highly defined tasks generally not only led to greater motivation and better performance, but they also required less effort on the part of management to direct.[3] When the task was well defined, the measurement system could be better defined. Their findings support our observations that when the objectives and measurement systems are well defined, three things occur: The intrinsic budget becomes defined, the extrinsic budget develops a self-funding rationale, and the employees are placed in a receptive and participative state.

Common sense provides another consideration in putting together a list of good objectives—quantity. The number of objectives should be few and easily understandable. Too many objectives confuse the purpose by diluting the attention of the employees. A major success component of a behavior-based incentive compensation plan is the ability to capture a large portion of the employee's mindshare. In addition, dividing the total cash incentive opportunity among multiple objectives can result in payouts that are too small to be meaningful or motivational.

Another element of a good employee performance objective is relevance. If the employees believe that they are able to have an impact on an objective, then they are able to see the objective's relevance to their jobs.

You can use the BBIC Fishbone diagram to provide direction as you cascade the objective-identification process down into the organization. But how do you identify the employee performance objectives on the foundation level? How can you identify those specific activities and elements that a local work group can focus on? Well, for one thing you can ask the employees themselves. All the experiential data show that controlled involvement of employees in the development of their performance objectives produces detailed, insightful, and accurate results.

Should that be a surprise? No. After all, it's common knowledge that the individuals who are actually involved in doing the job know best how to perform the tasks, produce the results, and even measure the progress. If this is indeed the case, then why haven't they come forward with this valuable information? The answer, of course, lies in the history of the general work environment. In the past, employee input was neither solicited nor desired. Or, if it were, employees were reluctant to participate because data were generally used to highlight problems and nonconformance issues. Participation was used as a device to develop accountability and, subsequently, punishment. Rarely, if ever, was employee input used to celebrate the successful completion of work that had been scheduled or planned.

As you begin to use measurement, and the accountability that it provides, to reward performance and celebrate success, you will first need to win the trust of the employees. Human nature tells us that the employees will provide unlimited input as to objectives and measures by which they can be rewarded if they perceive it as being in their own best interest. The best way to cultivate this trust is to have them experience the success of an incentive program that provides opportunities to fulfill their needs. This means that, at least initially, you will have to take the leadership role in establishing the objectives and measures at the grass roots level. To help you do this, there is a matrix technique that can be used in the identification of local employee performance objectives.

The Matrix Family of Measures

The matrix family of measures is a technique that has been borrowed from the discipline of industrial engineering. It is the last step in the process of identifying the why-pay elements of a behavior-based incentive compensation plan. Like the objective-identification process, the matrix family of measures can be applied at both executive and nonexecutive management levels. It is a micro-focused process that identifies the specific elements that make up the organizational and employee needs that were identified through the objective-identification process. As they act to fulfill these needs, the employees will also fulfill the organization's specific functional needs by bringing about performance improvement.

The objective of the matrix process is to establish several criteria that collectively represent the purpose and mission of the work group. These criteria can then be prioritized (weighted) as to relative importance, thus allowing the calculation of a single score that will indicate the level of the group's performance and relate to the incentive payout. Another approach, depending on the design requirements of the payout structure, is to use the weighting of each objective as a stand-alone multiplier for the calculation of incentive earnings.

At this point, the process of developing a behavior-based incentive compensation plan has expanded to include skill sets that traditionally reside in the organizational development group, the industrial engineering group, the compensation group, and others. With each group contributing its expertise to the process, the probability of success will be increased.

The process of designing a matrix family of measures should begin in the organization at the first level below the executives. The objectives identified at this level can then serve as parameters for the next level down, just as the objective-identification process is used to cascade objectives into the organization. The first step in the process is to define the performance criteria. To do this, employee focus groups examine their job duties and work responsibilities, with assistance from the organizational development and industrial engineering functions. The reconciled employee needs and organizational needs that were developed as a result of the objective-identification process are used as parameters to guide this process. The BBIC Fishbone diagram should be explained to the focus group and used as a road map for the thought process. It is beneficial for representatives from work groups that are upstream and downstream to participate in each focus group in order to provide the perspective of interrelationships.

In 1989, *Incentive* magazine reported in its annual FACTS survey of nonsales incentive programs that the main objectives for such incentive plans are driven by productivity.[4] Indeed, nearly all focus groups develop criteria that include quantity, quality, cost, employee utilization, financial contribution, and time utilization. This traditional approach will result in the majority of the objectives being identified and defined as specific functional needs that fall under the organization's key performance indicators. These will be financially oriented objectives that will become part of the extrinsic compensation formula. They will measure the impact of the employees' performance on the organization's profitability and will identify the source of incentive funding based on performance improvement.

The BBIC Fishbone and the needs parameters that were identified by the objective-identification process can be used as tools by skilled group facilitators to expand the employees' thinking into other areas, specifically those oriented to intrinsic compensation. The group can then identify criteria relating to the organization's intrinsic factors of unity, superior execution, and management skills and to the employees' intrinsic factors of focus, positive reinforcement, and empowerment. These factors will become part of the intrinsic compensation budget, the source of opportunities that management must provide for the employees to fulfill their intrinsic needs. In effect, there will be two matrices—the extrinsic matrix, with criteria to use in measuring and rewarding improvement to the organization's economic value, and the intrinsic matrix, with criteria to use in measuring and rewarding improvement to its organizational effectiveness.

Measurement

At this level of detail in the identification process, the definition of an objective becomes, to a large degree, the definition of how performance will be measured. These measurements can normally be grouped in three major categories:

1. Objectives that apply to the operations, such as output per employee hour, percent of schedule attainment, or comparison of budget to actual cost
2. Objectives that apply to the employees themselves, such as number of lost-time accidents, turnover rate, or comparison of hours worked to hours paid
3. Objectives that apply to customer evaluation, such as a customer satisfaction index

Most traditional methods of measurement revolve around dollars, units, or some kind of ratio relationship. Using the latter requires a good understanding of the marketplace or overall environment. For instance, the "percent of plan" ratio will be effective in a dynamic environment, where growth can be expected, but in a flat market, where little growth is possible, a more effective measurement may be "percent improvement over same time last year."

In establishing measurement for incentive compensation, there are eight steps to keep in mind:

1. Measure all the key indicators. Fulfillment of this guideline is assured through the objective-identification process and the cascade process.

2. Establish the measurements in a participative manner. The focus group approach ensures that the system is acceptable to the participants.

3. Keep it simple. The fewer the measurements, the more focused the effort.

4. Create new measurement systems only when the necessary data are not being collected. In all other instances, use the systems that are in place. However, it may be necessary to enhance current reporting systems to provide data feedback to employees in a more timely and direct manner.

5. Focus on group measures that encourage cross-departmental cooperation and identification with the organization's mission.

6. Establish realistic baselines, using historical data whenever possible. Baselines are a critical element of behavior-based incentive compensation plans because they determine the degree of perfor-

mance the employees must contribute in order to start earning extrinsic incentives. Baselines require a high degree of maintenance. Second only to feedback on performance, baselines require the most communication to the employees.

7. Strive to maintain stability, but be prepared to change when necessary. Accept the reality that the measurements will change as the business environment changes and the employees become more comfortable with the concept of determining their standard of living based on their performance.

8. Work in reality. Design the program for improvement based on where the organization is, not where it "should be." Use behavior-based incentive compensation to achieve sensible goals, steadily moving the organization toward where it should be.

Figure 5-5 shows a representative matrix that includes some of the elements associated with the matrix family of measures. The objectives and the measurement methods have been identified and have been assigned a weighted value. The latter will act as a focal guideline, an indicator of where management wants to place emphasis. As we will see in the design of the payout structure, employee contribution can be focused by applying the weighted factor to the incentive earning opportunity. For the elements in the matrix that relate to the intrinsic compensation factors, the weighting will assist

Figure 5-5. Representative matrix elements.

Objective	Measurement	Weight		Base	Actual	Increment	Value
		100%					

management in identifying those areas of intrinsic needs that will require the most attention and effort on their part. Using the weighting to identify and emphasize the employees' incentive opportunities is the most effective approach to enhancing employee motivation.

Part of the measurement process involves establishing a baseline to help identify improvement. Depending on the objective, this baseline can be an average of historical performance or of current performance. Or it can be some desired level of future performance. In establishing the baseline of measurement for behavior-based incentive compensation, it is helpful, first, to remain in reality, and second, to view the structure from the eyes of the participant. Ask yourself the question, Would I want to be measured that way?

Once the base has been defined, actual performance can be compared against it and the incremental improvement identified. In the extrinsic compensation matrix, a value for each increment of improvement can be established with the assistance of the financial group within the organization. Now the compensation development team includes organizational development, industrial engineering, and finance. (And you thought this was a single-function project!) In Japan, the concept of *Kaisen* is the effect of small, day-to-day improvements as they accumulate over time. Behavior-based incentive compensation is really out of the same mold. It should be designed to emphasize and reward the cumulative effect of small day-to-day improvements.

A portion of the value of incremental improvement should be set aside to fund the incentive compensation. Figure 5-5 shows how this portion, in dollars, can be plugged into the elements in the matrix that relate to the extrinsic compensation factors and thus used to calculate the incentive payout. If the matrix process has identified an objective that has no measurable dollar value, management could assign an incremental value to it and, in doing so, increase the ratio of improvement that is shared with the employees. More on this later.

There Is a Measurement for Everything

One of the biggest concerns in an organization that is considering incentive compensation is how to measure the performance of the support employees. Of course, the answer lies in the identification techniques and in the fact that this process is not performed in isolation. Rob Chestnut demonstrated this as compensation manager at US Sprint. His challenge was to include cost containment as an objective in the incentive compensation plan for the field sales force. The problem was how to encourage cost containment in a manner that would not discourage or reduce the selling effort. The answer

Figure 5-6. Cost containment coefficient.

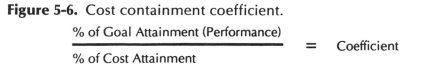

$$\frac{\%\text{ of Goal Attainment (Performance)}}{\%\text{ of Cost Attainment}} = \text{Coefficient}$$

was not in the weighting of cost objectives against sales objectives, but in the method of measurement.

Figure 5-6 shows how Rob Chestnut resolved the issue. He established a relationship between sales performance and costs that resulted in a coefficient that could be applied toward the incentive payout structure. The cost-containment objective became demotivational only when the salesperson exceeded the cost-of-sale parameters that management had established. On the other hand, if the salesperson's cost-of-sale total was below the parameters, his or her incentive payout increased. This ratio approach allowed the sales force to manage the selling process and make cost/benefit tradeoff decisions that would maximize both incentive compensation and revenues.

Notes

1. Linda Applegate, James Cash, Jr., and D. Quinn Mills, "Information Technology and Tomorrow's Manager," *Harvard Business Review*, November-December 1988, pp. 134–136.
2. Rosabeth Moss Kanter, "Fortune Forum II: Quality Leadership and Change," *Quality Progress*, February 1987, pp. 45–47.
3. Stephen X. Doyle and Benson P. Shapiro, "What Counts Most in Motivating Your Sales Force?" *Harvard Business Review*, May-June, 1980, pp. 133–140.
4. "Facts Survey: Nonsales Incentives at Work," *Incentive*, June 1989, pp. 45–47.

6

The What-Pay and How-Pay Factors: Extrinsic and Intrinsic Motivators

Most designs for compensation strategies are based on the market practices of companies with whom the organization competes for personnel. An additional consideration is the ability for fluid movement of employees throughout the company. In the traditional incentive compensation plan, positions that have higher potential impact on results will normally have commensurately higher incentive opportunities.

A behavior-based incentive compensation plan takes exception to these traditional positions. Instead of being based on market practices, the strategy is based on the organization's needs and the potential of the employees to fulfill those needs. In a broad-based incentive plan, strong consideration is given to the issue of equity by using a variety of ratio techniques related primarily to base compensation. These techniques provide the flexibility for easy movement of employees throughout the organization. An organization that subscribes to the philosophy of behavior-based incentive compensation will provide the most attractive compensation plan to the labor marketplace as well as maintaining flexibility within the organization.

In Chapter 5, we examined the extrinsic compensation factor of why-pay and its relationship to both the organization's and the employees' needs. In this chapter, we will discuss the issues of incentive compensation as they apply to motivation. The key motivating factors in any incentive compensation plan are the amount of opportunity available to the employees and the manner in which it is presented or made available to them. We will examine these factors and utilize the BBIC Fishbone diagram to evaluate case histories that illustrate the effectiveness of applying the factors of what-pay and why-pay. This process will develop our understanding and ability to design the most effective plan from both motivational and cost standpoints.

Short Term vs. Long Term

W. Edwards Deming, the statistician who has become an internationally renowned champion of quality, took the position that any employee's job can be distilled down to two basic factors: (1) from the long-term perspective, keeping the company in business, and (2) from a short-term perspective, improving his or her performance a little each day. Dr. Deming advocated the use of statistical process control techniques to affect an organization's short-term performance and thus, in turn, affect its long-term objectives. We should take heed of Dr. Deming's teachings because they have proved to be quite effective. As we relate compensation to quality, the question we should ask ourselves is, how can we use incentive compensation on the general employee level to support and reinforce short- and long-term performance?

From a participating employee's point of view, current compensation programs that are defined as "pay for performance" tend to emphasize individual contribution. They are normally designed around a unique approach to the redistribution of wages rather than sharing of the benefits of improvement. As a result, they tend to encourage competition among employees. They seem to be most effective with employees who are intrinsically motivated and, as a result, could result in increased turnover of dissimilar employees. A performance objective that is often used for this type of plan is goal attainment.

On the other hand, the plan design that is collectively referred to as "group incentive" tends to emphasize teamwork. These programs are normally designed around a funding process that adds to the base compensation budget. This process results in a more cooperative environment where the contribution of an army of good solid performers results in an improvement of overall performance.

Behavior-based incentive compensation blends these two incentive plan designs, incorporating both intrinsic and extrinsic rewards that are contingent upon performance rather than on a fixed budget. Because of this, BBIC creates superordinate goals that provide a reason for the team to work together and a reason for each employee to take individual action for the betterment of the group. This synergy results in higher levels of performance and also creates a consensus, or focus. The participants are committed to participation and wedded to the solution because the success of the group is in their individual best interests. With this understanding, it is easy to see how behavior-based incentive compensation provides motivation for both the day-to-day improvement produced by individuals and the longer term growth provided by groups working in concert for the good of the organization.

Application

The rest of this book will be devoted to analysis of the application of behavior-based incentive compensation. The first step in this process is to understand that a behavior-based incentive compensation plan is not a panacea; it is a compensation tool that is effective specifically in the areas where employees, performing in their workplace, can make a difference. Examples of objectives that can be appropriately addressed by this approach are increased performance, cost control, acting as a catalyst for change, alignment of pay with results, and communication of values.

The process of designing an incentive plan includes the formulation of what compensation (quantity and form) will be paid to the employees and how it will be paid to them. Included in this process is the identification of who will participate, the development of payout formulas, the definition of baselines, consideration of the need for a deficit reserve, and selection of employee-involvement techniques necessary to support and nurture the process.

What Portion Do They Get?

The BBIC Fishbone diagram shows that the primary element of the what-pay factor is the funding strategy. The first consideration in establishing the incentive compensation payout is how it will coincide with the company's pay philosophy. In general terms, the addition of incentive compensation below the top level management will require an organization to rethink its pay philosophy. Issues such as pay compression will lead to basic questions like, Will we maintain the integrity of our compensation ranges? Management's answer to this question will determine whether the incentive opportunity will be open-ended or not.

The compression issue is a difficult one, and its resolution will send a specific signal to the employees. Special consideration should be given to employee perceptions. As we have seen, behavioral psychology plays a significant role in the effectiveness of behavior-based incentive compensation. A closed-ended incentive pay range will limit the maximum amount an employee can earn in incentive compensation and thus could be used to control a fixed budget and manage the issue of compression. However, a cap on incentive earnings sends a subliminal message to the employees that there is a performance level beyond which management is not interested in going. The question that management needs to answer is, How important is the issue of compression? The performance range is the range in which incentives will be paid. The closed-ended performance range is a near relative to the closed-ended base pay range, but the same logic that supports one may not apply to the other.

A closed-ended base pay range is established with consideration for such elements as job levels, market pricing, administrative burden, and budgets. We have seen that these issues are not necessarily the driving factors for incentive compensation. Figure 6-1 graphically depicts the message that is conveyed to the employees by each approach. The diagram for a closed-ended plan shows odds of attainment where 80 percent of the employees are participating and 20 percent are bumping up against the ceiling. While this philosophy would be effective in motivating the employees, it has in effect told 20 percent of the workforce that there is a limit (maximum) to the amount of performance the organization requires to be successful.

The diagram for an open-ended plan design is established with consideration for the operating advantages that will accrue to the organization. Historical or current performance is used as the threshold, and the goal is set as a stretch in performance that can be realized if everything goes right. In this example, 20 percent of the participants surpass the goal. They receive compensation in relation to their contribution and are viewed by the rest of the employee

Figure 6-1. Performance range options.

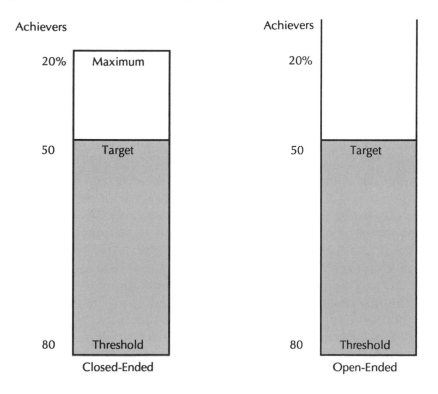

population as role models. The closed-ended approach limits the amount of intrinsic and extrinsic compensation available to the employee, and the open-ended approach provides a substantial amount of both types of compensation. Bringing behavioral psychology and consideration for the needs of the employees into the design of an incentive compensation plan forces senior management to make difficult decisions concerning the organization's pay philosophy. Fortunately, the benefits well warrant the tough decisions.

Where Will It Come From?

As we have noted before, an incentive compensation plan should be self-funding based on the incremental value of improvement. This funding is normally established by a formula that determines the amount of the incentive funds that will become available based on performance improvement. This formula can be established with consideration for physical criteria or financial criteria or a combination of both. The selected measurements that make up the formula are usually weighted or prioritized. But since we are coming from a background of cost containment into an environment of participation and sharing, we should make sure that the weighting assigned to the measurement does not emphasize controlling the incentive payout over the earning opportunity.

In the late 1980s and early 1990s, Metropolitan Life Insurance Company initiated an incentive compensation for employees below the top management level. The plan had three measurement aspects, based on corporate objectives, department objectives, and individual objectives. For payment purposes, the individual objectives were weighted most heavily, then the department objectives, and then the corporate objectives. While weighting the corporate objectives most heavily would have ensured the corporate gains prior to paying any incentive, Met Life realized that the individual has little control over the corporate results. By placing the emphasis on individual objectives that were tied to the department's goals, management encouraged the day-to-day performance improvement that culminates in the company achieving its objectives. The individual and departmental objectives make the plan meaningful to the employees, and the financial objectives address the investors' interests.

Physical Formulas

Physical formulas represent the traditional concept of employee performance improvement. They are normally some measure of unit output per labor hour. An example of a physical formula would be an agricultural co-op that measures performance based on tons processed per hour. In a more detailed application of this formula with an organization that has multiple products, each product would be assigned a standard that expressed the expected output of that product within a uniform time frame (hourly, daily, weekly, etc.). These standards help to factor the changes in product mix into the formula and ensure the integrity of the units-per-labor-hour formula. In incentive compensation practice, the standard is a ratio used to compare the output value of the product mix. For example, in an electronics assembly plant, one memory board assembly may equal three terminal board assemblies because it requires three times the labor input to produce. The financial and industrial engineering disciplines are normally enlisted to assist in identifying these standards and the associated value of an increment of improvement. Normally, unless management wants to place emphasis on a special product, each product will add to the incentive earning opportunity in the same ratio as the standard that it is assigned.

The physical formula is designed to reward employees for performance improvement in areas that they can directly impact. This formula has very little relationship to market conditions or pricing strategies, which the employees cannot directly impact. Thus, it provides a high level of fulfillment to the employees' intrinsic needs of empowerment, positive reinforcement, and focus. The ability of the employees to affect the outcome directly and to receive immediate performance feedback is a powerful psychological force that makes this a very effective approach.

It is important to note that the profitability of the organization as a result of activity in the marketplace does not have a direct relationship to the physical formula. Using a physical formula, it is possible to pay incentive compensation for performance improvement during a period of declining profitability. Once again, the design of a behavior-based incentive compensation plan becomes a matter of balance between the identification, prioritization, and fulfillment of employee needs and the identification, prioritization, and fulfillment of the organization's needs.

Financial Formulas

Financial formulas are most often utilized in an organizational culture where the well-being of the employees and the well-being of the company are considered one and the same. In this formula, individuals (or groups) are measured against the company's performance. The relationship of input to output is expressed in terms of dollars. Examples of this are the ratio of payroll costs to sales revenues or of a combination of operating costs, such as labor and materials, to sales revenues. Financial formulas have been used in traditional gainsharing programs to link the compensation of the employees to the welfare of the organization.

These formulas can be an effective approach to generating a sense of teamwork and shared fate, as well as improving profitability. However, in order to capitalize on these positive elements, the incentive plan must provide the employees with opportunities to fulfill their intrinsic needs. This is due in part to the fact that the extrinsic compensation offered by the traditional financial formula is neither immediate nor certain. Elements beyond the control of the participating employee, such as taxes, interest, nonrecurring adjustments, pricing decisions, and marketplace conditions, act to weaken the extrinsic motivational impact of the financial formula. In the late 1980s, the Borden Company tried to initiate an incentive plan that utilized the financial indicator of return on equity. According to a Borden executive, management eventually concluded that this financial indicator was too difficult for the hourly employees to accept. Instead, the plan was revised so that workers at 180 different plants were given the opportunity to win cash bonuses depending on how their plants performed against indicators in such areas as attendance, quality, safety, and productivity.

The Combination

We have seen that the physical formula can be applied to a variety of performance variables. The matrix family of measures discussed in Chapter 5 is a technique for doing this. In addition to using a physical formula, an organization could include a financial formula in the overall incentive compensation structure. This would serve the dual purpose of enhancing a sense of teamwork and ensuring that a portion of the payout was contingent upon improvement of the organization as a whole. The Xerox office products division utilized this approach in a program that incorporated physical formulas, such as productivity, cost, quality, and timeliness, and paid out monthly on a departmental level. A portion of the total earned incentive pool was set aside, and a financial formula was used to calculate the amount of this payout that was to be awarded at year end. We examine this case history in Chapter 9, in a section on noncash incentives.

Extrinsic Compensation: The Payout

Funding schedules relate payout to performance and define the incentive earnings opportunity of the employees. Such schedules have a threshold and a target (goal) and are either capped or open-ended. Increments of improvement are assigned that reflect the employee's ability to impact the objective and the value of improvements to the organization.

Each performance-improvement objective should have a schedule with a threshold to indicate the baseline above which the incentive earnings begin to accrue. The threshold is a reflection of the organization's needs and, under normal circumstances, should be the acceptable level of nonincentive performance. However, it is not uncommon to find low-level thresholds (30 percent) in an open business environment where there is strong opportunity for growth and management wants to encourage it. High thresholds (90 percent) are found in environments where there is a mature level of performance and management wants to encourage the attainment of the business plan.

A threshold can be a historical number or a baseline that is set by management as required by business conditions or the business plan. When historical performance is used as the threshold, there is a powerful message sent to the employees: "We are going to improve over last year's performance and pay out handsomely when we do."

When the organization's needs dictate that a certain level of growth must be achieved prior to the activation of incentive opportunity, the BBIC Fishbone diagram can help identify the intrinsic needs of the employees that can be utilized to support this approach. In this situation, these needs would most likely center on the elements of empowerment and positive reinforcement. Anytime that management dictates performance standards that are not substantiated by historical fact, the employees will experience a need for empowerment to reassure themselves that they are more than "voice-actuated robots." The reason why the practice of involving employees in the setting of thresholds and targets is so effective is that it provides them with an opportunity to earn this intrinsic compensation.

Occasionally, an organization may utilize a stair-step method that raises the threshold with each subsequent year's improvement. The difficulty of this approach is that, unless the earning opportunity increases proportionately, the employees may perceive it as a scheme to make them work harder and faster for something that soon escalates out of reach. If economic considerations or technological advances make this approach a necessity, the negative aspects can be offset by involving the employees in the business rationale for doing so. Whatever the threshold settings, they will require annual maintenance and review. Along with this business case analysis will be the need for extensive employee involvement and communication to maintain the employees' perception that the plan is fair and equitable.

A target is normally a performance goal that is established for each objective. However, the best plans are designed to encourage unlimited improvement. Semantics are important in a compensation environment so loaded with psychic power. The word *target* may be inappropriate for behavior-based incentive compensation plans because it conveys a limit. The normal word association is that targets are "hit." Perhaps the use of the word *goal* would better convey the concept of continual performance improvement.

Funding Schedules

The funding schedule is the rate at which the employees share in the incentive earnings based on some relationship of incentive pool earnings to their contribution. Much can be revealed about the emphasis of an incentive compensation plan by examining the slope of the funding schedule. The following examples of nonexecutive employee incentive schedules have been developed to illustrate this point.

The schedule in Figure 6-2 is not all that encouraging to the participants. It indicates a situation where the plan design has conveyed to the employee that it is more important to go from 95 to 96 percent than to go from 85 to 95 percent and that there is only a small range of improvement available. This may be the right plan for an organization such as a utility company that is in a mature marketplace. However, with such a steep slope, if the unleashed potential of the employees resulted in performance above management's expectations, the payout would be out of control.

Figure 6-2. Too hot.

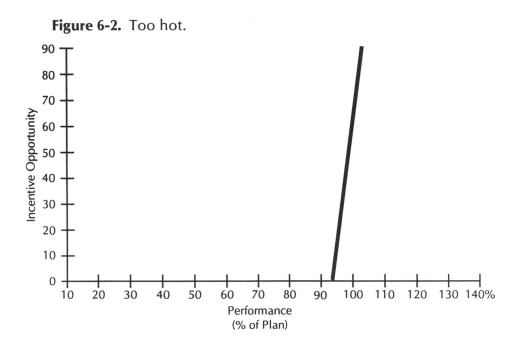

The schedule depicted in Figure 6-3 is encouraging to the participants, but the limited incentive opportunity conveys to the employees that achieving the target is all the improvement that management is interested in. The slope of this funding schedule is designed to penalize failure to hit the target more than it is designed to reward outstanding performance.

In Figure 6-4, the incentive opportunity conveys to the employees that performance from base toward goal will be rewarded at a rate that will result in a significant increase to base pay for achieving goal. In addition, an accelerator that applies to the funding schedule communicates to the employees that performance beyond goal, while increasingly difficult to achieve, is possible and will be handsomely rewarded.

The ability to set a realistic goal plays a significant role in establishing the right slope for the funding schedule. There will be pressure from senior management to set aggressive goals that will result in significant profit improvement. But what is important here is not the potential that the goal represents but how realistic the prospects are that it can be obtained. A goal of 15 percent that is attained provides a much greater contribution to the organization than a goal of 30 percent that the employees quit striving for. Goal setting is a bit like forecasting the weather—you get better with experience. Some questions that are critical to ask during the goal-development process are: Where are we starting from? How hard is it to achieve the performance that we are targeting? Are we dealing with performance reality as indicated by the historical data?

Figure 6-3. Too cold.

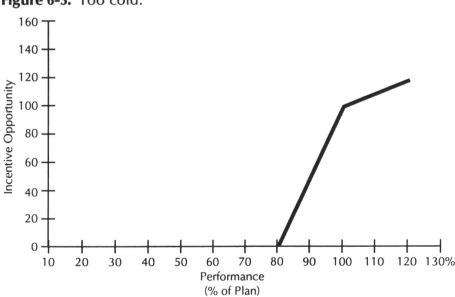

Figure 6-4. Just right.

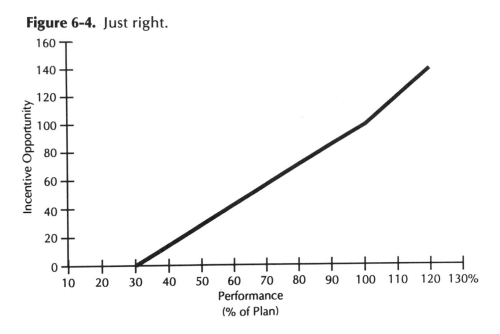

Equity: Distributing the Rewards

Once the performance objectives have been identified, the methods of measurement established, the value of an increment of improvement determined, and a formula developed that will accrue monies into an incentive pool, the next step is to determine how the incentive dollars will be distributed among the participants. Assuming that the incentive compensation plan is based on groups rather than individuals, one approach is to provide everyone in the group an equal share. On the one hand, this approach is in conflict with the traditional concept of compensation being related to the worth of the job. On the other hand, this approach contributes heavily to the psychic income budget because every employee becomes aware of exactly how much an increment of improvement is worth to them. In addition, equal distribution reinforces the team concept, creates a degree of peer pressure, and encourages employees to share information and assist one another. A variation of this approach is to equate the available incentive pool to dollars per total hours worked. Then each employee receives incentive based on hours worked. This approach attempts to associate incentive earnings with contribution just as base pay is associated with time spent at work.

A more traditional approach would be to provide everyone in the group a share based on some base compensation determinant such as percent of midpoint. The use of this approach provides control and equity but tends to emphasize the value of the job rather than the concept of the employee as a contributing human being. Because behavior-based incentive compensation is focused on tapping the human potential of each employee, this traditional approach may send a confusing signal to the participants.

Yet another approach is to incorporate a personal performance measurement in the group payout calculation. The application of this approach may be in keeping with Edwards Deming's short-term/long-term philosophy described at the beginning of this chapter. Incentive compensation has a definite impact on the day-to-day performance of employees. The formal performance-evaluation process, on the other hand, emphasizes long-term employee development, creating a workforce that will serve the company well over the long run.

Performance Evaluations and Incentive Payouts

Performance evaluations have traditionally been used to determine the amount of merit increase that an individual will receive. With that related background, what is to prevent us from using these evaluations to determine how much, or at least a portion of how much, of an incentive payout an individual should receive? The answer is, nothing except the employee's current perception of the process as being subjective and divorced from performance. In order to use the performance-evaluation process in a behavior-based incentive compensation plan, it is necessary to change the nature of it. It will need to become more closely based on data and more timely. This means that the process would include specific objectives—measures, thresholds, and goals—in effect, all the data included in an incentive compensation plan. Conceptually, then, the incentive compensation plan becomes the performance evaluation. The evaluation process, as it currently exists, is then free to become more focused on human development. Its design could evolve to emphasize those skills and pinpoint those behaviors that the employees need to develop in order to maximize their incentive earning opportunities. The performance evaluation process is thus transformed into an action plan for employee development. As such, it becomes much more meaningful to the employee and much more beneficial to the organization as a tool to bring about long-term development.

The drawbacks of the traditional form of employee evaluation—subjective in nature, emphasis on the individual, and lack of timeliness—normally preclude its use as an objective in the family of measures developed for a behavior-based incentive compensation plan. Figure 6-5 shows the impact that including performance evaluation in the family of measures could have. In this example, an organization could miss its financial objective and still pay out 36 percent based on the personal evaluation.

Figure 6-5. Performance evaluation.

Objective	Weight (%)	Performance (%)	Share Multiplier (%)
Financial	40	0	0
Physical	20	100	20
Personal	40	90	36
			56

Using the results of the performance evaluation as a multiplier to the individual's incentive earnings could make a motivational contribution to the plan design. If average performance is rated as 100 percent and the evaluation process has a high level of integrity and timeliness, then an above-average performance rating could have a positive effect on the amount of incentive compensation that an employee earns. However, this places conflicting value measures on the evaluation system and is confusing to the employees, telling them that average performance is 100 percent of expectations. All in all, it may be better to have the evaluation process evolve into a developmental tool.

Budgets

One of the questions relevant to any incentive compensation plan is, Where will the money come from to pay the employees? We have seen that the process is self-funding and that the incremental improvement will generate the extrinsic incentive budget. But where do the funds come from? Do they drop like manna from heaven when performance exceeds threshold? We all know that organizations run their annual operations based on preestablished budgets, so that even if you were to initiate a program that was self-funding, the money generated would be part of operational revenues and probably inaccessible as a source of compensation funding.

Thus, it is necessary to calculate budgets and gain approval to fund a behavior-based incentive compensation program prior to the implementation of the plan. There are basically two ways to calculate an incentive budget, top-down and bottom-up. Which approach you use depends on the method of sharing the improvement.

Bottom Up

In the bottom-up approach, the incentive opportunity is presented as an individual opportunity to be achieved through teamwork.

A fixed dollar value is set for each increment of improvement—for example, $50 per month to each participant for every 1-percent improvement in productivity for the month. The budget is calculated by establishing the improvement goal for each objective, adding all the payout values at goal together, and multiplying the total by the number of participating employees. This monthly total is then multiplied by twelve to become the program's annual budget for performance at goal. This budget is based on the assumption that each employee will earn at the goal level (see Figure 6-6). If performance falls below goal for the year, then the budget is underspent. If performance exceeds that goal, the budget is overspent. It is important that senior management realize this and accept the "downside" of exceeding goal.

A variation of this approach involves assigning a percent of midpoint to each increment of improvement. This provides equity from a pay administration standpoint, but because the incentive opportunity is stated in terms of percent rather than cash, the relationship between reward and performance becomes diluted. To the employees' perception, an even greater dilution takes place in a structure that provides a percent of midpoint for a percent of improvement. The design challenge is to present the incentive in terms as concrete and meaningful as possible so that it remains attractive to the employees on a continuing basis.

The bottom-up approach to distributing incentive compensation is very effective in an environment where performance can be

Figure 6-6. Bottom-up payout schedule.

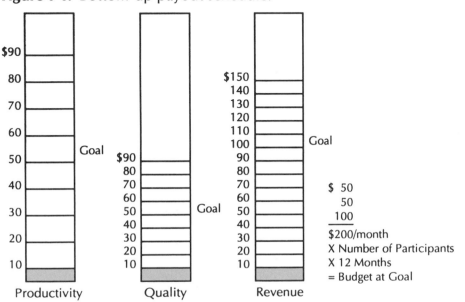

tracked monthly and accurately reported on a relatively timely basis (within thirty days). This approach adds significantly to the employees' intrinsic compensation because it is easy for them to understand. Normally, physical formulas are used, and there is a direct correlation of results to reward. The incentive is positive, immediate, and certain. There is also a combination of the individual and team elements at work in this design. Each individual knows that he or she will receive the dollar level assigned to the performance level. Yet they all know that the performance improvement that is achieved will be a function of team effort.

The downside of this type of an approach is that the organization may pay out for performance one month and the next month experience losses that more than offset the gains. Thus, on an annual basis, the employees might receive incentive compensation even though the organization suffered a net loss. Because the bottom-up approach couples the motivational power of intrinsic compensation with the financial impact of extrinsic compensation, a situation of this type is very rarely the result of poor employee performance. Rather, it is most often a result of a change in the economy or the business environment. The bottom-up approach is probably more appropriate for use in a start-up environment or a labor-intensive industry that functions relatively independently of minor fluctuations in the economy.

Top Down

The top-down budget calculation is the more traditional approach to the distribution of extrinsic incentive compensation. With this approach, the incentive opportunity is presented as a group opportunity, with the payoff to be distributed at a later date. Normally, financial formulas are used, and the increments of improvement are expressed in total dollar value to the organization. As an example, say that each percent of return on capital over goal is worth $10,000 to the company and that 50 percent of this profit will be allocated to a pool for the employees to share either quarterly or annually. This approach is safer for the organization because it provides the opportunity to design in safety nets to prevent paying incentive compensation when the performance of the organization as a whole has not improved.

There is certainly a fiduciary rationale for the top-down approach, which is appropriate for use in many situations. Nonetheless, it is important to point out that the potential savings to the extrinsic incentive budget can be offset by the costs to the intrinsic motivation budget. With the top-down approach, employees feel farther away from the incentive opportunity and, in some instances, may even have improved their group's performance and received no payout for it. The imbalance created by the reduction in the intrinsic budget may need to be offset by an increase in the value of the extrinsic incentive opportunity.

In effect, a bottom-up approach may deliver more bang for the buck by requiring less extrinsic incentive compensation because of its high level of intrinsic compensation. In turn, the top-down approach may require a higher level of extrinsic incentive compensation because of its lower level of intrinsic compensation.

The Rule of Thumb

As a professional who is involved in the application of the compensation process to stimulate the growth of the organization, you must guard against the development of a plan that is so conservative that it incorporates a top-down design in conjunction with insignificant payouts. If the payouts for individual objectives are insignificant, as could be the result of too many objectives in the family of measures, the employees' efforts will be spread too thin. If the employees are unable to achieve the overall performance improvement needed to generate a significant incentive payout, they will perceive the incentive opportunity to be lacking.

If the payouts are insignificant as a result of incremental values not being shared equitably, then the employee response to the incentives may be less than total and less than long-lasting. The rule of thumb for what makes a good annual incentive compensation budget ranges from 5 percent to 20 percent of either annual income or midpoint. Whatever figure is chosen should reflect a balance of the competitive nature of the base compensation, the benefits package, and the intrinsic compensation opportunities available to the employees.

Who and How

Now that we have established the factors of why-pay and what-pay, the next step is to establish the factor of how-pay. To do this, we must identify the employees who will participate in the incentive compensation plan. Will the plan be implemented throughout the organization or will it be confined to a few locations or departments that will be the site of pilot projects? (There is considerable wisdom in the use of testing to work out the difficulties inherent in any prototype system.)

Once the location has been identified, the next question to ask is, Will everyone at the location participate? In other words, will the executives participate in the same plan as the nonexecutive employees? Joseph Scanlon, the originator of the gainsharing concept, believed that all employees should participate in the plan because this assures rank-and-file employees that the concept has been sanctioned by senior management and that the structure is valid.

While there may be some rationale not to have all the employees participate in the same plan, doing so adds to the psychic benefits of incentive compensation. It sends a message to all employees that "it's us against the competition." It may be necessary to define executive management's goals in broader terms, but in general, the organization should be portrayed as a single entity. This approach is supported by the Japanese concept of *Kaisen*, where management is responsible for improving the systems of the organization and the other employees are responsible for improving their own performance. A business question to ask when identifying the participants is, Who can impact the results? This question provides a natural sorting of employees to identify those who can participate. The first rule of incentives is that each participant must have the capability to impact the results.

A behavioral question to ask once the pool of participants has been identified is, Based on the objectives, what form of organization will add most to the psychic budget? Will group dynamics be more effective than an individual emphasis? Will a grouping of cross-functional employees with the same grade and incentive opportunity generate a higher motivational level than a grouping of employees separated in reward opportunity by grade? Or, is dividing the organization into departments or logical work groups with a common earning opportunity the way to proceed? There is no set answer as to how the participants should be organized. Much of that will be determined by the objectives and by who can impact them. However, it is important to note that the use of grade or title to determine participation or to establish the degree of incentive eligibility can result in a ridged demarcation that may work counter to the concept of teamwork that makes behavior-based incentives so effective. In short, another rule of thumb is that, in a behavior-based incentive compensation plan, teamwork produces the business success that creates the incentive compensation.

Pay at Risk

To facilitate the process whereby the nonexecutive employees put a portion of their pay at risk, the organization can initiate a salary range holdback or a payline reduction. With the range holdback, the employees' salary range is frozen until the industry payline surpasses it. We saw this approach in the GTE case history in Chapter 4. With a payline reduction, the merit increase budget would be reduced, thus retarding the growth of the employees' base compensation. Either approach, singularly or in unison, can create a pool of undistributed compensation funds to use as a hedge against cyclical swings in the organization's revenues. This improves the competitive position of the company because it lowers costs in the area of base compensation and benefits. In Japan, many businesses have utilized these methods to develop a competitive edge, putting as much as 25 percent of their employees' compensation at risk.

The philosophical rationale for pay at risk is that it makes the employees feel more like owners. This may be true, but the reality is that the employees are going to be quite skeptical about participating in such a plan. When using an at-risk approach, the question to ask is, What is at risk, a portion of the employees' compensation or the success of the program? Placing the employees' pay at risk (an uncomfortable term), at least initially, is an issue of perception. In order for employees to accept this approach without reservation, it is necessary for them to understand compensation practices and the rationale behind their specific program. Without this, the locker room talk will be that "they reduced our pay." In addition, the incentive opportunity must offset the at-risk portion by a considerable amount, so that when the employees perform the mental cost/benefit tradeoff analysis (and they all will), there is no question in their minds as to the benefit of participation.

One way to develop a positive cost-benefit profile is to establish the incentive payout threshold at some point below the current level of performance. This would allow the employees to add incentive compensation to the reduced base compensation at a rate that would make them whole when the current level of performance was reached. While this approach may have some of the elements of a shell game, it has some merit, too. It not only protects the company in the event of a downswing in the economy, but it also allows the employees to experience success with incentive programs. This "running start" design has shown itself to add momentum to an incentive program and to propel it into the realm of performance improvement.

When pay is put at risk, special attention should be paid to the type of work involved and the performance objectives being addressed. In a service environment, where emphasis is on satisfying the customer, the measurement systems are more subjective and less able to reflect true performance. In this situation, any pay at risk should be kept to a minimum. On the other hand, in an environment of strong measurement and high opportunity, such as special projects, it may be appropriate to place a high portion of pay at risk in order to stimulate activity. What about equity in a situation where the two programs are installed simultaneously in the same company among employees of the same grade level, and the low-base/high-risk group receives a higher total cash compensation? Is this an issue? Yes. Although it is not an equity issue—after all, greater risk should provide the opportunity for greater reward—it is definitely a communications issue because there is the problem of misperceptions about equal treatment among employees.

In general, putting pay at risk among employees that have not experienced it before and are unfamiliar with the concept is, well, risky. The term itself could be perceived to imply that the total compensation has been secured, and all that's left to be done now is to minimize its erosion. With a novice audience, it's better to focus on the rewards for exceeding the performance threshold.

Add-On Incentives

Add-on incentive compensation is a pure function of performance improvement. As such, it is relatively easy to introduce. The base compensation becomes the terms of employment for adhering to policies and procedures and for performing up to threshold. The incentive compensation focuses on the business issues of improving results. While perhaps not ideal from a purely financial standpoint, this approach does have the benefit of operating in an environment that is uncluttered with potential employee relations issues. Perhaps the best solution is a compromise . . . a balance. An add-on design could be used to develop experience on the part of both management and employees and to develop accurate performance data that everyone is comfortable with. Then, one or two years later, the plan could shift into an at-risk design with an associated increase to the incentive opportunity.

Qualifiers

In a behavior-based incentive compensation plan, go/no-go qualifiers—those events that are required either to happen or not to happen before the earnings are shared—should be avoided if at all possible. This design is not encouraging to the participants because it presents the incentive as a form of cost control rather than an earnings opportunity. Figure 6-7 presents an example of this all-or-nothing matrix. One axis represents a financial objective, and the other axis represents a physical objective.

From a motivational standpoint, this approach has three areas of weakness. First, it has maximum levels of incentive opportunity beyond which the employees receive no payout (and the organization receives full benefit). Second, it is possible for the participants to

Figure 6-7. All-or-nothing matrix.

	Financial Objective			
	Below Threshold	Threshold	Par	Maximum
Physical Objective	12	18	24	36
Below Threshold	Percentage of Midpoint Opportunity			
78	0	0	0	0
Threshold				
150	0	2	3	4
Par				
228	0	3	4	5
Maximum				
300	0	4	5	6

improve their performance significantly in one area, providing benefit to the organization, yet receive no payout. Third, the level of incentive opportunity assigned to the combined objectives borders on insignificant. If the plan were unbundled and each objective assigned its portion of the incentive, it would be insufficient to stimulate interest in the program. But if we apply a bit of hyperbole, we can find one positive element in the plan: Putting any pay at risk in this approach would not be appropriate because of the small size of the maximum upside opportunity.

Modifiers

Modifiers are elements of the plan that can be used either to increase or to decrease the amount of incentive compensation. From the perspective of the participants, modifiers, like qualifiers, can add an element of question to the pure legitimacy of the payout design. Unlike qualifiers, however, modifiers can be either positive or negative. In the perception of the participant, a modifier that has a downside—if it can negatively impact the earned payout—removes the certainty of the incentive being delivered as a result of performance improvement. In this instance, the payout is no longer perceived as guaranteed.

Caution should be exercised in choosing any modifier. Certainly, there will be situations where you will want to use a modifier, but try to use only positive modifiers. One example of a positive modifier that drives both awareness and, to some degree, performance is the customer satisfaction index. This indicator measures how the customers perceive the organization. If this number is used as a multiplier to the incentive earned and no downside (negative multiplier) is utilized, then customer satisfaction will be perceived by the employees as a positive (though somewhat subjective) element of the plan.

Accelerators

The funding schedule in Figure 6-4 illustrated how an accelerator could be utilized to maintain the momentum of an incentive plan so that performance exceeds the goal. As performance improves and extrinsic compensation is earned, the balance of the behavior-based incentive compensation formula shifts. Performance improvement becomes more difficult, and the incentive opportunity loses some of its attraction, because the employees' cost/benefit perception shifts. At this point, accelerators can be used to fine-tune the balance of the behavior-based incentive compensation formula. We have seen in earlier chapters that extrinsic incentive compensation is quantity-sensitive. Therefore, if we want to increase—or, in this case, maintain—the attractiveness of this incentive, we can do so by increasing the quantity of the incentive offered.

Accelerators can be applied to the intrinsic compensation as well, but because the intrinsic incentive element is quality-sensitive, the application of an accelerator to this element requires a high level of understanding of behavioral psychology and dexterity in the use and interpretation of the BBIC Fishbone diagram. It is particularly important that the employees' psychic needs be accurately defined.

An example of applying an accelerator to the behavioral element of the formula would be the case of an organization with a specific functional need to develop a sense of ownership and accountability among all employees. In general, as performance improvement reaches goal, there is need for more front-line supervision in response to the increased need for facilitation and administration in a faster-paced environment. If the employees' intrinsic needs include the need for empowerment, then using an intrinsic accelerator could afford the opportunity for nonmanagement employees to assume the role of supervisors and team leaders. This adds intrinsic incentive to the formula, offsetting the difficulty of the incremental improvement.

Safety Nets

Safety nets come in two types, nets for the company and nets for the employees. A safety net for the company, otherwise known as a deficit reserve, consists of a portion of the earned incentive compensation that is withheld from the employees and placed in escrow. This reserve protects the company from paying out incentive compensation to the participants only to find at year end that overall performance was negative. This can happen when a department performs well and receives incentive but other areas of the organization fail to perform as expected, or when the organization as a whole performs well for part of the year but not well enough to offset the negative periods. Normally, deficit reserves are utilized in an organization that is sensitive to the economy. Another form of safety net for the company is the Improshare concept, where the payout is based on a rolling average of several pay periods. This tends to smooth out any downward trends that may occur.

The safety net for the employees takes a different form. One type might be utilized in a situation where the employees have a relatively high amount of their base compensation at risk. The safety net in this case would guarantee a minimum payout in the event of circumstances beyond the employees' control. This element of the extrinsic incentive compensation also has significant value from an intrinsic incentive standpoint. It sends a signal to the employees that the organization has a need for unity and partnership on all levels, and this need supports the fulfillment of employees' needs.

Frequency

Frequency of payout is one of the most powerful elements of the how-pay factor. This is because it is a first-level, real-world manifestation of behavioral psychology. In Chapter 2, we saw that an incentive is most effective in developing motivation if it is positive, immediate, and certain. The frequency of the payout determines how immediate the incentive is perceived to be.

The most desirable frequency, from a behavioral standpoint, is immediately after the performance has taken place. From a business standpoint, however, the frequency of payout is constrained by availability of performance data and the related administration. However, the age of electronic data processing may soon make this constraint a thing of the past. Other considerations are fluctuations in the economy and the size of the incentive payout. Longer periods may be desirable from a business standpoint as a means of smoothing peaks and valleys or if the plan has been designed to produce a sizable payout only after a considerable period of time.

In general, the most effective payout frequency would be to alternate incentive pay with base pay. For example, if base compensation checks are issued biweekly, the incentive compensation payout could be issued on the alternate weeks. This would provide an opportunity for managers and supervisors to celebrate success and discuss business issues with a fully receptive audience. In looking for ways to increase the intrinsic budget of the behavior-based incentive compensation plan, the element of frequency is one of the first places to turn.

The intrinsic incentive value of frequency is often overlooked or underestimated and sacrificed for the sake of administrative convenience or to limit potential overpayments. This unnecessarily weakens the motivational strength of the incentive compensation plan. For instance, the delivery of extrinsic incentive compensation is least effective when combined with the normal issuance of base compensation. Incentive pay, added to the base paycheck, is so anticlimactic as to be all but lost in the process. When you keep incentive compensation separate from base compensation, on the other hand, the employees receive a significant message about the importance of their performance in relation to the well-being of the organization and to their standard of living. It would be better to add staff to the payroll department than to provide incentive compensation as an addition to base compensation. The increase in performance that is realized by the timely and effective delivery of incentive compensation will more than offset any potential additional costs.

Performance Feedback

At the beginning of this chapter, we discussed Edwards Deming's two factors of an employee's job: (1) from the long-term perspective, to keep the company in business; (2) from a short-term perspective, to improve performance a little each day. The question is, How can we use incentive compensation to achieve this? We have seen that it is possible to fulfill the employees' needs for empowerment and positive reinforcement by making them partners in the business results and by providing timely rewards. In doing this, we address Deming's job factors. In providing timely performance feedback, gathered by means of the incentive compensation measurement structure, we fulfill the employees' needs for focus and positive reinforcement.

In a classic study of motivation conducted by Stephen Doyle and Benson Shapiro and reported in the *Harvard Business Review*, it was found that the degree of definition of the task and the amount of time between performance and the feedback of the results had more impact on repeat performance than did extrinsic rewards.[1] The more clearly the task was defined and the more timely feedback was provided, the more motivational was the impact.

Does this tell us that we can forgo the extrinsic incentive compensation element and achieve our objectives solely through the use of communications? Unfortunately, it does not. The BBIC formula clearly shows the need for extrinsic incentives. What this study does tell us is that we can maintain the momentum of daily improvement by providing timely performance feedback as short-term, high-intensity, intrinsic compensation. The capability to provide this information should have a high priority in the design of any behavior-based incentive compensation plan because it is a significant contributor to the intrinsic budget.

Note

1. Stephen X. Doyle and Benson P. Shapiro, "What Counts Most in Motivating Your Sales Force?" *Harvard Business Review*, May-June, 1980, pp. 133–140.

7

The Quality Connection

From the perspective of evolutionary management styles and human resources management techniques, if the 1960s was the decade of "productivity improvement," and the 1970s the decade of "employee involvement," and the 1980s the decade of "quality improvement," then the 1990s could become the decade of "behavior-based incentive compensation."

Behavior-based incentive compensation combines the critical elements of all of these human resources management techniques under a single umbrella that provides the employees with a long-term reason to participate in making their organizations successful. From productivity-improvement techniques comes the business case and financial rationale. From employee-involvement techniques comes the structure that enables the employees to make a difference and the psychic incentives to do so. From the quality-improvement process comes the tools to identify performance issues, measure specific results, and formulate specific actions to impact those results.

In effect, it could be said that the quality-management process that exists in the early 1990s is the culmination of those processes and programs that came before. The heart of this form of quality management is the concept of employees, working in teams, using a structured process to identify and resolve problems. The process starts with a statement of why the improvement is desired or necessary. Then, using specific problem-solving tools and statistical analysis, the employees define the problem, identify its underlying causes, and develop, test, and implement solutions. Then the process starts anew.

The Incentive Question

This team process and these tools—checksheets, graphing, histograms, Pareto diagrams, and control charts, to name a few—can be utilized in the incentive compensation process with extreme effectiveness. On a micro level, these tools can be used to answer the questions, "How can I impact the results? What can I do to participate?" As we have seen, these are critical behavior-based questions. Leaving them unanswered or unaddressed will result in a well-designed payout matrix that exists only on paper, in the incentive compensation file drawer. Fortunately, the quality-management process provides the wherewithal to answer these questions and turn an incentive matrix into a motivational process that taps the source of human potential.

The Quality Question

Incentive compensation, with its promise of an increased standard of living, answers the critical question that attends this quality-management process: "Why should I participate or continue to participate?" Left unanswered, this question will shorten the life of the quality-management process. So we see that there exists a symbiotic relationship between quality management and behavior-based incentive compensation. This relationship is mutually beneficial, as the combination of the processes produces a better result than is produced by the two if each stands alone.

The total quality-management process and behavior-based incentive compensation both utilize "people skills," including problem solving, statistical analysis, communications, employee involvement, and group dynamics to work toward the same ends. We will examine case histories of plans that have merged the quality and incentive compensation processes into a single culture. According to their own accounts the people involved did not start out with this combination in mind. But they soon discovered the mutual similarities and the benefits of combination.

Because these are real-world plans, they will all display the truism that there is more than one way to produce an end result. Each one is unique, designed as they all are for their own organization's culture, industry, and management style. They employ elements of the total quality-management process, behavioral technology, and incentive compensation mechanics. None will be a classic, clearly defined plan, but they all are based on incentive compensation principles. By studying these case histories, you can develop valuable insights that will be of assistance in developing your own behavior-based incentive compensation plan.

Vista Chemical

Vista Chemical is a chemical processing and manufacturing company with headquarters in Houston, Texas. It has 1,700 employees in nine plants located in the Gulf Coast area. Originally, Vista was the chemical division of the Conoco Company, then was spun off and became part of duPont, and in 1984 became independent as the result of a leveraged buyout. Throughout all these changes, management maintained a history of sharing with the employees.

Vista's quality-management process, their formal approach to incorporating quality into employee performance, emphasizes several different skills. All employees are trained in statistical process control, in managing performance through identifying specific (pinpointed) behaviors that are observable and measurable, in positive-reinforcement techniques, in team management, and in other quality-process management skills. The company's vice-chairman and executive vice-president, John Weidner, is a strong supporter of the quality-management process and of the philosophical concept of sharing gains with the employees. In his view, gainsharing would provide a significant reason for employees to make use of the tools the quality process provided.

Weidner and his executive team appointed a cross-sectional project team to research gainsharing and other ways of sharing the benefits of performance improvement with the employees. After a year and a half, the team presented its findings that a gainsharing approach would best fulfill the charter to: (1) enhance the organization's overall effort to improve customer satisfaction, quality, and productivity; (2) maintain Vista's competitive edge; and, (3) provide increased opportunity for job ownership and employee rewards.

A second team of cross-sectional line management was assembled to develop a pilot gainsharing plan on a business unit basis. Members of this team consisted of representatives from the marketing, manufacturing, legal, finance, human resources, and plant management areas. As we have observed, multifunctional skills come into play in designing a compensation plan.

Vista calls its plan Quality Management Process Gainsharing. Because the process of developing and maintaining a behavior-based incentive compensation plan requires the same skills as the quality-management process, it was quite natural for them to merge the two in a mutually supportive process. The final plan, which was designed to meet the specific needs of the organization and its employees, appears to be a blending of gainsharing, where group performance is focused on improving productivity and reducing costs, and goal-driven profit sharing, where the formula encourages employees to identify with the organization's success.

Wayne Hilgers is manager of quality development at Vista and has been involved with both the quality-management process and incentive compensation almost from the start. According to Wayne, the company has always had benefits and savings plans more generous than most. It also has had a classical executive incentive compensation plan and stock option awards that extended deeper into the organization than most traditional plans.

The Financial Formula

One of the initial observations of the project team was that there was a high degree of interdependence among the business units. Wayne says, "Vista is a continuous-process, integrated chemical company with significant upstream and downstream relationships. We had to exercise caution not to develop a system that would break us apart but one that would bring us closer together." To assist in formulating a balanced plan, Vista hired a consulting firm with experience in both behavioral psychology and incentive compensation to work with its in-house committee.

After much research, the committee proposed an incentive compensation plan that utilized a financial formula based on return on investment to share the results of the organization's performance improvement. This method was chosen, in part, to ensure that the shareholders received at least a minimum return on their investment before sharing with the employees.

A threshold level for return on investment was established using a formula:

$$\text{ROI} = \text{net operating profit after taxes} \div \text{capital employed}$$

Of the financial performance in excess of this return on investment threshold, 7 percent was allocated to fund the incentive plan. The extrinsic incentive compensation opportunity was open-ended. The greater the return on investment over threshold, the more incentive compensation was available to the employees.

The Role of Quality

In conjunction with this incentives effort, Vista was also involved in a quality-improvement process based on Edwards Deming's principles. The company's emphasis is on natural work teams, consisting of a supervisor and his/her reports, with a focus on improving external customer satisfaction. "The philosophy is that everyone improves their actions on a continuous basis and the organization improves as a result of lots of small steps," said Wayne. "The gainsharing plan wasn't originally focused on quality, but as it evolved, it became evident that the quality-improvement process and the gainsharing process were intertwined."

As a result of this observation, a modifier, a customer satisfaction index, was added as a multiplier to the financial formula. This index could impact the financial formula either positively or negatively by as much as 10 percent. Based on customer satisfaction, the amount of incentive compensation funds available to the employees as a group could range from 6.3 percent to 7.7 percent of the improvement over threshold. In an effort to ensure fairness and to reduce the subjectivity of the customer satisfaction indicator, a family of measures was developed that included direct customer input, internal quality measurements that impact customer satisfaction, and measures of results, such as complaints, that are influenced by customer satisfaction.

Top-Down Objectives

Senior management provided the direction by identifying areas that were important to the company. These objectives were communicated to the natural work teams, who then met to define their specific performance objectives and assign a weighting to each one on a document called the Q Score Card. As this process cascaded down through the company, all employees became aware of the company's performance needs and how they, as individuals, could impact those needs.

Bottom-Up Objectives

Vista's quality process emphasizes the natural team concept. These natural teams were rolled up into thirty-nine work units for the purposes of the incentive plan. These work units are each responsible for their own local program objectives. "Work units develop their Q Score Card by putting together the elements of the cards from each natural team. This roll-up of specific objectives creates awareness and a willingness to help," Wayne tells us. "Each work unit has a payout based on the performance against their objectives.

"Approximately 50 percent of the Q Score Card must deal with the key objectives that were defined by executive management. Another 10 percent should be tied to some measure of performance of the group they serve. The remaining objectives can apply to the local things that the work unit may want to improve for the year." Wayne points out a key element that is a function of a financial formula: "Irrespective of the work unit's performance, a payout can occur only if the company's financial target has been exceeded."

The work units vary in size and composition. For example, a plant consisting of several natural teams all working together for a common end may make up one work unit. On the other hand, in an organization like the headquarters operation, a natural team in marketing may make up a work unit because of the singular nature of the function.

Wayne's experience has shown him some of the tradeoffs that have to be made to conform the concept to reality. "You want the payout teams to be as small as possible. This way they can focus on the tasks they have control over. They can measure their impact and receive their reward. In our situation, due to the type of business we are in, we had to go with larger groups to avoid problems such as internal competition that would create discord."

The Payout Formula

On a work unit level, each objective in the family of measures was assigned a weight percentage, the total of which equaled 100 percent. The objectives on this card combined to make up the formula that determined how the gains of improvement were shared with the employees. Each score card was evaluated and approved by two levels of management. Performance ratings for the objectives were reported each month. Thus, it was possible for the members of the work unit to calculate their scores by multiplying the performance rating times the weighting for each objective. The performance score was the sum of these calculations. The payout was issued to all employees once a year after the annual return on investment had been calculated.

The overall extrinsic incentive compensation budget was developed through the financial formula that calculated the total improvement over the return-on-investment threshold. The portion of this budget that was available for each team was based on the ratio of the team's payroll as a percent of the organization's total payroll budget. "This was done to assure that the incentive opportunity was the same for all work units," says Wayne. The same equity logic was applied in distributing the work unit's incentive earnings to individuals based on percent of salary.

Incentive payout began when the team achieved a Q Score of three performance points. This equates to 30 percent of the total incentive opportunity available to that team. At a Q Score of 10, the team received 100 percent of the total incentive opportunity. In order to make full use of human potential and to encourage overachievement, Vista extended the payout ceiling. A team that produced a Q Score of 13 would earn 130 percent of the total incentive opportunity as calculated by the payroll ratio. In other words, the financial formula established the budget, but management added a contingency to maintain the motivational appeal of the plan.

The maximum incentive compensation opportunity available to the employees equates to 10 percent of the return on investment in excess of threshold. At a 7 percent share of the improvement, with a positive customer satisfaction index modifier of 10 percent, the total improvement budget is 7.7 percent. A team that earns a Q Score of 13 will receive 130 percent of the 7.7 percent, for a total incentive compensation opportunity of 10 percent of the performance improvement. This is in addition to the employees' base pay. There is no pay at risk, and the incentive that is earned is not added to base pay or included in the calculation of benefits. There are four union locations, and all of them are participating in the plan. However, once established, the payout is outside of the bargaining process.

The figure of 10 percent was chosen as the incentive cap based on the traditional compensation rationale of industry standards and practice. In its research, Vista found that the average incentive opportunity for programs of this type among capital-intensive companies was around 10 percent. Vista also found that in labor-intensive companies the incentive compensation opportunity tends to be higher because the return on investment dollars tends to be lower.

Communications

The program was introduced to the management group during a day-long launch process that was facilitated by a consultant. The process was designed to get buy-in from the line managers, who had an opportunity to evaluate the plan and provide their input. According to Wayne Hilgers, "The cross-functional nature of the design team resulted in a good solid structure. There were only minor modifications as the result of the line management's feedback." Wayne thinks that there is another reason for the high degree of acceptance. "Our culture emphasizes the team. I'm sure that the members of the design team communicated with their functional teams during the design stage to solicit their input. I don't think anyone was surprised with the design when we announced it."

The plan was rolled out to the employees in natural team meetings conducted by the team leaders. Each supervisor was provided with a script and overhead projection presentation materials for the meetings, which took place over a period of days. Wayne thinks that the employees were comfortable with the concept in part because company policies had prepared them for it. "Before we installed our plan, we had seen three successful years where executive management had issued discretionary payments to the workforce at the end of the year. There was no formula and no formal commitment, but, as a result, the employees were experienced in sharing the gains of improvement."

Current performance is communicated to the employees throughout the year by a variety of methods. The company newsletter provides coverage, and the status of the financial indicator is reported quarterly in a letter from the president. The Q Score Cards are the basic method of performance feedback in this plan. Because these cards were developed by each work unit as a result of input from the natural teams, all employees are aware of the system and are involved with the process. The Q Score Cards are displayed in a highly visible location in the workplace and updated at least every month.

Broad-Based Training

As part of this plan, Vista has developed a four-day training seminar that all employees must attend. Wayne's group conducts most of this training, and the trainers in the plant locations carry it down into the organization. The training is called team management. "It should really be called management of team activities," comments Wayne. "The purpose is to make the employees aware of how to make their teams effective." Wayne tells us, "The training is a combination of the research that we did. It's the result of a lot of talking and a lot of listening. It contains elements gained from discussions with quality consultants and behavioral consultants, from visits to other organizations, and from a lot of reading."

The training provides a detailed picture of how all the elements of the culture work together. Employees learn about the concept of natural teams using the quality-management processes, the techniques of providing positive reinforcement on a timely basis, the use of performance data to manage the process and people, and tying it all together under an incentive umbrella that shares the gains of improvement.

Management Commitment

Management has taken a highly visible role in participating and supporting the total culture at Vista. Wayne says that the team management training in most sections "is taught by high-level managers in the company." At the classes for the headquarters employees, the chairman visits and talks about his team and its objectives and accomplishments. In the field operations, the plant manager teaches a section of the course.

Emphasizing Quality

Natural teams are the essence of the culture at Vista Chemical. In both the total quality-management process and the gainsharing plan, these teams are the heart of the operations structure. Seizing the opportunity to integrate these activities and benefit from the synergies, a category has been established on the Q Score Card to encourage the natural teams to maximize their participation in the quality process. Going forward, the quality process will be a line item on the score card.

So How Is It Going?

The Vista plan was introduced in December 1989, and all the Q Score Cards were installed by February 1, 1990. "The employee interest is high, and there has been lots of progress so far. As an example, the work unit that I am a member of currently has a Q Score of 10.2," says Wayne. "As a company, we expect to see even more improvement over time. The Q Score Cards for next year have already been submitted and approved. From the standpoint of maximizing our human potential, we are well focused."

Vista Chemical's nonexecutive incentive compensation plan is a clear picture of a goal-driven gainsharing design. The incentive budget is funded by the return generated by the operation, thereby ensuring that both the company and the employee gain. The organization's priorities are communicated to the workforce, and all employees participate in a process that results in a better understanding of the business. The performance of work units against multiple, localized objectives determines the amount of incremental incentive earnings. Before an incentive payment can be made, not only the return-on-investment threshold but also the local performance threshold(s) must be exceeded.

Is There a Downside?

Wayne points out that under this type of plan it is possible for the employees to score well and receive no incentive compensation as a result of such influences as the economy or poor performance of the organization overall. From a motivational standpoint, this uncertainty of payout represents the downside of this design. Another problem is that the plan is somewhat complex and may not be easy for the average hourly worker to understand. Performance is disassociated from the source of incentive funds, although there is a payout relationship. Finally, the incentive compensation payout is infrequent, being on an annual basis.

Is this reason for concern? From the perspective of a behavior-based incentive compensation plan, there are several ways to balance the problem of the extrinsic payouts being uncertain and infrequent. Vista Chemical worked to those strengths as a result of its consultant's expertise in the field of behavioral psychology and its involvement in total quality management. In effect, Vista designed a behavior-based incentive compensation plan that provides opportunities to fulfill the employees' intrinsic needs.

Strong Intrinsic Compensation

"The heart and soul of Vista's plan is people meeting in small groups to review their performance, evaluate the progress, provide recognition and encouragement for improvement, and take corrective action when it is necessary," says Wayne. "We have found that in order to positively reinforce the idea of daily, continuous improvement, it is necessary to interact with the employees on an ongoing basis rather than just once at the beginning of the year."

In an industry where oil prices and economics have such a significant impact on revenues and profitability, what if there is no payout at the end of the year?

"Our employees understand the economics," says Wayne. "They know that if there is no share for the shareholder, there will be no share for the employee. They also understand that they are putting something in place today that will reward them down the road. But more than the reward is the fact that we communicate with each other, support each other, and provide performance feedback and positive reinforcement all year long. We have developed the systems to track performance and communicate results. What makes this process work? What makes the employees participate? It's as simple as talking to them!" It is also important to note that the employee compensation packages are competitive and that no pay is at risk.

Total Effectiveness Rating Analysis: Vista Chemical

Armed with an understanding of the environment, culture, and compensation plan design, we can use the total effectiveness rating model developed in Chapter 4 to analyze the design of Vista's plan. Looking at the numeric relationship developed as the result of the analysis, we can see that the incentive compensation plan has an effectiveness rating of twelve points, equivalent to a basic nonexecutive incentive compensation rating. (See Figure 7-1.)

Examining the intrinsic and extrinsic incentive elements of the plan, we find a normal relationship between the factors of why-pay and focus. The natural team process drove the performance objectives down to the individual level and created a strong sense of focus on the part of all employees. In the analysis, this portion of the design was effective, combining the basic weighted values of the two factors for a subtotal of two points.

The relationship between the factors of what-pay and positive-reinforcement appears to be unequally balanced. The factor of what-

Figure 7-1. Total effectiveness rating for Vista Chemical.

Extrinsic Factors		Intrinsic Factors		Subtotal Rating		How-Pay Modifier		Total Rating
Factor	Weight	Weight	Factor					
Why-Pay	1	+ 1	Focus	= 2	+	0	=	2
(weak)			(strong)					
What-Pay	1	+ 3	Positive Reinforcement	= 4	+	0	=	4
(weak)			(strong)					
How-Pay	2	+ 4	Empowerment	= 6	+	0	=	6
						Total Points		12

pay has lost much of its motivational impact because the financial formula is subject to outside influences. This removes the element of certainty from the reward process, and performance is disassociated from the incentive compensation. This can be represented by bringing one point, only half the basic weighted value (two points) of the what-pay factor to bear in the model.

This motivational weakness is offset in the relationship by the additional emphasis that the organization has placed on intrinsic compensation. The management commitment, training, team emphasis, and timely, data-based performance feedback all contribute to an environment that provides plenty of opportunity to fulfill the employees' need for positive reinforcement. This can be represented by bringing three points, 150 percent of the basic weighted value (two points) of the positive reinforcement factor to bear in the model. As a result, this portion of the design balances out and results in a subtotal rating of four points.

With so much emphasis placed on the factor of positive reinforcement, if the factor of what-pay had been designed to be more immediate and certain, its overall motivational effect would have been increased. For example, if the financial formula had been designed to be unaffected by outside influences, the effect on the motivational power of the plan could be represented by the addition of the basic full weighted value of the what-pay factor (two points) for a subtotal of five points.

Normally, the modifying factor of how-pay can add considerable weight to the overall total score because it affects each of the intrinsic factors. In this situation, however, it could be considered underpowered. Placing the payout on an annual basis and making it uncertain removed the last two of the three key motivational elements: positive, immediate, and certain. This can be represented by bringing only two points, 66 percent of the basic weighted value (three points) of the how-pay factor to bear in the model. Here again, the culture and environment carried the day by providing intrinsic compensation sufficient to offset the underpowered extrinsic elements of the design. The team and quality elements of the culture provided the employees with a high degree of empowerment. This can be represented by four points, bringing 133 percent of the basic weighted value (three points) of the empowerment factor to bear on the model for a subtotal rating of six points.

The analysis indicates that the extrinsic compensation portion of the formula lacks the motivational strength that it could have produced. Offsetting this is a very powerful intrinsic compensation portion. While this type of design requires a high degree of application effort on the part of management, it does result in a functioning program. Does this plan have sustainability? Can it be considered an extrinsic incentive compensation plan if a change in the economy causes it to fail to pay out compensation? Is it possible to increase the amount of intrinsic compensation enough to keep the formula balanced in the event that there is no extrinsic payout? Only time will tell. For now, according to Wayne Hilgers, "it's working fine."

In an update to this case history, Vista was acquired by a German company in mid 1991. According to Wayne Hilgers, this means that Vista will need to reevaluate the financial formula used to fund the incentive pool. Additionally, Hilgers states they are developing a mechanism that will allow adjustments to the Q cards to be made during the year in order to maintain focus on changing business issues.

Corning Incorporated

Corning Incorporated has been involved in the quality-management process since the early 1980s. James Houghton, chairman and CEO, has gone on record as being committed to the process. The company has identified the overall cost of quality as a significant organizational need in terms of both economic value and organizational effectiveness. In 1988, the economic value was between 20 percent and 30 percent of sales. Organizational effectiveness was included as an objective based on Corning's definition of quality: meeting the customer's requirements. To Corning, this means that everyone has a customer, and therefore everyone in the company must be involved in the quality process.

James Houghton believes that improving quality is a process that must be established for the long term. In any long-term drive, the question is one of how to keep the employees committed to and involved in the process. The answer, obvious to us, is to offer them a share in the gains of improvement that result from the application of the process. The other alternative—asking the employees to participate in a process that will provide substantial benefits to the organization but will not provide them an opportunity to participate in those benefits—fails to answer their question, "Why should I participate?"

Commitment to the intent of an organization requires an understanding of what that intent is. It also requires an understanding not only of the importance of the organization's direction, policies, and goals but also of the process for measuring progress toward implementing them. The quality-management process develops this understanding. Commitment is a unique attitude that is produced by a combination of rational thought and human emotion that makes employees "feel good." Unfortunately, this feeling can ebb as the day-to-day work effort takes its toll.

If the process is extended one step further and the employees are given the opportunity to earn rewards for the improvement, they will develop personal interest in continuing the application of the process. Total quality management involves employees changing their habits, attitudes, and thinking. Not only does incentive compensation seem to be an element in the process that can address the issue of sustainability, but it also seems to be a means of facilitating initial, sincere acceptance and implementation of the process.

Corning is committed to a culture that emphasizes gainful employment, the opportunity to grow, and job security as it relates to the health of the organization. Incentive compensation is a logical outgrowth of this type of culture. Claude Sullivan, director of human resources services for Corning, tells us about his company's incentive compensation philosophy: "We want our employees to relate more closely to the success of the company, and we know we can accomplish that if we tie pay more closely to performance."

The Individual and the Group

Corning has taken a holistic approach to performance improvement. The company has both a quality-management process and a compensation philosophy that encourages improvement on the individual and group level. On an individual level, there is the merit increase plan and a division cash award. At Corning, performance evaluation is a developmental tool that creates an action plan for individual improvement.

Once a year, each individual receives an evaluation called the performance development and review, which is kept independent of any salary action. "The focus is to conduct a constructive evaluation that recognizes strengths and formulates action plans to work on weaknesses," says Claude. The salary action follows three months later, along with another discussion of performance.

The other compensation element that encourages individual improvement is the division cash award. "The purpose of this award is to provide positive and immediate reinforcement to those employees who exhibit behavior that is considered important to the organization," says Claude. "It may not be the cash that has such a positive effect, it may be the recognition of going up to an employee and saying, 'Here, this is in appreciation for that exceptional contribution you made.'" This program has a budget equal to 1 percent of the salary budget, and funding is passed down to the department level for distribution. A supervisor can nominate an employee for the award anytime and with as little as a single written line of explanation. The approval authority is one level up, and the check is generally awarded within one week of recommendation. In consideration of the other programs that exist at Corning, there is an annual cap on the division cash awards of 8 percent of the recipient's base salary. The employee pays the taxes on the award. (The issue of taxation is discussed in more detail in Chapter 10.) "We see this award as supporting the philosophy of our business," says Claude. "We have a very active quality process, and variable compensation is a logical outgrowth of that. It's a way of getting the employees involved and empowered. Our quality process and our variable-compensation process are intertwined."

Improvement on the group level is encouraged through the use of two reward programs, the corporate performance bonus plan and the goalsharing plan. The bonus plan is based on the organization's improvement. It includes all salaried employees and has a financial formula that funds the process based on performance against return on equity. The payout has a range of between 5 percent and 10 percent of base salary. The payout is annual, and all salaried employees receive the same percent of base compensation. In the two years the plan has been in existence, the payout has been 7.5 percent and 8.75 percent. According to Claude, "Our employees are quite happy with the bonus plan."

Goalsharing

In 1988, Corning initiated its "goalsharing" plan, which, as Claude is quick to point out, "is not gainsharing. In this plan, if you meet your goals, if you improve performance in your operation, you receive a payout." The reward portion of the plan consists of an annual payout based on the combination of a corporate financial indicator and team performance toward specific objectives. In 1990, the goalsharing plan was in place at one plant and scheduled to be

installed in all facilities by the end of 1992. It takes in all salaried and
hourly employees, including managers. According to Claude, it is
being introduced into the union environments with a high degree of
receptivity.

The fundamentals of the plan revolve around the plant as the
team. A committee identifies performance objectives for the plant and
sets improvement goals for each objective. Payout is based on performance against these goals. The committee consists of the plant
manager and a cross section of salaried employees and hourly
workers. As a result, the objectives are meaningful and relevant to all
participants. They are objectives that the employees can have a direct
impact on in their daily work efforts.

On average, there are five objectives, or goals as they are called at
Corning, per plant. These goals must contribute to the corporation's
objectives and be issues of significance to the local business. Most
often they will consist of such measures as cost per piece, quality,
customer service, and safety. In keeping with the corporation's
philosophy, the goals place emphasis on daily, continuous improvement. The corporate staff reviews the plans of each plant to ensure
consistency of purpose with the corporate goals and equity of opportunity between facilities.

The Payout

The same techniques that are part of the quality process are used
to identify the objectives and measures for incentive compensation.
Once the objectives have been determined, the process utilizes a
matrix measurement similar to the measurement matrix discussed in
Chapter 5. Each objective is weighted according to its value to the
organization. A base level and goal are established for each objective.
Performance is calculated as a percent of goal attainment and
multiplied by the weighting to arrive at a performance indicator for
that objective. These performance indicators are added together, and
the sum is expressed as a percentage of total goal attainment.

An amount equal to 10 percent of the total salary budget is
allocated for the goalsharing incentive compensation. The incentive
compensation payout range is from zero to 10 percent with a payout
target of 5 percent. As an example, if performance against all objectives is at 100 percent, then the payout goal of 5 percent is multiplied
by 100 percent (the sum of all of the performance indicators), and
each participant receives 5 percent of base salary as the incentive
compensation. Figure 7-2 illustrates the relationship between payout
and performance.

"We issue the incentive compensation payout once a year to
maximize the impact of the check," says Claude. "We very consciously

Figure 7-2. Example of a Corning-style goalsharing matrix.

Performance Objectives	Monthly Percentage of Goal												Weight	Performance Indicators
	1	2	3	4	5	6	7	8	9	10	11	12		
													10%	
													10%	
													20%	
													10%	
													15%	
													15%	
													20%	

Base Goal Cap

Incentive Range = 0% 5% 10%

Incentive Payout = goal (5%) X Performance Indicator

100% | Sum of Performance Indicators

developed a program that will focus our activity on setting *future goals* rather than rewarding improvement over past performance. This type of a plan gives us the opportunity to revisit our decisions every year. This ensures that the objectives that we work on and the goals that are set will be fair and equitable for the business situation at that facility. The goalsharing element builds teamwork and commitment to the success of the unit."

The 75-25 Split

Figure 7-2 does not depict the total process for calculating the incentive compensation payout. The payout structure in the goalsharing plan is based on two factors: a physical formula, which is made up of a family of measures at the plant level, and a financial formula, which is related to the corporation's overall success. The physical formula contributes 75 percent of the earning opportunity, and the financial formula contributes 25 percent of the earning opportunity. Using the physical formula, at 100 percent of performance goal, the participants earn an amount equal to 3.75 percent of their base salaries (total incentive payout opportunity goal is 5 percent with a cap at 10 percent for a total performance of 200 percent).

Twenty-five percent of the employees' earning opportunity is tied to the financial formula of return on equity. At a performance goal of 100 percent in this category, the participants earn an amount equal to 1.25 percent of their base salaries, with a maximum incentive opportunity of 2.5 percent, for performance at 200 percent. Claude states, "The financial formula was developed using a model that would forecast a what-if scenario. We applied data for the last 20 years to develop a formula that would equitably reflect the company's performance."

The return-on-equity formula contains a base level below which no funds will be contributed to the incentive compensation budget. It also contains a return-on-equity goal, at which 12.5 percent of the total incentive compensation budget will be contributed to the goalsharing budget, and a cap, at which the full 25 percent of the total incentive compensation budget will be contributed. "The calculation is easy," says Claude. "In either category, the performance is calculated as a percentage of goal. That percentage is then multiplied by the incentive payout that is budgeted for performance at goal (5 percent of base salary). This calculation brings you to the gross incentive payout for that performance indicator. If the indicator is the physical indicator, the plant's goals, the payout is then multiplied by 75 percent to arrive at a net payout number for that category. If the indicator is the financial indicator, the return-on-equity goal, the payout is multiplied by 25 percent. Those two net numbers, added together, form the net payout that each participant receives."

In effect, this is really two plans in one. In one plan, 25 percent of the incentive opportunity is based on a profit-sharing concept that ties the employees' fortunes to the organization's success. This approach provides strong financial justification for the incentive payout. In the other plan, a form of objective-based, large-group incentive focuses employees on specific, more localized criteria. Financial justification is more difficult to establish with this approach owing to the nature of the objectives.

Claude tells us, "This is not a complicated calculation for our employees. The secret is to communicate and educate. If you do that, the program will be understood and well received. As a result of our communication process, our employees at all levels know what they can do to impact the return on equity. We are also very careful to communicate to our employees that this is not profit sharing," says Claude. "We emphasize the fact that this is goalsharing. We let them know that 'If the company performs in a certain way, you will receive a percent of your salary in variable pay,' and we work with them to identify how they can make an impact."

Putting Compensation at Risk

Question: When is at-risk compensation not at-risk compensation? Answer: When the merit increase would not have been issued to begin with. When Corning suffered the effects of a downturn in the industry, management decided to forgo the planned 5 percent merit increase for that year. Rather than play compensation catchup, Corning decided to take advantage of the situation and modify the corporation's payline philosophy by installing incentive compensation. The incentive compensation payout structure was developed so that performance at goal would provide the "missing 5 percent." As a result, the corporation has a payline that is 5 percent below that of the industry average and a pay philosophy that can result in compensation up to 5 percent above that of the industry average, based on performance.

Have the employees put some of their compensation at risk? As is so often the case with incentive compensation, it is a matter of perception. From the technical compensation standpoint, the answer may be yes. From the employees' standpoint, the answer may be no. After all, you can't put something at risk that you don't have or will not be getting. It depends on how the information was presented to the employees.

Communications

According to Claude Sullivan, Corning's human resources community was a strong supporter of the design, development, and implementation of this incentive compensation philosophy. The roll-out was conducted by the division manager, who held a general meeting to emphasize to all of the employees that this was a local program with objectives that could be impacted by the plant. To ensure uniformity of message, the human resources organization developed and provided the division manager with a script, a video, overhead projection material, and brochures for each employee. Worksheets were provided along with copies of the company's annual report. Each employee was coached through the calculation process to determine what his or her individual incentive compensation would have been for the previous year if the plan had been in place. Compensation professionals were on hand to assist in answering questions.

The quality teams were utilized to enhance the education process. Group activities were scheduled, and quality-process techniques such as brainstorming and problem solving were utilized to identify what would be done to impact the performance objectives from both a work-group and an individual basis. The same process was used to identify how to measure performance improvement and how to calculate incentive earnings. One of the results of all this was the realization on the part of the employees that the quality process provided the means for them to earn incentive compensation. This opportunity provided the daily motivation to perform in a quality manner, to make the small improvements that would culminate in the organization reaching and surpassing its objectives.

The Next Generation

Looking backward, would Corning have done anything differently? According to Claude, "We wouldn't change it. Our program communicates the message to our employees that it is important to improve and that if they improve they will receive a share." He did add, "We are working to make our payout opportunity at goal more substantial. I would like to see a range of from zero to 20 percent with a 10-percent incentive opportunity at goal. We are also considering increasing the amount available for the division cash award."

Summary

Corning's nonexecutive incentive compensation plan is a hybrid design that is customized to the company's own environment. Examining the goalsharing element of the plan using the BBIC Fishbone diagram, it is easy to see that the extrinsic factor of why-pay contains key elements that are relevant to the employees. The physical formula provides specific objectives that they can impact. While there may be a financial rationale to the productivity and cost objectives, other objectives make no financially defined contribution to the incentive budget. This is not uncommon in a physical formula design. Often there will be one or two objectives that generate the revenue to fund the payout. This provides management with the opportunity to include in the plan other objectives that may be more oriented toward organizational effectiveness than economic value. The same rationale that economically justifies the quality-management process applies to this type of incentive payout design. All the little, constant improvements and daily contributions will add up. If the improvement is there on the local level, then in the long run the improvement will be there for the organization as a whole.

What about the financial formula, the return-on-equity element of the plan? This factor addresses the organization's need for economic value. It is management's buffer to ensure that the performance improvement is there for the organization in conjunction with the incentive payout for the employee. As in most financial formulas, the objective is remote from the employees' daily performance. The management at Corning understands this and works hard to address the employees' need for focus and empowerment. As a result, the employees understand how they as individuals fit into the formula. But by the very nature of the formula, the outside influences that affect the payout are beyond their control. As a result, this element of the plan is not a strong supporter of empowerment. But at 25 percent of the payout, this may be an acceptable tradeoff to cultivate employee identification with the organization's success.

Total Effectiveness Rating Analysis: Corning Incorporated

Based on what we know of Corning's environment, culture, and the nonexecutive incentive compensation plan called goalsharing, we can use the BBIC Fishbone diagram and the total effectiveness rating model to analyze the plan design. (See Figure 7-3.) Looking at the numeric relationship developed as the result of the rating analysis, we can see that the incentive compensation plan could be given a rating of sixteen points. This is four points above the effectiveness rating established for a basic incentive compensation plan. This high rating indicates that the incentive compensation plan design contains elements that are present in a behavior-based incentive compensation plan.

Examining the intrinsic and extrinsic incentive elements of the plan, we find that the factors of why-pay and focus are above average in strength. This is the result of the utilization of the quality-management process and associated problem-solving/performance-improvement tools. The application of these tools and the team-oriented process resulted in establishing clear, precise performance objectives with well-defined measurements and goals. According to Claude Sullivan, all employees were well focused on what they needed to do to impact the objectives. The combined motivational effect of these elements could be considered almost double the effect of a basic incentive compensation plan with no behavioral elements. This can be represented by bringing twice the basic weighted value (one point) of both the why-pay factor and the focus factor to bear in the

Figure 7-3. Total effectiveness rating for Corning, Inc.

Extrinsic Factors			Intrinsic Factors		Subtotal Rating	How-Pay Modifier	Total Rating
Factor	Weight	Weight	Factor				
(strong) Why-Pay	2	+ 2	(strong) Focus	=	4	+ 0	= 4
(strong) What-Pay	3	+ 3	(strong) Positive Reinforcement	=	6	+ 0	= 6
(weak) How-Pay	2	+ 4	(strong) Empowerment	=	6	+ 0	= 6
					16	Total Points	16

model. Each factor is assigned two points and as a result, this portion of the design results in a subtotal of four points.

Continuing with this analysis technique, we see that the plan has an unusually strong relationship between the factors of what-pay and positive reinforcement. The goalsharing strategy emphasizes payout for performance improvement and provides assurance to the employees that the incentive will be received if performance improves. As part of the positive, immediate, and certain elements of motivation, the goalsharing funding strategy assures that the payout is certain.

The extrinsic incentive opportunity, with a range of from zero to 10 percent, may be a little weak and therefore not as "positive" as it could be. Increasing this extrinsic incentive opportunity, as Claude Sullivan wants to do, would certainly increase the positive motivational power of the plan. But as it stands, it does not hurt the plan because of the high degree of intrinsic compensation that it is associated with. The positive reinforcement factor is extremely supportive as a result of the quality-management systems that are designed to provide measurement and performance feedback. Each of these factors is more developed in this plan than in a basic incentive compensation plan. This can be represented by bringing 150 percent of the basic weighted value (two points) of both the what-pay factor and the positive reinforcement factor to bear in the model. Each factor is assigned three points and as a result, this portion of the design results in a subtotal rating of six points.

We know that the factor of how-pay is a modifying factor because it has a significant impact on each of the intrinsic compensation factors. A critical element of how-pay is the payout process, which is where theory meets reality and the organization actually gives out cash money. As such, this element of the plan may be treated in a conservative manner. Yet, there is very little reason to be timid at this point. If the plan is well thought out and management has confidence in the design, then there is much to be gained by acting boldly.

In Corning's design, however, this factor was developed conservatively. The payout is delivered on an annual basis in combination with what could be interpreted, in concept, to be at-risk compensation. This results in diminishing the effectiveness of the incentive from the standpoint of being positive and immediate, two of the three key elements of motivation. If the range of incentive opportunity were raised from 10 percent to 20 percent, then the rationale for holding payment to make the checks large enough to be significant is no longer a consideration, and the payout process could be accelerated to a monthly level. This would have a significant motivational impact on the intrinsic factors of focus, positive reinforcement, and empowerment.

As it stands, the factor of how-pay is underpowered and has a modifying impact only on the factor with which it is linked, empowerment. This can be represented by bringing just two points, 66 percent of the basic weighted value (three points) to bear only on the intrinsic factor of empowerment. As it did with the other factors, the quality-management process carries the day. It provides sufficient intrinsic compensation in the form of empowerment to offset the underpowered extrinsic factor of how-pay. This can be represented by bringing four points, 133 percent of the basic weighted value (three points) of the empowerment factor to bear in the model.

The combined effect of the incentive compensation and the quality process generates a solid overall effectiveness rating of sixteen points. With some minor modifications to the factor of how-pay, the motivational impact would soar. That may be the next step for this leading-edge program, but for now it looks as if the success of the behavior-based incentive compensation plan at Corning is assured.

The Grand Unification Theory

Don McAdams, executive vice president of the American Productivity and Quality Center, notes that out of extensive research performed by the center has come the following conclusion: American business is moving toward a concept of management that emphasizes quality in every aspect.

Organizations pursuing this management approach exhibit elements that have been identified as critical to its success:

- Strong and visible commitment from the CEO
- Lots of employee involvement, and the systems to support it
- An understanding of the customer's needs and the process of how those needs are met
- A plan for change
- Ample training for the employees in such areas as:
    Just-in-time inventory management
    Statistical process control to identify and eliminate variables
    Data-based problem solving
- Cycle time analysis to reduce response time to the market
- Job redesign/enrichment
- Incentive compensation to reinforce the desired performance

The intuitive observation, supported by case history data, is that incentive compensation will act to integrate all the quality-improvement elements into a single process in the perception of the employee.

In total quality management, all changes and training are focused directly or indirectly on a measurable family of issues such as productivity, quality, timeliness, and service. When rewards are tied to this family of measures, the employees understand how each element is a necessary part of a process that will yield personal reward based on participation.

8

The Organizational Environment and Employee Involvement

By now it should be obvious that you cannot design and implement a successful behavior-based incentive compensation plan in a vacuum. Certainly, the familiar compensation matrix that maintains the financial relationships is as important as ever. But it is only a small part of a more complex matrix that includes such elements as management style and the cultural environment of the organization. And the closer we look the more we find these elements to be mutually supportive.

The Symbiotic Loop of Incentives and Employee Involvement

Being a combination of motivation and compensation, a behavior-based incentive compensation philosophy cannot be successful based solely on the payout structure. Just as a hazardous work environment makes it more difficult for employees to focus their total commitment to the task at hand, so will an incentive compensation plan be unable to effectively motivate employees if it fails to provide the proper environmental support.

Behavior-based incentive compensation is dependent upon a culture of active employee involvement. Such a culture stresses contribution to the bottom line and provides ways for the employees to participate in making improvements. There is a strong relationship between employee involvement and incentive compensation. As with the quality process, incentive compensation provides the reason to participate in the available systems.

For that reason, it is necessary to understand the support matrix that exists throughout the organization. This matrix consists not only of such relatively tangible elements as the organization's structure, communication systems, and training programs, but also of such relatively intangible elements as corporate culture and the attitudes of both employees and management toward the quality process. To the degree that employee involvement has a sufficient support matrix, behavior-based incentive compensation will act as a multiplier on the results of that process.

The fact of the matter is that compensation philosophy needs to include the environmental element as well as the financial element. We know from experience that changes in the business, organizational, or human resources environment will initiate changes in compensation plan designs. Conversely, we can intuitively see that changes in the compensation philosophy will change the environment, at least on the organizational and human resources level. An organization that has an incentive compensation philosophy will, by nature, gravitate toward a culture where excellence is expected and rewarded.

In such an environment, the intent of the organization will be clear to everyone. Accountability is a cultural factor that comes into being as the result of the pressure to perform. This pressure will be the result of two elements: (1) active, formal communication and performance-feedback systems that provide intrinsic reward; (2) the extrinsic financial compensation itself. Feedback of both types is critical because without feedback there can be no fine-tuning of performance by the employees and no means by which the change can be managed. This means that behavior-based incentive compensation is a group effort, requiring the stewardship of those who are skilled in such disciplines of change as organizational development, training, and employee relations.

Until employees are fully informed as to where they and the organization are going, they will not feel confident enough to unleash their full potential by taking the initiative. They will not feel empowered to act because they are not sure that they know where the organization is headed.

The organizational environment and the involvement systems that exist in that environment all address the factor of empowerment. Empowerment seems to exist in an environment of management support where systems are in place to capture and channel the unleashed human potential.

The Chicken and the Egg

If there is no empowerment, there can be no behavior-based incentive compensation. Empowerment in a BBIC situation is driven by the fundamental powers of self-interest and needs fulfillment. This translates on a higher level into total commitment to the organization's intent on the part of the employee. For that reason, behavior-based incentive compensation drives employee involvement. Conversely, the quality of employee-involvement systems determines how successful behavior-based incentive compensation will be in affecting the organization's performance.

Assessment Surveys

Incentive compensation of any kind will probably not work in an environment where the employees perceive initiative as being risky. In such an environment of mistrust, any program that requires the employees to contribute additional resources will be viewed with suspicion. Therefore, it is necessary to gather sufficient data about the employees' perception of the culture and environment of the organization in order to answer the question, "How ready are we to begin the installation of behavior-based incentive compensation?"

As we have observed, compensation interacts with a company's culture. Surveys can be used to gauge the well-being of the employees and their readiness to participate in the cultural change associated with behavior-based incentive compensation. Internally focused audits that measure quality of work life and externally focused audits that measure customer satisfaction will both be beneficial to achieving a total understanding of the environmental issues.

There are many organizational development consultants who can assist in the development and implementation of the surveys required to capture and analyze this information. In many instances, this will be the most cost-effective and objective approach. Whether outside assistance is utilized or not, the recommended process should consist of a comprehensive organizational survey and a survey of the perceptions of senior management. The organizational survey should consist of a core element, to compare to industry norms, and a flexible element, which should address the unique concerns of groups within the organization.

In assessing the organization's readiness for BBIC, both readiness of operations and readiness of culture should be investigated. In the area of operations, it is a question of whether or not the existing work system and process are amenable to a behavior-based incentive compensation philosophy. To what degree are the current performance-evaluation systems and the operational systems associated? Will a change in one require a significant adjustment to the other?

In the area of culture, there are several questions: Do people at all levels feel free to express their ideas without fear? Do the employees relate to the organization as a group or as individuals? Do people at all levels know what the goals are and what is expected of them? Do the employees have a sense of pride that is associated with the pressure to perform? Is there trust between management and non-management employees? Is the work environment in constant crisis, or is it calm and organized?

These categories can be explored through the use of surveys or focus groups. Whatever technique that is used to evaluate readiness, one of the results should be a list of constraints that, properly addressed, will ensure the smoothest installation of the incentive compensation plan. These constraints should be viewed in light of the BBIC Fishbone diagram, which will provide the necessary insight to overcome the constraints by balancing the BBIC formula with the proper mix of intrinsic and extrinsic rewards.

Designing a plan just to address the company's need for organizational effectiveness through a cultural environment of employee involvement may not provide the hard dollar results that are necessary for survival in the business world of the 1990s. On the other hand, emphasizing the purely numerical approach of the compensation matrix ignores the vital issues of leadership and people. The answer is to create a culture where the human element feels supported by the financial elements. After all, it is the human element that produces the results.

Commitment and Congruence

Having examined several case histories and having heard from a score of experts on the matter, we can conclude that the design process for a nonexecutive incentive compensation plan starts with support from top management. It is a well-known fact of business life that the normal organizational environment fosters a reluctance on the part of most employees to experiment with anything that might jeopardize their current success. But if such behavior changes are actively supported by the managers, the situation turns around, and the employees, on all levels, are free to act. On the mid-management level, senior executives must set the standards and expectations to be met.

It is not surprising to find that the first step in the design process is for management to exhibit active, involved leadership, visibly committed to the effort. This will in turn foster active, involved, committed participation on the part of the employees. What is a good indicator of the true level of top-management commitment? In a word, funding. Are the executives willing to put their money where their mouths are? If the factor of what-pay in the BBIC Fishbone diagram shows an equitable and motivational distribution of funds, then employee perceptions are strong that the top management is totally behind the philosophy. If ample funding is actually and realistically available to the employees, incentive opportunity will rise, and foot-dragging, or passive resistance, will decline.

The factor of why-pay also carries significant weight when it comes to demonstrating executive commitment. Putting aside the altruistic overtones, management becomes committed to behavior-based incentive compensation because of the short- and long-term financial impact such a compensation philosophy will have on the bottom line. What is important here is the degree of commitment.

Management will also have to commit to sharing financial and performance information with the employees. The degree of this sharing is proportional to the degree they will be able to "walk the talk" in front of the employees.

Once executive support has been developed for behavior-based incentive compensation, the next step is to ensure that the specific tactical goals of the incentive compensation plan are congruent with the compensation philosophy's objectives. In order to do this, it is necessary to establish a clear link between the organization's strategic plans and the program design. We have seen how the BBIC Fishbone diagram can act as a tool to identify the relationships and build the linkage between the organization's needs and the employees' needs. The Fishbone diagram can also act as a communication tool to gain top management's understanding and agreement.

It is critical for all levels of management to understand the linkage between their unit's objectives and the compensation plan design. Incentive compensation can be a bittersweet development, especially to middle management, so the more benefit they perceive in it, the easier it will be for them to accept it. The sweet part is the positive effect that incentive compensation has on performance results. The bitter part is that those performance increases attack the traditional role of middle management. As described in the following section, this attack is two-pronged and cuts to the heart of established methods of managing.

In order for you to help managers cope with change, it is important for you to have a good understanding of the management style that exists throughout the organization. In the world of sales, the reference is to "know your buyer." Identifying the overall management style and the substyles that exist by department will enable you to communicate the benefits of behavior-based incentive compensation in terms that are meaningful to the individual manager.

Management's Readiness for Equal Pay and Empowerment

In an article in the *Harvard Business Review*, Rosabeth Moss Kanter described the disturbing effect of incentive compensation on the perception of the organizational chain of command.[1] Traditional hierarchy relationships, by definition, are based on a degree of in-equality. Traditional compensation evolved to support this system through two specific relationships. One relationship is that between pay and the value of the position to the organization. This is the obvious process of controlling compensation costs. The other rela-tionship is that between pay and the organizational structure; this appears to be the process of using compensation to establish or define authority. The compensation concept of "pay compression" could be considered a manifestation of this thinking.

Providing employees with the opportunity to augment their pay through performance improvement creates the potential for a subor-dinate to make more than a superior ("pay compression"). In an in-centive compensation program, where performance objectives are clearly defined, contributions are clearly measured, and rewards are contingent upon performance rather than personalities, the tradi-tional bonds of hierarchical authority tend to give way to relationships based on respect. (For this reason, incentive compensation would be extremely difficult to install in a military environment.) There is also the potential for middle managers to perceive a threat to their job security. After all, in behavior-based incentive compensation, the idea of employee involvement is to provide empowerment to the em-ployees. As a result, the role of middle management is changed. Instead of managing by directive, first-line supervisors must be coaches. This takes away some of their management prerogatives, a difficult issue for them to address. Also, there is a real potential to flatten the organizational structure over time by changing the func-tion and, in doing so, to phase out a significant quantity of this level of management.

In a functioning environment of employee involvement, the em-ployees have received information, training, and been given permis-sion to take calculated risks. They are expected to think for them-selves as opposed to asking permission. They are encouraged to change their thinking away from the roles of reactive individuals, receiving instructions and filling predefined job functions. They are encouraged to think of themselves as owners, aware of and respon-sible for clearly defined results. As owners, they have the opportun-ities to investigate how their actions and results affect the owners of adjacent departments or organizations and adjust their actions to maximize results.

Naturally, all this is quite difficult for middle management to ac-cept. They can perceive the situation as one where they are caught in a top-down, bottom-up squeeze. To alleviate this perception, they need the training and support that will help them deal with and manage this threatening change to their environment. More ad-vanced employee-involvement cultures will have provided this type of training to their managers as part of an ongoing process. However, if you are embarking on the journey to improve the performance of the organization through the use of incentive compensation for the nonexecutive employees, you must institute training in the art of change management.

Middle managers must be provided support in order for them to be successful with this new management style. Their responses will be in direct relation to the degree that senior executives have exhibited their commitment. Their success will be determined, to a large degree, on how comfortable they are with the concept and process. Their comfort level, in turn, will be based on training, understanding, and how much involvement they had in the design process. In addition, they must be included in the incentive compensation, because they, too, will ask the question, "What's in it for me?"

Employee Readiness

Will the employees buy this stuff? Will they act according to the observed laws of human nature and respond to the opportunity to earn intrinsic and extrinsic compensation? Yes, they will. But the real question is, Will they do so automatically, or will they need assistance in the process?

Figure 8-1 is a graphic depiction of the various states that employees may be in prior to the implementation of a behavior-based incentive compensation plan. Their location on this scale will determine the balance of intrinsic and extrinsic incentive compensation that the initial plan should contain. Normally, the lower they are on the scale, the more intrinsic incentive opportunities will be available for inclusion in the plan design and the more impactful these opportunities will be.

Before introducing any new plan, it is important to understand the employees' current state of mind. One of the best ways to do this is to utilize an attitude survey to solicit and reflect the employees' perceptions. In the process of designing the survey, it would be well to consult focus groups of the employees who will be surveyed. This will assure that the survey, no matter what the process or how it is conducted, will include issues relevant to the employees. Such a format should result in a relatively accurate reading of employee perceptions and attitudes toward a change of this magnitude.

An accurate assessment of employee readiness is important for many reasons. For example, if they are hostile as the result of a history of mistrust, it will be necessary to conduct some major communications and team-building interventions prior to initiating an incentive compensation plan. If they are in the range of unaware, or

Figure 8-1. Employee readiness meter.

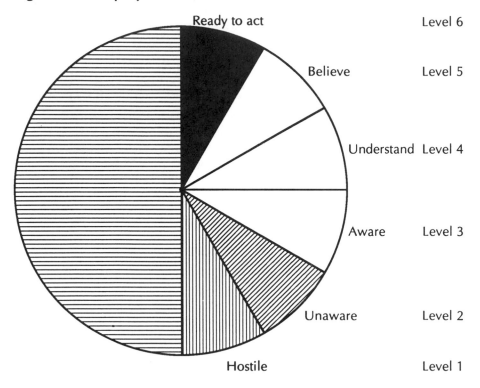

just aware, they may view incentive compensation as a destabilizing threat. Remember, most of the employees who will participate in such a plan desire a stable, fixed-income environment around which they can plan their lives. The initial reaction from many could be, "If I want to gamble, I'll go to Las Vegas."

It is necessary to raise the level of the employee readiness meter at least to level 4, that of understanding, prior to initiating the extrinsic portion of the compensation plan. At that level, the employees should understand the mechanics and financial relationships that benefit them and the organization. Moving the organization's awareness up to that level is really part of the program-implementation process. The intrinsic compensation factor in a behavior-based incentive compensation plan contains a wide variety of psychic tools that can be utilized to manage the changing perceptions of the employees. A partial inventory of this psychic toolbox includes employee involvement, training, communication, information sharing, performance feedback, promotional activities, honor, recognition, and management support. These tools may be the primary compensation vehicles used during the initial stages of implementation. Once a receptive environment has been cultivated, extrinsic compensation opportunities may be initiated.

How to Get Them Ready

Arthur Brief, professor of management and corporate culture at New York University's Graduate School of Business, has a performance formula: Productivity *equals* training *times* motivation. We have added the element of communication to that formula and displayed it in Figure 8-2. The pyramid illustrates that communication, training, and motivation are essential to any effort to improve performance. These are psychic tools in the incentive professional's toolbox that can be used to maintain the dynamic nature of behavior-based incentive compensation.

There is a story about the professor of business who was discussing the performance pyramid with her students. Having covered the topic of communications, she proceeded to discuss the value of the other two elements, training and motivation. In preparation, she asked a student if he could tell the class the difference between ignorance and apathy. The student responded, "I don't know and I don't care." Like the student, employees without training or direction may have a high level of activity but will tend to produce few results. On the other hand, trained and aware employees who lack motivation may be difficult to move to action.

Communicating the Concept

It's been said that vision *plus* self-management *plus* communication *plus* action *equals* empowerment. Generally speaking, when incentive compensation is first introduced to nonexecutive employees,

Figure 8-2. Performance pyramid.

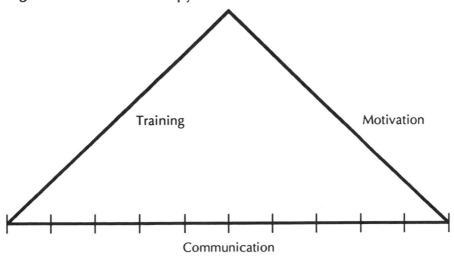

many of them may be reluctant to embrace it either because they don't believe that they can impact the measurement or because they don't understand the process. Communicating these two key elements is a significant undertaking, and because the process is somewhat detailed and often technical in nature, there is a real potential to lose the attention of the participants.

Speakeasy, Inc., with offices in Atlanta and San Francisco, is a consulting firm that provides training in the art of interpersonal communications and public speaking. Sandy Linver is the president of Speakeasy and the author of *Speak Easy* and *Speak and Get Results*. Her organization works with the fact that listeners decide at the beginning of any discourse how much attention to pay. Like anything else, paying attention requires effort (that's why it's not called *giving* attention). So the audience quickly performs a mental cost/benefit tradeoff analysis to determine what kind of an investment to make. The degree to which the employees will pay attention to what management is communicating to them is a function of how much they perceive the material to be of benefit to them.

This concept is worthy of consideration during the program communication process. Issues that are of great importance to the individuals who are responsible for the design of compensation plans are not necessarily of interest to the participating employees. You are familiar with compensation terms and techniques that the general employee has little or no knowledge of. Thus, you must be careful to communicate information about the plan in a manner that is easy to understand. Unless it's clear to participants what the new compensation system is all about, the plan's objectives will not be met.

The design of the information package and the process of how it is communicated to the employees should be a function of the environmental and readiness assessments. These assessments will tell you what the employees view as the most important elements of the package. When you include the key attributes of the behavior-based incentive compensation plan in the attitude surveys, the employees will be able to express their attitudes toward them and toward the delivery process. The material will be perceived as having value if it is designed and presented as a solution to specific problems or as an opportunity to fulfill specific needs. (Sounds a lot like the element in the total quality-management process that deals with understanding the customer, doesn't it?)

In short, the communications strategy should start with a benefit premise that states the positive consequences of the change to the employee. This is an excellent foundation from which to start the movement from unawareness to understanding and belief. Compensation is a personal subject, and the employees will view any discussion of it from an individual perspective.

Communications should cover both the micro and the macro elements of the compensation plan. There are the small details of the pay system, and there are the broader issues that affect pay, such as inflation, the state of the business, government regulation, and competitive issues. All of the elements need to be communicated in a process that will raise the consciousness of all employees to at least level 4, the level of understanding, on the readiness meter. Because there is a correlation between understanding and perception, this is an excellent approach to impact the employees' perception. The more they understand about the incentive compensation process, the more they will perceive it as an opportunity.

Communications are necessary to educate and to establish direction. In the roll-out of most traditional compensation plans, communications inform the employees as to the mechanics of the plan and the impact it will have on their pay. This information usually takes the form of a matrix, with the circumstances of the employee's pay applied to that matrix. This individual application assists in making the process meaningful to the employee. Great care is normally taken to assure that the employees understand the change and that their questions are answered. In general, the first announcement of a change in the pay philosophy is delivered to an audience that will be either negative or passive.

Behavior-based incentive compensation creates an additional avenue of communication that can be used to provide intrinsic compensation to the employees. They have the opportunity to participate actively and to benefit from that participation. There is the opportunity for communications to be used to generate enthusiasm for the incentive opportunity that is presented.

In a communications strategy for incentive compensation, the elements of awareness, acceptance, promotion, and excitement are all needed. The communication elements of promotion and excitement can make the difference between a static plan and a dynamic one. There is a real danger that, left to traditional thinking, the communications and administrative procedures will be designed to require a minimum of management effort. While nobody likes the thought of an administratively intensive program, it is important to understand that too many bureaucratic structures and too many management systems can drain the life from a dynamic process.

A behavior-based incentive compensation plan needs to remain dynamic in order to address the changing needs of the organization and the employees. When it comes time to design the communications element of a nonexecutive incentive compensation plan, it will be necessary for the incentive professional to don another hat and start thinking like a marketing professional. First, it will be necessary to develop a marketing strategy, and second, to translate that strategy into a campaign. The information obtained from the environmental analysis and the employee-readiness assessment can be used to develop a promotional campaign to "sell" the compensation package to the employees. Here, compensation managers could learn something from specialists in the field of consumer promotions, who design plans to get people to take action. In doing so, they create habit patterns such as brand loyalty that are desired by the organization. By the same token, getting employees to take action and to develop new performance habits is exactly what an organization desires as the outcome of behavior-based incentive compensation.

Incorporating promotion techniques into the incentive compensation plan design and communications can help achieve the organization's objectives. As an extreme example, this merchandising approach can take the form of a gamelike environment where the compensation is offered in a nontraditional form such as merchandise or travel. (We will see how this can be done while maintaining a businesslike environment when we examine a noncash case history in Chapter 9.)

You need a marketing strategy that identifies and addresses employee concerns. Who within (and without) the organization needs to know what information? The content of the message will have to be tailored to meet the needs of each separate employee group; managers have different needs than do nonexempt employees. Whatever the communications needs are, it is important that all employees be informed as to the behavioral psychology that is the foundation of the incentive compensation philosophy. This will provide them with the ethical reassurance that it is OK to be interested in the end results from an individual perspective.

The marketing strategy should also include a plan for delivering the communications. In most instances, this will take the form of small group meetings. Individual and multishift communications are also effective. An often-overlooked approach is to send communications directly to the home. (Such communications base their effectiveness on the type of incentive program that is planned; we will examine more of this, too, in Chapter 9.)

Because communications can be used to deliver intrinsic compensation, the element of frequency plays a part in their effectiveness. The Fishbone shows that communications will be most effective if they are designed into the plan to be ongoing and of a frequent nature. The more methods of communication that are utilized, the greater the chances of the message being retained. Methods include video, interpersonal questions and answers, booklets, brochures, and even CRT data displays that can provide the most up-to-date performance information. Remember, in a dynamic system, the information needs of the employees will be changing on a continual basis. Communications delivery systems should be designed to address these changing needs.

Because incentive compensation programs deal with current performance, they are dynamic systems that require ongoing attention and maintenance. Communications plans are necessary to establish direction, to generate enthusiasm, and then to maintain momentum. We have seen how this latter function can be accomplished through the use of performance feedback, thus fulfilling the need for positive reinforcement. Feedback also helps the employees to evaluate their current performance and make adjustments that improve results and generate higher incentive payouts. Without communications, performance is left to stumble around in the dark.

Employee Training Needs

A good working definition of *training* is "the exchange of knowledge and skills needed to execute the behavior required to achieve the desired result." For our purposes in this context, training encompasses the concept of education as well. The goal of training is to make all of the employees knowledgeable as to the mechanics, economics, and benefits of the incentive compensation system. It is also important for them to understand what their roles are and how to be successful in those roles. In order to accomplish this, it is necessary to identify the educational needs of the organization. For instance, nonmanagement work groups, made up of individual employees, will have specific training needs different from managerial and supervisory needs.

Employees need to understand the reasoning behind management's decision to implement an incentive compensation philosophy. They have probably seen other human resources programs come and go, so they will need some reassurance as to the permanence of this approach, in order to overcome their initial reluctance. For that reason, it is important that the employees receive an education in the fundamentals of behavioral psychology. This understanding will help explain why management is pursuing this new compensation philosophy.

Once the employees understand the compensation philosophy, they will want to gain an understanding of what they can do to impact the results. Problem-solving techniques, statistical analysis, analytical thinking, and group dynamics are just a few of the many skills that the employee population will demand in their quest for performance improvement. Looking at the side of the BBIC Fishbone diagram that addresses the organization's needs, we can see that this is exactly the type of positive impact that a company with a need to improve organizational effectiveness would like to achieve.

In some situations, especially where the employees have been empowered through self-managed work teams and where their performance responsibilities have been increased, it may be necessary to go so far as to provide behavior-based training in the basic skills of their new job performance. By showing the employees how to perform the tasks, by measuring the results, and by rewarding performance, the progress of the employees along the learning curve will be greatly accelerated. In this way, they will realize their potential and the organization will realize the benefits of their performance improvement much more rapidly.

Management Training Needs

Managers and supervisors will need to have their capabilities upgraded. Once employees realize that they can vary the amount of their paycheck through their involvement, commitment, and participation, they will begin to put pressure on the organization for more responsibility and opportunity. Management will have to make a quick shift from overcoming the inertia that exists when employees are reacting to directives to controlling, channeling, and focusing the momentum that occurs when employees benefit from their own actions.

The BBIC environment places a premium on the professional skills of the managers and supervisors. Front-line and middle managers have the most responsibility for transforming the strategy developed by executive management into reality on the job. A workforce that is pushing for more opportunity and support will require managers who will not act as obstacles but who can and will be facilitators. Clyde Guinn, an executive with the Marriott Hotels, stated in a quality leadership conference in Kansas City in November 1989 that the keys to empowerment are feedback, training, and recognition. Managers who have been trained to support the employees are vital in helping the employees to gain empowerment.

Most managers will at least be familiar with the concept of incentive compensation and with employee-involvement techniques. Probably the most important, and perhaps the most foreign, element of management training for most organizations is behavioral psychology. Training in this field will provide the needed rationale as to why this approach is being implemented for all employees. It makes a lot of sense to the employees when senior management says the company is going to utilize a basic law of human behavior to improve its competitive position. This training should also include a working knowledge of how to use the compensation process as a tool to provide focus, positive reinforcement, and empowerment to the employees.

Recognizing and addressing the need for new and improved management skills will provide a needed base of stability for a concept that is difficult for all but the most progressive managers in a nonsales environment. But the training in behavioral psychology will help managers to become facilitators.

As we discuss the issue of readiness, it becomes apparent that the training we are talking about is training that addresses the cultural issues, belief systems, and values of an organization. This training must be designed to bring about a change in these beliefs and values so that they support the new compensation philosophy.

Motivation

Motivation provides the energy that drives the effort toward completion. Without motivation, performance will be lackluster. We have seen that humans will continue to establish needs that require fulfillment. For that reason, it is prudent to consider developing an environment that is maintained by a three-stage incentive compensation philosophy. The first two stages are (1) long-term incentive programs of the type most commonly used at the executive level and (2) short-term incentive programs that provide reward on a much more timely basis. Mainly because of the timing of the delivery of the reward, these two stages lend themselves to the application of extrinsic compensation. The final stage is (3) a motivational tactic that is based on the delivery of daily incentives. This stage lends itself to the application of intrinsic compensation. Properly trained in behavioral technology, all employees in the organization will have the capability to provide fulfillment to the needs of positive reinforcement, focus, and empowerment on an almost immediate basis.

Once they realize the impact that they can have on their income, employees will demand, and management will want to encourage individuals to participate actively in, functions peripheral to their actual work function. Systems to accommodate this should be in place or at least be in the process of development. All this is part of the change in the organization's culture and values. Employee-involvement techniques are another subject, worthy of a separate book to cover the topic adequately. Although we cannot do the topic justice here, we will offer some generalities to convey the concept of the topic as it applies to behavior-based incentive compensation.

The basic concept of employee involvement is empowerment. The intent is to provide a means for all employees to contribute effectively to the company's business objectives and overall well-being. These means are generally methods of group participation within functional units, between functional units, and with customers and suppliers. There may also be individual opportunities to contribute, such as suggestion systems. Whatever form these means take, their purpose is to enhance the employees' ability to contribute. The systems should result in increased employee responsibility and enhanced authority to take action and bring about innovation.

Self-managed work teams offer an excellent way to support employee involvement. As the term indicates, these are groups that have the authority to manage their own work processes. As a team, the employees plan and schedule their own work flow and take responsibility for their output or other results of their efforts. These teams provide the opportunity for the employees to fulfill their need for a sense of identity.

A good example of self-managed work teams in the service sector is found in the Associates Financial Services Company of Dallas, a consumer finance operation. With over 500 branch locations throughout the United States, it provides over $3 billion in consumer financing annually. Each branch acts as an independent entity, advertising, sourcing, processing, administering, and collecting loans. The concept is to provide local service to the local market niche by acting as the "neighborhood" finance company.

As a result of this localized approach, there is a strong sense of identity among the employees in each branch. Success is measured by how well the individual offices perform in loan placements and collections. Everyone works as a member of the team to support this end. Group incentive programs that include all the branch employees are part of the productivity strategy of the Associates. These programs are nontraditional in the sense that they are short-term "spurt" activities. They are focused on specific business objectives that are measured at the branch level and normally last no more than three months.

As reward vehicles, they use merchandise, travel, and cash. As we will see in Chapter 9, noncash awards provide a promotional opportunity that is not available with the use of cash. In an industry such as the one the Associates is in, growth is necessary on a daily basis, so there is real value to the stimulus that a highly promotable reward medium can bring.

The noncash approach permits incentive programs to be designed so that branches compete against each other and that individuals share equally in the rewards based on the performance of their branch. It is in the competition between branches where the real impact of self-managed work teams can be seen. When the author was the director of sales incentives for the Associates, the incentive programs that built competition between branches generated the best results. The sense of identity that exists within self-managed work teams tapped into the source of human potential and resulted in that extra effort on the part of all branch employees to be the best.

Quality Support

Hand in hand with self-managed teams goes the ability of each team member to perform all tasks that the team requires. Cross-training and job rotation provide employees with the opportunity to fulfill the need for empowerment in a job that is more rewarding from a personal standpoint. From a business point of view, this cross-trained capability has shown itself to result in greater productivity and lower turnover.

Quality councils, or any forums where the employees can meet with senior management, represent an important element in a program of employee involvement. A pipeline to the decision makers is often perceived by the employees as an indicator of management commitment and a real opportunity to gain approval for recommendations. The motivational value of exposure to senior management has been well documented in the development of the quality process. Quality circles had their foundation in this concept. Conversely, incentive compensation supports the quality-improvement process by providing a reason to maintain individual interest while the slow growth of the process takes place.

As stated, the administrative process must remain flexible and dynamic in response to changing needs. There are, however, general guidelines for such plans. There should be a formalized system, such as the objective-identification process, for planning performance improvement and setting goals. There should be a system for tracking improvement and providing performance feedback. And there should be some method of delivering the incentive via the payroll system.

All this makes it necessary for the compensation function to interface and work cooperatively with the organization's employee records systems group, financial reporting group, and information management group to develop the initial systems and processes.

Pilot Program Design

Behavior-based incentive compensation is more than a compensation philosophy; it is really a management philosophy that utilizes the discipline of compensation as a tool. If your organization is not familiar with the application of this management style, a prudent approach would be to develop a pilot project to help everyone become comfortable with the mechanics of the process, to gauge the receptivity of the employees, and to evaluate the impact to the organization's profitability. As some of the case histories have shown, one approach to developing a test is to create a complete program design based on the existing cash compensation administration process. This is a complicated and time-consuming process, however. Executive management must first commit its support, then consensus must be gained on the objectives of the program. Research will need to be conducted to determine the organization's readiness and the likelihood of a new plan's success.

In preparation, committee(s) must be assigned that will be responsible for the design. The level of employee involvement in the design process should be identified, and the employees' role spelled out. The review and approval process should be defined in order to keep the project on track and to facilitate decision making. Then the scope of the program must be identified and agreed upon. The expected outcomes must be clearly defined, and any constraints identified and addressed.

Once the process is agreed upon, the design of the program can commence. This is the often grueling task of specifying the plan elements that fall into the BBIC Fishbone extrinsic incentive categories of why-pay, what-pay, and how-pay. These details encompass many key questions: Who will participate in the pilot? How will the participants be grouped and rewarded? by individual? by team? by organization? What will the compensation strategy be? Will the employees receive cash or stock? Will the incentive be at risk or added on? What will the performance objectives be? How will they be measured? What are the reasonable expectations of improvement? What will an increment of improvement be worth? What portion will be shared with the employees, and when? All these questions and more must be answered and then modeled under various scenarios to identify the impact on the employee and the organization.

This is a methodical and effective process for developing an incentive compensation plan for nonexecutive employees (or for any employee group, for that matter). It is the only way to design a cash-incentive compensation plan that will stand the test of time. But, as we have seen, there are more perspectives to incentive compensation than just the development of the compensation matrix. Prior to going through the detailed process necessary to develop a payout design, it might be beneficial to apply another perspective, one that deals with the organization and its environment.

Before embarking on the development of a pilot program, you might find it beneficial to stack the deck in favor of success by providing a positive incentive experience to both employees and management in a nonthreatening manner. If the process is couched in a familiar framework and is of a defined, short-term nature, employees would be more inclined to participate. In addition, managers would feel less as if their careers were at stake based on the performance of the program. In effect, we are talking about a process that is lighthearted rather than dead serious. This approach combines the concept of group incentive compensation with classic employee-involvement technique: the suggestion program.

An Ideal BBIC Employee-Involvement Technique

The suggestion program is a traditional employee-involvement technique. All but the most disengaged employees have been exposed to the process at some point in their working lives. It is a win-win concept where employees are rewarded for voluntarily contributing job-based observations that benefit the organization. Everyone is familiar with the concept and the mechanics of the process. Rarely, if ever, are there any negatives associated with the process, and therefore suggestion programs are perceived as nonthreatening by the employees.

So what we have is an individual, voluntary incentive program that in most situations exists as an aside to the primary purpose of the business. Because this basic employee-involvement process is a form of incentive compensation, we can evaluate it using the Congruent BBIC Fishbone diagram that we developed in Chapter 5. By viewing Figure 5-2 we intuitively see that it is possible to improve the effectiveness of this type of plan by adding specific elements of intrinsic and extrinsic compensation.

First of all, keep the voluntary aspect of the program; this makes the process familiar and comfortable to the employees. Next, define the scope as a pilot program for group incentive compensation. If you want to improve organizational effectiveness through increasing the elements of active participation, common aim, and creativity, then one of the design elements should be team participation. Another consideration is the length of the commitment. If you keep the time period short, employees are more likely to volunteer because they can see an end to the process should it lack the positive reinforcement needed to fulfill their needs. Ninety days seems to be sufficient time to achieve performance results and complete the test.

From the employees' perspective, this pilot design contains several intrinsic compensation factors and elements. Because the plan solicits ideas for cost reduction and performance improvement from the employees, they have an opportunity to fulfill the need for focus by contributing their job knowledge to solve work-related problems and improve the work environment.

The design element of teamwork provides the employees with the opportunity to fulfill the intrinsic need for empowerment and the company's need for organizational effectiveness. There is comfort in numbers, along with the synergy and strength to solve larger issues. This comfort level encourages active participation, open communications, and partnership on all levels. Participation is a matter of choice, so the perception is that there are probably no hidden management agendas.

So you have a voluntary, short-term, team-oriented, data-based, empowering program. From an employee-involvement standpoint, it is rather attractive. All it needs is the extrinsic compensation factor to jump-start the process.

The National Association of Suggestion Systems is an organization that keeps track of the statistics relating to suggestion programs. Their data show that employee participation and the performance of the programs will increase in relation to the amount of the suggestion savings that are shared with the employees . . . up to a point. Their data indicate that sharing more than 20 percent of the first year's net savings with the employees does not seem to achieve proportionately more incremental performance. Of course, 20 percent is a significant amount of extrinsic compensation, probably more than you would want to include in a pilot program associated with base compensation. But this approach is so divergent from base compensation that it would be possible to add a payout of 20 percent of the first year's net savings to the program design without endangering the overall compensation process.

Now we have a powerful behavior-based incentive compensation pilot program that incorporates a familiar employee-involvement technique as the vehicle. With the proper mix of training and communications, this type of program is an excellent opportunity for the employees to experience the benefits of group incentives. They have the opportunity to earn meaningful incentive compensation and receive a positive experience in the process of team dynamics and group problem solving. For management, a pilot program of this type provides experience in using incentive compensation as a tool to encourage and reward employee contribution. This is accomplished in a form that removes the pressure of failure and enables everyone to learn from the experience and acknowledge the benefits. Managers should also be included in the incentive opportunity, to increase their commitment and to demonstrate the validity of the process to all employees.

From the standpoint of organizational effectiveness, a team suggestion program would accelerate employees' progress along the learning curve. In little more than three months, all employees in the organization could be brought to the point where they would be ready for the introduction of more sophisticated employee-involvement, quality-improvement, and incentive-compensation programs. With this short-term experience behind them, employees would be much better prepared to provide input into the design process of a longer-term, nonexecutive cash-incentive compensation plan.

From the standpoint of economic value provided to the organization, the process identifies and removes obstructions within the organization that have constricted the productive flow of work and impeded the employees in the course of their daily activities. As a result, the environment after such a pilot program is one that is prepared to make the most of employee contributions and provide the least amount of frustration to the employees in return. This is a valuable point to note in the analysis of environmental factors. In an environment where the processes conspire against the employees, an incentive compensation plan will only encourage frustration and then anger. By cleaning up the systems, procedures, and processes in advance, management sends a clear signal indicating solid support for the employees.

Suggestion programs often use noncash rewards such as merchandise or travel as the extrinsic compensation. As we will see in Chapter 9, the use of such awards permits a flexibility that is not available through the normal compensation paradigm. But are these awards effective. Can merchandise be a valid compensation vehicle? The answer is yes. There exists a multibillion dollar incentive industry that is built on this concept. Programs of this type have been documented to generate a net return on investment of at least three to one and often much greater, based on payout caps and other design factors.

Note

1. Rosabeth Moss Kanter, "The Attack on Pay," *Harvard Business Review*, March-April, 1987, pp. 60–67.

9

Cash or Noncash?

Behavior-based incentive compensation is an emotionally charged process. Management views it with suspicion and trepidation. It will change the status quo, and there is no assurance that it will work. The employees view it with suspicion and anxiety. Until they have been brought to the level of understanding and acceptance, employees can perceive this form of compensation as having the power to disrupt their security and standard of living. It will change the amount of their paychecks and the structure of their jobs and heaven knows what else. And they don't know if these changes will be good or bad.

From the employees' perspective, there are things that can go wrong in the implementation of the program. What if the objectives are the wrong ones? What if the measurement is inaccurate? What if the thresholds are set incorrectly? What if there is no payout, or too much payout? From the standpoint of the managers associated with the implementation the main question is, What happens to the organization and to their careers if the program fails to perform as expected?

These are all valid concerns and must be addressed prior to implementation of any incentive compensation plan. One approach is to get all employees, from the boardroom to the mailroom, to accept the initial program as a good-faith effort where management and nonmanagement employees will work together, using the tools of open communication and performance data, to strive toward performance improvement and the equitable sharing of results.

One way to achieve this acceptance is to eliminate the perception that the initial program is a permanent approach to compensation. This can be done by utilizing a medium of extrinsic incentive that is not cash or related to base compensation. In doing so, it is possible to infuse into the initial effort a sense of extracurricular activity that puts it outside the sober realm of base compensation. As explained in Chapter 8, initiating behavior-based incentive compensation into the organization through a pilot program that is not attached to the base salary administration plan provides the opportunity to develop accurate objectives, performance data, and personal experience on all levels in a less threatening environment. If incentive compensation isn't the right approach for the organization, if the program design isn't right, or if the return doesn't justify the investment, the program can be discontinued at the end of the timeframe without significant negative repercussion.

At this point we enter the world of noncash incentives.

A Balance of Values

Looking around us on a daily basis we can observe the social change that has taken place. The postwar population explosion has matured into a working population that maintains what can be classified as neotraditional values. These values are a balance of new and traditional values that support the goal of an enriched quality of life. Among the core values that support this goal are material security, upward mobility, personal fulfillment, and freedom of choice.

The emphasis on quality in the business world is a direct response to these neotraditional values. As consumers, these employees demand products and services that provide personal recognition and satisfaction. An incentive compensation system that provides extrinsic noncash rewards can provide fulfillment to the needs of these employees. By providing both extrinsic and intrinsic satisfaction, noncash rewards are a viable approach to a pilot program.

Noncash Incentives

Will employees respond to noncash incentives? You bet they will! Just look at the success of the frequent-flyer and frequent-user programs (at least those that have been designed properly). There is no disputing that we live in a materialistic society. This society, in many ways, judges people by the standard of living they have achieved and the material symbols of success that they have acquired. In 1988, *Newsweek* devoted an article in the business section to the movement of companies toward the use of noncash rewards.[1] American Airlines, Shell Oil, Campbell Soup, AT&T, Ford, General Motors, and Chrysler were among the companies experimenting with this approach in an effort to balance their overall compensation formula.

In May 1990, *Personnel* magazine published an article stating that incentives have moved out of the sales environment into the workplace and employers are using travel to exotic places and consumer merchandise as awards to motivate employees.[2] Companies from Branch Banking and Trust Company of Wilson, North Carolina, to the Marriott Hotel Corporation report a positive employee reaction to the material opportunities and the promotional activities that surround them.

According to *Premium/Incentive Business* magazine Florida Power and Light has switched to using merchandise as an incentive in its suggestion program after using cash for over sixty years.[3] In the first year of usage, the program had greater employee participation and more suggestions implemented than in the total sixty years combined! Florida Power and Light has 15,000 employees, and over half participated in the program. Previous participation rates had hovered around 2 percent. FP&L has an extensive quality improvement/management process and patterned the valuation of the ideas along the lines of how overall employee performance is evaluated. More than just the quantity of savings was considered. Elements such as how well an idea was documented and thought out were also included in evaluating how much the employee(s) received. The method of reward was to give points that could be redeemed for merchandise out of an awards catalog. The company used a sweepstakes, a common consumer promotion, to jump-start the program and gain motivational momentum.

What Are They Using?

Noncash incentives can be placed into one of four major categories: merchandise, travel, recognition, and status. As we will see, merchandise and travel (individual or group) are most often used to drive performance and capture short-term improvements, while recognition and status most often contribute to the cultural environment and to long-term change. Noncash incentives are as varied as the employee base that they are designed to stimulate. They range from tuition credits to shares of stock to charitable items to consumer merchandise to paid time off to health services.

Psychic Income

Cash is undisputedly a powerful element in the extrinsic compensation portion of the BBIC formula; after all, it is our accepted medium of exchange. Because of what it represents, however, cash has a kind of secretive nature that makes it difficult for the organization to promote and difficult for the employee to display as recognition for performance. When is the last time you went into a supervisor's office and saw a wall chart of the merit increase matrix? Check stubs or W-2 forms are difficult to display in the course of normal conversation. In short, cash isn't much fun in and of itself.

On the other hand, noncash items such as consumer merchandise have tremendous promotional appeal. They can be shown in glossy photographs and even made available for physical testing. What this provides to the organization is visibility. With the tangible reward attached to the needs of organizational effectiveness and economic value, the employees have a real-world sense of focus. It adds excitement to the daily routine. If you are considering a pilot incentive compensation program designed to operate in an environment that is removed from base compensation plan, then noncash rewards could be a viable short-term alternative.

Perhaps one of the more significant attributes of noncash incentives is that they are experiential rather than transactional. This experiential attribute, tied as it is to emotions, is the source of psychic income for the recipient and a powerful source of motivation. Incentive travel, either group or individual, is almost purely experiential and as a result has proven to have very high motivational appeal. Merchandise has what the sales and marketing professionals call "trophy value." It provides social esteem because it can be displayed and discussed with family and friends. A materialistic society responds well to the offering of material rewards, and merchandise items are tangible symbols of success.

Noncash incentives provide the opportunity for guiltless buying. In this area of heavy leverage, many employees are carrying a heavy burden of personal debt. If they receive incentive compensation in the form of cash, there is a good chance they will use it to pay off some of the debt. Merchandise, on the other hand, provides what could be called forced frivolity.

When was the last time you purchased something substantial on a whim? Maybe it was a new wardrobe while on vacation or a new set of golf clubs or . . . . Think back, can you remember the feeling of controlled abandon that you had? Can you remember how good it felt? Faced with no alternative but to choose a merchandise or travel reward, the program participant experiences that same sense of guilt-free buying. All the issues just mentioned are reasons, on the personal level, noncash elements can be used in a pilot program to develop strong motivation in an incentive compensation plan.

Even as an element in a pilot program designed for the short-term objectives of orientation, familiarization, and database verification, the use of noncash rewards is a difficult concept to accept. Being aware of this, we must look past historical paradigms and consider new options.

The Business Case for Using Noncash

The American Productivity and Quality Center's report *People, Performance, and Pay* summarized the results of a nationwide survey on nontraditional reward systems. The data show that, in the area of generation, noncash provided a higher return on investment than did cash by almost three to one. Thus, in a commission environment, where sales representatives have substantial control over the amount of compensation they receive, noncash incentives provide a better return on investment than cash. If we could understand why these employees respond the way they do to noncash incentives, it would be much easier for us to accept the use of noncash in a nonsales environment, at least on an interim basis.

The answer may be in what economists call the marginal utility of a dollar. The concept of value is based on the individual's perception of how an item under consideration will fulfill current needs. We have seen in Chapter 2 that the priority of a need changes and reduces as the need becomes fulfilled. The return-on-investment results found in *People, Performance, and Pay* indicate that the sales employees perform a mental cost/benefit tradeoff analysis when they reach a certain level of compensation. The data indicate that their perception of the value of a dollar decreases as their income increases. This is, at least in part, due to the very strong definition of the real value of a dollar.

Incorporating noncash awards into the compensation paradigm can relieve the pressure on the perceived value of cash and introduces a perception of value that varies by individual. One of the powerful elements of noncash incentives is that, with a wide-enough selection, individuals can choose their own satisfier and, in this way, set their own goals. By allowing the employees to set their own goals contingent upon fulfillment of specific organizational needs, we have achieved every manager's dream. We have translated the organization's objectives into the employees' objectives.

The freedom to choose motivates the individual. Opening up the incentive compensation process in this manner shows appreciation for individual desires and keeps the energy and creativity in an organization at a high level. Conversely, dictating a set of options is often based on perceived stereotypes of employee profiles and has a tendency to perpetuate them. A plan that can fulfill individual desires will provide the strongest motivational appeal. In using noncash rewards, care should be taken not to impose a limited offering based on the plan designer's personal opinions. Whether or not an award is considered appealing is a function of how it is perceived by the recipient.

The trophy value of noncash incentives is beneficial to the organization as well as to the individual. Such incentives can enhance organizational effectiveness by capturing more of each employee's attention. Among their other attributes, noncash incentives, such as merchandise, have functional value. They exist in reality as something other than an abstract economic concept. As such, they can maintain within the employee two key performance thoughts: (1) the type of performance necessary to earn the incentive, and (2) a positive attitude about the organization that provided the earning opportunity outside of the cash compensation plan.

Tell Me Again How It Works

Developing the extrinsic compensation design element of an interim noncash incentive program is similar to developing a cash incentive payout structure. The procedures discussed in previous chapters—objective identification, weighting, and valuation—all remain the same. The same disciplines apply to both incentive plan designs. The contingencies for receiving the reward must be specifically defined. The employees must be able to impact the objectives. The objectives must relate to the organization's needs and be clearly stated to the employees. Whether the incentive mechanism is cash or noncash, the design must be such that the employees understand that it is earned based on performance against specific criteria that adds value to the organization. The difference is that noncash incentive programs normally utilize a token system.

One form of the token system is to assign point values to the various performance objectives. Such performance points are normally related to an increment of improvement, as measured by the performance reporting mechanism. An example of a quality/cost-related objective for a small group of employees is a plan for a paper mill. A group of five employees operates the papermaking machine that turns pulp into paper. There are several papermaking teams in the mill, each with its own performance history. For our purposes here, we will focus on one team whose objective is to reduce pounds of scrap per shift as defined and measured by the team's performance.

The team's historical level of scrap has been identified and an average of 700 pounds per shift has been established as the threshold. Each 100 pounds of scrap costs the company $150 in energy, materials, lost productivity, labor costs, and general overhead. Improvement is measured in increments of 100 pounds. Performance points are assigned to the increments of improvement. The value of these points is a function of the value the improvement has to the company and the portion of that improvement that the organization wishes to share with the employees. The same process for identifying the performance objectives and the family of measures discussed in Chapter 5 was used to develop the performance points payout schedule.

As the payout schedule in Figure 9-1 indicates, there is an accelerator applied to the schedule. A certain amount of scrap is an inevitable result of the papermaking process. Thus, the closer the

Figure 9-1. Performance points payout schedule at paper mill.

	Scrap Pounds Per Shift		Performance Points
	1,000		0
	900		0
	800		0
Threshold	700		0
	600		1,000
	500		2,000
	400		3,000
	300		5,000
	200		7,000
	100		10,000
Goal	0		15,000

team gets to zero scrap, the harder it becomes to reduce it. In addition to reducing costs, a team that manages to run a shift with no scrap would exceed the productivity standards established by the industrial engineering group due to the fact that the papermaking machine experienced no downtime. In such a case applying an accelerator is financially justifiable.

Scrap is tracked on a shift-by-shift basis. In this example, the employees can see at the end of each shift how much they have earned for their cost-reduction/quality-improvement efforts. Performance data are verified and reported on a daily basis. At the end of each week, the shift supervisor conducts a meeting to review the performance for the week and to issue the incentive compensation points earned. The employees collect these award point certificates until they have a sufficient number to redeem for the merchandise or travel award of their choice.

Token System Dynamics

From the standpoint of an interim, pilot program, a noncash incentive compensation plan addresses the need of organizational effectiveness by providing the mechanism for managers to develop their skills in delivering intrinsic compensation through social reinforcement.

The weekly issuance of points certificates provides a manager with an opportunity to discuss performance with the employees in a nonthreatening context that is meaningful to them. In this open forum, the employees' needs for social recognition and positive reinforcement can thus be fulfilled. These are opportunities to celebrate success and to identify what the activities and behavior were that resulted in success so that they can be emulated in the future and communicated to others. These meetings also provide the employees with opportunities to seek assistance from management in resolving the obstacles that prevent them from accomplishing their objectives. In effect, these meetings are natural employee involvement techniques that fulfill the need for empowerment, positive reinforcement, and focus.

Performance points may, at first glance, appear to be an unsophisticated award. However, they play a key role as a bridge between intrinsic and extrinsic compensation. In effect, they present the opportunity to reward the employees more than one time and in more than one manner for the same performance, thus providing multiple encouragement to keep improving their performance. The employees receive intrinsic compensation, that "good feeling" when they initially see the results of their performance at the end of each shift. They receive that same intrinsic compensation, this time in a more intense form, when their supervisor awards the points check. They receive intrinsic compensation a third time when they redeem their points for the reward and actually receive the extrinsic compensation.

Because of their nature, noncash incentives offer the opportunity to provide a unique form of intrinsic compensation. This takes the form of family involvement. Merchandise or travel awards, even time off, can be communicated to the family via promotional literature mailed to the home. By involving the family in the compensation process, performance improvement can be discussed at home in an environment that is interested, involved, and supportive. Benefits of this approach accrue to both the employee and the organization.

Too Much of a Good Thing

In keeping with our observations in Chapter 2 as to the hierarchy of needs, we should be aware that, like anything else, too much repetition can cause satiation on the part of the recipient. At some point, a program that has been set up to offer merchandise out of a catalog will lose its appeal. Whether you are using noncash incentives as an ongoing performance-improvement strategy (as it is in sales environments) or as a short-term transition strategy into a cash incentive plan for nonsales employees, you should be aware of this potential for satiation and the techniques available to counteract it.

Changing the incentives that are offered from program to program is the most obvious and most effective approach to avoiding satiation. Changing the promotional communications that create the excitement and awareness is another approach. Running a merchandise award program with its own uniquely focused theme for a period of time, then changing to an incentive travel award with a different theme, has proven for the author to keep employee excitement, awareness, and involvement at a high level.

The appeal of merchandise tends to be of an individual nature, but travel incentives can be designed to appeal either to the individual or to the group as a team. If the organizational need is to stimulate teamwork, then an incentive travel award where the employees travel as a group is an excellent choice. In keeping with the concept of noncash as a transitional approach to incentive compensation, changing the incentive media and promotional themes provides management the opportunity to change the performance objectives and payout schedule to adjust for flaws in the plan design or changing business objectives with minimal negative reaction from the participants. It's a matter of perception. Each change will be perceived as a new program with new objectives and rules, a new game that is unrelated to base compensation.

Budgets and Benefits of Noncash

While the use of such things as merchandise, travel, gift certificates, and time off may seem foreign, there are several significant benefits that justify such use, if only on an interim basis.

We have seen that noncash awards provide the opportunity to issue both intrinsic and extrinsic compensation to the employees. They are excellent for use as a change agent, to develop experience with incentive compensation in a nonthreatening manner. They are well established in the sales force and customer promotion arenas because of their ability to focus attention on specific activities and to get people to take action. They have even proven more cost effective in sales situations where the base compensation was not an issue.

Assuming that the human nature of salespeople is not so significantly different from that of nonsales people, we can extrapolate the same cost effectiveness into a nonsales environment. This would seem to indicate that at least in a start-up mode, the incentive compensation budget using merchandise would be less than the cash incentive compensation budget for equivalent levels of performance improvement. Of course, this holds true only if the base compensation is competitive and is perceived as equitable by the employees. As we noted in Chapter 8, part of the organizational assessment should be to determine how the employees perceive their compensation. If there is a problem in this area, it must be addressed and resolved prior to any other effort at establishing incentive compensation and employee-involvement systems.

Along this same line of thinking is the opinion that noncash should only be used in an add-on to the overall incentive compensation design. Understandably, we would be hard-pressed to find a single employee who would accept a reduction in base compensation—the regular paychecks that the household budget is based on—for the offering of merchandise or travel. This approach is in line with the thinking that a pilot program, focused at orientation and acceptance, should be as nonthreatening as possible.

How should the incentive compensation budget be established? This is a complex decision that hinges on such issues as the socioeconomic status of the employees involved in the program and the competitive pay strategy of the organization. As we discussed in Chapter 6, in the pages that explained the factors of what-pay and how-pay, the acceptance of a behavior-based incentive compensation pay philosophy may alter the organization's competitive pay strategy by applying traditional compensation thinking only to the base compensation element. In such a situation, the current income and socioeconomic levels of the participants are the critical factors in deciding the level of incentive opportunity.

Data collected for *People, Performance, and Pay*[4] indicate that, using noncash media, incentive opportunities of 4 percent to 6 percent of annual income have been effective in improving performance in a sales environment. The National Association of Suggestion Systems has data that indicate contribution and participation in a nonsales environment will increase proportionately as the incentive opportunity approaches 20 percent of annual base compensation. That's a pretty wide spread.

The use of noncash media throws a curve into the otherwise empirical process of establishing an incentive compensation payout because of the issue of perceived value. Personal experiences of the author have shown that a total incentive compensation opportunity using merchandise in a nonsales environment was effective at an 8%–10% annual level.

Interestingly, the token system of awarding points based on performance improvement has a cost savings element that provides economic value to the organization. In most token systems, points are of a cumulative nature. Like cash, each point can be added to the previous months' points until the employee has earned enough of them to purchase the noncash item. Unlike cash, the points are not used to purchase such daily items as gas or groceries. They remain in escrow until they are redeemed for the chosen item.

The cost advantage to the organization is in the form of improved cash flow. In most situations where points are issued to employees to be redeemed for merchandise or travel, there is no cost to the organization until they are redeemed. Points earned for performance improvement several months ago are only a balance sheet liability until they are activated by the employee. The benefit to the organization is the improvement in organizational effectiveness and economic value and the interest earned on the monetary value of the unredeemed points. This cash flow element of performance points makes their usage a good financial value for the organization. And the element of their perceived value makes them a good motivational value.

The Value of Points

The value of a point is best determined through a process we are all familiar with . . . by backing into it. First, you figure out the general potential value of the expected improvement. Then you decide what portion of that improvement should be shared with the employees.

Overshadowing this decision is the organization's pay philosophy. If such issues as compression and total compensation payline relative to industry standards are important, then these issues will serve to mitigate the total incentive opportunity. Consider a hypothetical company with all employees participating in a noncash incentive compensation plan that is an add-on to base compensation. The objectives have been identified, and it has been decided that a monthly performance-improvement goal of 10 percent is reasonable. The incremental value to the organization at a 10-percent improvement is equal to 25 percent of the base compensation budget. In consideration of the organization's pay philosophy, management has decided to share a portion of the incremental value up to 10 percent of the base compensation budget. It's roughly a 60-40 split. The total base cash compensation budget is $240,000, and the total incentive compensation budget is $24,000.

Once the budget has been established, the value of a point can be determined by choosing an arbitrary number of points and dividing it into the incentive budget. In our example, the group's annual earning opportunity for performance at goal is established at 24,000 points. Dividing this into the example budget, each point equates to $1.00. Should circumstances surrounding the how-pay factor (promotional perceptions) require an increase in the quantity of points available, the value of a point can be very easily reduced to $0.01 by multiplying the total number of points available at goal by 100. It is important to note that each group's earning opportunity should be equal.

By using the family of measures matrix process that was reviewed in Chapter 5, it is possible to establish the incremental value of improvement, in points, for each performance objective. In this example, the total earning opportunity for each employee in the group is set at 2,000 points for every month the group reaches goal in all of its objectives. Each objective is weighted and assigned a ratio (expressed as a percentage) as to its value to the organization, and that ratio is multiplied by the 2,000 points. Once each objective's total points at goal have been calculated, the point values for levels of incremental improvement on an individual objective basis are easily calculated by dividing the number of increments between threshold and goal into the total number of points available at goal.

A Balance of Usage

If we have learned anything in our examination of incentive compensation and motivation, it is that there is no single "right" plan design. Each organization has its own unique cultural environment and business needs. What we have established is that with the proper balance of base compensation, performance-related incentives, and behavioral psychology, an organization can tap into the wellspring of human potential and reap the benefits.

Fundamental to the process from a transactional sense is a strong base compensation plan. Second to that is an incentive plan that addresses the extrinsic factors of why-pay, what-pay, and how-pay. The use of cash as the incentive media most closely fits this criteria.

Fundamental to the process from an experiential sense is a strong background in the application of behavioral psychology and its related interpersonal skills. In conjunction with extrinsic compensation and as a multiplier to the motivational impact, the element of intrinsic compensation is important to the success of a balanced plan. Social recognition, performance feedback, and employee involvement are key elements in this category. Noncash media such as plaques and trophies have long been used to assist in the implementation of such behavioral approaches as honor and recognition. These awards have the capability to deliver both intrinsic and extrinsic compensation and, as a result, can be utilized as a bridge between the material world and the world of behavioral psychology. This is especially useful in the situation where the participants have not been exposed to incentive compensation and the introduction of such a compensation process would require the corporate culture to be reshaped.

A quick look at the psychic elements that can be used to enhance cash and noncash incentive compensation programs provides a strong insight as to how they are mutually supportive.

Cash Incentive Compensation

Perception:	Serious, a partner in the business
Acceptance:	Familiar, long-term
Communications:	Normally none at all or focused on payout matrix and mechanics
Timely Payout:	A function of performance reporting and payroll administration capabilities
Delivery:	Normally tied to payroll processing, associated with paycheck
Performance Feedback:	Timely if not tied to payout computations
Promotion:	Normally none; very low excitement level
Social Recognition:	None

Noncash Incentive Compensation

Perception:	Fun, innovative, a learning process, an earning opportunity
Acceptance:	Unique, short-term
Communications:	Focused on objectives, employee-performance activities that can impact objectives, unique reward opportunities
Timely Payout:	Generally on a monthly basis, a function of performance-reporting capabilities
Delivery:	Unique "points" check
Performance Feedback:	Timely, highly visible
Promotion:	Exceptionally high visibility; reward opportunities tied to performance levels

Social Recognition: High and ongoing, in both work-
                             place and home environments

This list shows that it would be easy to create a situation where financial income could be equated to base compensation by the
recipient no matter how it was earned. The psychic elements of a
reward system seem to be the source of the communications and
promotion opportunities, the excitement and fun that are the stimulating elements of an incentive program.

   A conclusion you can draw here is that noncash media are a valid tool in the effort to improve organizational effectiveness and
economic value through human resources. To limit yourself to cash
as the only tool in the application of incentive compensation will limit
the potential impact that incentive compensation could have on your
organization. As for the proper usage of cash and noncash incentive
media, it is a matter of balance. There is no perfect plan. Behavior-
based incentive compensation is a dynamic process that changes over
time based on the experience of management and the participants
and the sophistication of the plan design. The use of noncash media
provides you with the flexibility to experiment with design and to
develop skills.

The Xerox Office Products Division: Case History

Merchandise and travel have been used as motivational incentives in
the sales environment for over fifty years. But not until very recently
have they been accepted in the nonsales environment as a valid
approach to motivating employees and focusing their energies on
specific business objectives.

   One of the notable earlier uses of merchandise as incentive compensation for a nonsales workforce was in 1982 at the Xerox Office
Products Division, then located in Dallas, Texas. The division was
developing and introducing memory typewriters, document-creation
devices with a memory, and information-processing systems that were
advanced word processors with computerlike capabilities. While these
products may seem commonplace today, in 1982 they were technolog-
ically on the cutting edge. For perspective, it has been said that if
capabilities in aerospace had developed at the same pace as the
electronic information processing capabilities, the Wright Brothers
would have landed on the moon in 1912.

   Phillip Cooke, currently a senior human resources executive, was
then manager of human resources assigned to the office products operation, and he remembers the challenges. "At that time IBM, with
their ball typewriter, dominated the world of word processing. The

business strategy was to enter the electronic typewriter marketplace with a product that could compete due to its breakthrough technology.

"There were other players that were poised to enter the marketplace with similar technology. The window of opportunity was small due to the fact that these companies were all using similar technology and were competing on their ability to execute. The organizations that could execute exceptionally well would be the ones that seized the market share. What we had from a product standpoint in the early 1980s was expensive, and our execution was not as good as some of the competition. This was a start-up operation, and we were experiencing the difficulties that you have with a start-up situation. Volume and quality were our two major challenges. We were performing at 50-60 percent of running production plan, and the product wasn't performing as well as we wanted it to. Our margins were such that we needed sales volume to support the operation. As part of the Xerox Corporation we had an excellent introduction into the marketplace, but the other side of the coin was that our customer loyalty was at stake."

Tom Skelly, who was vice-president of operations for the Office Products Division at that time, led the effort to change this. The objective was to produce a memorywriter every seven minutes. To do this he installed a sophisticated materials-handling process to handle the volume. It was completely paperless, with lasers and computers sorting bar-coded parts bins. "Tom also recognized that you can't change behavior by just going after the biggest issues," says Phil. "He realized that we needed to establish the proper environment first. At that time, we were just beginning to develop our employee involvement techniques. If you remember back to the early 1980s, employee involvement wasn't as established as it is today. We realized that employee involvement was good and that we should have this, but it was a hit-or-miss process with very little team emphasis.

"As with many start-up and growth ventures, there was a period of time where we experienced constant reorganization. In addition, with most of the management coming from the parent organization, there were elements of a big-company mentality that made it difficult to function in an entrepreneurial mode. As a result, after a few years of significant organizational change, the employees in our operations group began to reduce their initiative. While they liked the new employee-involvement techniques that we initiated, they were skeptical of our commitment to them. Therefore, they took on low-risk projects, ones that had a low profile, and waited to see what management wanted."

Bruce Rismiller, Xerox Corporation's vice-president of human resources, provided strong support for the improvement effort, and

Mike Randals, his manager of human resources, provided a large portion of the conceptual design. It could be said that they and Tom Skelly formed one of the earlier, informal, cross-functional incentive compensation design teams.

The first step was to develop a perfect-attendance award. Phil recalls, "The perfect-attendance program was a quarterly cash payment with a tangible award that symbolized the culture we were in the process of developing. The union wasn't exactly supportive, but they went along because there was no takeaway associated with it. The Office Products Division management in general felt somewhat uncomfortable with the concept. The overall thinking was 'you pay 'em to come to work.' But Skelly was a pragmatist. We had somewhere in the neighborhood of 1,300 employees. He took a look at the cost of absenteeism as it translated into lost productivity and reduced quality. He then compared it to the impact on these performance indicators that perfect attendance would have. The net of the analysis was that perfect attendance cost less than absenteeism and, as a result, we had a perfect-attendance program."

Did it make a difference? Can a minimal amount of cash and a trophy make an impact on a buffeted and benumbed workforce? Phil Cooke saw several benefits to the approach. "The power of the program was that it got the employees to relate to a sense of team rather than a bureaucracy. It sent the message that 'we need you, every person is important.' In doing that, we provided our employees with a sense of self-worth and focus."

The positive response to the perfect-attendance award gave support to additional creative thinking, and in early 1982 the Office Products Division initiated a behavior-based noncash incentive compensation plan for all employees who were not on commission. The decision was to use a token system in conjunction with a merchandise catalog. The program was to run for a full year as an add-on to base compensation. In keeping with the focus of the business effort, the program was given the promotional theme "The Leading Edge." At that time, the author was doing developmental work in the field of noncash behavior-based incentive compensation for a major incentive supplier and was the consulting account manager for this program.

Behavior-Based

"A reward is only a reward in terms of the recipient. The reason for choosing noncash was to try to have fun with the process. Skelly wanted to put fun into the workplace and remove the accumulated tedium," Phil recalls. "By the very nature of the work, manufacturing has a hard time relating to the customers. Design and product changes, quality issues, production schedule changes, all these are perceived, from an assembly line point of view, as outsider intrusions to the process of 'getting the work out.' We wanted to overcome this type of thinking.

"Middle management was uncomfortable with this change in attitudes, environment, and perspective. It was new and perceived as gimmicky, with too much rah-rah. In a sense, it was somewhat threatening to them." To overcome their anxiety and to gain their commitment and participation, the company provided training in the basics of behavioral psychology. The initial phase of the training provided these managers with an understanding of behavioral psychology and the concepts behind a token system. Once that was accomplished, on-the-job coaching developed their skills in delivering intrinsic and extrinsic rewards to their employees for performance improvement. The training emphasized the relationship between the extrinsic pay factors and the intrinsic factor of positive reinforcement. To the author's knowledge, this was the first combination of behavioral psychology and incentive compensation in an overall performance-improvement plan.

Design Overview

A task force of analysts was assigned to develop the incentive compensation structure that would address the needs of improving organizational effectiveness and providing economic value. Employees were formed into teams by department. The overall objectives were to reduce costs and solidify team spirit. Each team had performance objectives that related to the organization's business needs and were impactable by the employees.

The teams were assigned performance thresholds in the areas targeted for improvement in their respective departments. Owing to the newness of the organization and the significant business problems that the organization had been experiencing, historical performance levels were not used as the performance thresholds. Each objective had a threshold that was assigned by management as the *expected* level of normal performance. The employees earned performance points for improvement over threshold. They could then redeem these points for merchandise from a catalog that offered over 2,500 items.

A communications campaign was designed with the threefold purpose to inform, involve, and motivate. The campaign focused on the incentive opportunity and communicated the rule structure, explained what types of performance earned performance points, promoted the incentive award opportunities, and recognized superior performance.

Systems were set in place to measure and report performance on a timely basis. Performance-feedback charts were established in each work area and were updated on a regular basis. These charts provided the employees with several forms of intrinsic compensation, helping to keep them focused on the performance objectives and providing positive recognition and encouragement for their efforts. These charts also displayed the number of performance points each team had earned.

The budget for this incentive compensation investment included both fixed and variable costs. The fixed costs were associated with training, communications, and administration. Based on the findings of the task force, the areas of concentration that would best address the organization's needs were found to be: operating budget reduction, productivity improvement, and quality improvement. The variable costs constituted the bulk of the incentive budget and were the contingent costs of the employee awards, to be paid only if the employees exceeded performance thresholds. The program design was considered an investment rather than a compensation cost because the break-even point was very low; at program goal, net savings were expected to be in excess of $11 million.

Program Structure

Employees were assigned to one of eight teams that were, in effect, logical work groups. Approximately 60 percent of the organization was employed in some form of manufacturing. The organizational chart placed these employees in one of four small manufacturing units (SMUs). Three of these units focused on producing products, while the fourth performed a remanufacturing function. Each SMU became a performance team. The fifth performance team was the material assets team. It consisted of the employees in the materials, procurement, and quality-control functions. The sixth team was composed of the employees in the logistics and distribution functions. The seventh team was comprised of the human resources employees, and the eighth team, the support departments, including senior management, operations analysis, and finance.

Each team had a small number (three to five) of key performance indicators that were to be the focus of their performance-improvement efforts. In an effort to provide insight and an understanding of the process, the teams and their performance objectives are listed at the end of the next paragraph. Before you review these objectives, remember that they were not mandated by senior management. The task force of analysts spent a considerable amount of time with each department manager, working to identify the correct performance objectives. These analysts provided financial, industrial engineering, and productivity improvement consulting expertise and the department management provided the detailed operating knowledge. The end result was a set of performance indicators that the department management accepted as the key output indicators.

Once the performance indicators had been identified, lengthy and involved negotiations established ownership of the total program on the part of management. The indicators were discussed in management meetings where executives from departments upstream and downstream could comment on how their organizations would be affected. One major concern addressed in this negotiation process was that a department might choose an objective to focus on that would prove detrimental to another department. Several of these indicators were discovered and adjusted as a result of this process.

Team Objectives

☐ Small Manufacturing Units
  - Schedule attainment: weighted weekly average
  - Quality: weekly installability
  - Spending/production: spending performance below budget

☐ Material Assets
  - Spending: actual below budget, three-month rolling average
  - Purchase price variance: favorable against plan
  - Availability: percentage fulfillment of customer spares request
        —Code-1 work orders
        —Percentage spares fulfillment
  - Performance inventory: reduction of monthly level against planned level

☐ Logistics and Distribution
  - Expense reduction: percentage below budget
  - Availability: response to emergency orders
  - Investments: reduction of monthly inventory level versus planned

☐ Human Resources
  - Expense reduction: actual versus plan, 3-month rolling average
  - 50 percent of average SMU earning

☐ Support Departments
  - 100 percent of the average monthly earnings of the three SMU teams and the material assets team

The support departments included the top management in the division and their direct reports, all operations analysis and manufacturing system employees, and the finance and accounting specialists. While management continued working to define direct methods of measuring the support groups efforts, they did not want the difficulty of this process to slow up the implementation of the program. Using a general indicator allowed all employees to be included in the program. It also acknowledged the fact that these support functions did contribute to the success of the line functions and therefore should share in the gains. Including senior management in the program provided legitimacy to the program and secured top-level involvement.

The Reserve

Tom Skelly wanted to ensure that all employees focused on the overall objectives of the organization as well as their team objectives. He also wanted to use the incentive compensation program to communicate the fact that the organization's success hinged on everyone working together. To achieve this, he decided that 25 percent of each employee's total incentive opportunity at goal would be provided in the form of a plant-wide stock plan. All Office Products Division program participants earned performance points based on the plant-wide reduction of the operating budget.

In addition to providing focus and emphasizing teamwork, this design element served to reduce the potential cost liability in the unlikely situation where a team would earn incentive compensation for performance above its threshold but the organization as a whole was unable to reduce operating costs. This reserve was in actuality a backoff of the employees' total incentive compensation earning opportunity and was largely beyond their immediate control. To avoid any misperception, care was taken to present this plan to the employees as yet another earning opportunity. Those employees who became part of the organization during the program received pro rata shares according to number of active months in the program.

Payout Schedule

Each team received earned performance points on a monthly basis. All the team members earned equally based on the team's performance. The points were distributed in a unique check at a special monthly meeting. Supervisors and managers utilized this opportunity to put into practice the behavioral techniques they had learned, by providing positive reinforcement through tangible rewards. During the rest of the month, they used performance feedback and the merchandise award media to provide intrinsic compensation.

The monthly checks for points provided timely and tangible re-inforcement for performance that the teams could control, and the plantwide stock plan provided more deferred compensation. Performance in the area of plantwide budget reduction was reported on a monthly basis, providing intrinsic compensation, but the point checks were issued on a semi-annual basis. As you will see, the budget design was such that the monthly earning opportunity was large enough to be attractive to the employees. The plantwide stock plan was not used to bring the incentive opportunity up to attractive levels but, instead, to add to an already attractive opportunity. In this way, the focus on cost was maintained without losing the motivational impact of the incentive opportunity even though it was delayed.

A breakdown of the payout schedule for the small manufacturing units demonstrates the process used to measure performance improvement and calculate incentive compensation earnings on a monthly basis.

Objective: Quality

Percentage Installability

Incremental Improvement	Performance Points	Cash Value
11%	5,500	$27.50
10	5,000	$25.00
9	4,500	$22.50
8	4,000	$20.00
7	3,500	$17.50
to base of 1%	to base	to base

Objective: Schedule Attainment

Percentage of Schedule

Incremental Improvement	Performance Points	Cash Value
3.0%	2,750	$13.75
2.4	2,200	$11.00
1.8	1,650	$ 8.25
1.2	1,100	$ 5.50
0.6	550	$ 2.75
base%	0	base

Objective: Spending

Percentage Below Budget	Measurement Performance Points	Cash Value
10%	4,500	$25.00
9	4,500	$22.50
8	4,000	$20.00
7	3,500	$17.50
6	3,000	$15.00
5	2,500	$12.50
4	2,000	$10.00
3	1,500	$ 7.50
2	1,000	$ 5.00
1	500	$ 2.50
0	0	base

You can see by this payout structure that the objectives matched the performance issues of the organization at that time. Each objective was weighted as to its overall importance. The message this payout structure communicated to the employees was that quality was the most important objective, followed by cost and then schedule attainment.

The Budget

Because the behavior-based incentive compensation plan was perceived as a tool to improve performance, management considered it an investment. As a result, the budget was calculated based on the assumption that each team would perform at goal and receive earnings at goal for every month of the program. The payout thresholds were the performance goals that management had in the business plan. This was aggressive thinking because up to that point performance had not been meeting business plan. The thinking was that a noncash, behavior-based incentive compensation plan would be unique and powerful enough to pull performance up to and beyond the plan.

Management understood the process was self-funding based on payout for performance in excess of plan threshold. If performance did not meet plan, there would be no payment of incentive compensation. If performance exceeded the business plan thresholds but did not reach performance improvement goal levels, then only a portion of the budget would be spent. If performance met the incentive compensation payout goals, then the entire budget would be spent. There was a payout cap to the plan. If performance exceeded the performance improvement goals, the employees would not receive any additional payout.

The total noncash incentive opportunity at goal for the eleven months the program was scheduled to run was approximately $1,100 per employee. This budget number was calculated by backing into it. The primary question that management asked was, What will it take to motivate the employees? Based on previous experience, on the socioeconomic level of the employees, on the type of work, and on the fact that noncash awards were to be the incentive media, an intuitive value of $100 per month per employee was recommended to, and accepted by, senior management.

At first glance, $100 per month total cash incentive opportunity at goal may not seem significant enough to motivate a workforce. But keep in mind that the program occurred in 1982 and that the incentive opportunity was an add-on to base compensation. Even so, offering cash in amounts as small as in the SMU payout example would be open to question as to the attractiveness to the employees. This is one of the difficulties of designing a plan that rewards incremental improvement. The perception of the value of an increment of improvement to the participant becomes a determining factor. One of the reasons for choosing merchandise as the medium for this program was its attribute of perceived value and the additive element of performance points.

While no effort was made to hide the cash value of a performance point (½ cent), all earning opportunities were presented in point values rather than cash. The program communications and promotional activities were designed to emphasize the incentive opportunity to the employees and deemphasize the cash cost of the awards so all merchandise purchase costs were presented in points.

The total eleven-month noncash incentive opportunity at goal for the small manufacturing units looked like this:

Schedule attainment	$180
Quality	$335
Spending/production	$305
Plantwide stock	$280

A financial rationale was established for each of the performance objectives where possible, and a return on investment was calculated for each team as well as for the overall organization. The return on investment for the organization, with all teams at goal-level performance, would be in excess of eleven to one. This ROI did not include the financial impact of improved quality or schedule attainment, because the ability to track the dollar savings was not in place at the time of the program.

Communications and Promotions

Effective communications form the backbone of a good behavior-based incentive compensation plan. They are a key provider of the intrinsic factor of focus. In order for a behavior-based incentive compensation plan to be effective, all employees must know what is expected of them and what incentive opportunities are available in exchange for their contribution and involvement.

Communications can provide intrinsic incentive by translating the organization's needs into each participant's personal goals. This can be done by: (1) pinpointing and defining performance objectives, (2) prioritizing the objectives as to importance and value to the organization, and (3) providing direction and insight as to how performance improvement in these areas can be achieved.

A campaign of communications and promotion was developed to provide focus and to generate the fun and excitement necessary to the program's success. A full-time coordinator was assigned to manage the process and to act as a resource contact for employee questions that arise during a program such as this. Phil Cooke discusses the value of a well-thought-out communications campaign and a designated coordinator: "We never let the process be reduced to pure mechanics. The coordinator was truly enthusiastic in his pursuit of promotion and communications. The result was that we took our responsibilities conscientiously but not overly seriously. It helped keep things in perspective. The campaign also provided the opportunity to communicate the big-picture information to all employees."

In order to communicate the objectives of an incentive program in a highly visible format, it is necessary to develop a theme. "The Leading Edge" was chosen as the program theme because it tied into the concept of the overall business product and focused on the program's objectives. Custom graphics were designed and became the visual representation of the program.

An awards catalog was produced with a cover customized with the program's theme and logo. This catalog showcased a wide range of merchandise and travel opportunities that were within the earnings capabilities of the payout structure. (The plan rules and payout structures were printed inside the catalog.) The entire employee population was bused to a five-star hotel, where Tom Skelly announced the program. A specially produced video was shown, and each employee received a copy of the awards catalog. Upon return to the workplace, employees found promotional banners and progress charts displayed in their work areas. The total effort was designed to appear as a division-generated effort. Vendor and supplier references were conspicuously absent.

Prior to the launch, senior executives had conducted an orientation seminar for all managers. While most managers had been involved in the development stage of the plan, Tom Skelly wanted to make sure that they understood his level of commitment to the plan. He also wanted to address any questions or concerns that might exist. At this meeting, each manager received a copy of the program operations manual.

As part of the ongoing communications program, a monthly newsletter titled *The Wally Street Journal* (after the program coordinator, Wallace Watson) was published to keep the employees up to date on the value of their shares of plantwide stock. The *Journal* also communicated performance data for each of the teams and served as the forum for management to provide social recognition and intrinsic compensation by highlighting exceptional team performance and individual contributions. Success stories were promoted, and suggestions were provided as to how to maximize the earning opportunities. There were columns, too: Views, What's News, Editorial Comments, and even Personals.

Program promotional mailers were sent to each employee's home quarterly. These mailers restated the performance objectives and earning opportunities. They also offered discounted specials on seasonally attractive merchandise to add motivational momentum to the program. The purpose of these mailers was to involve the family and to provide the employees with the opportunity to convert performance points into merchandise.

As a tie-in with other company activities, a contest was held in conjunction with the company picnic. Employees were encouraged to submit designs for a T-shirt that was to be produced and distributed to all employees at the company picnic. The designs were judged by a community art group, and the winner and runner-ups received 10,000 additional performance points. There was some concern on the part of management that the use of discretionary points for special projects would develop an undesirable behavior pattern on the part of the employees. For that reason, discretionary points were used only for activities not directly related to the work.

Results of Noncash Incentives

Is this a joke, or did it really work? Was this unique and "leading-edge" incentive compensation plan successful in addressing the needs of both the employees and the organization? Phil Cooke thinks it was quite successful. "The Leading Edge program dovetailed into and supported our quality circle effort. That is, it fit with the other employee-involvement initiatives we were implementing such as the newly developed computer-aided training, where employees could advance at their own pace. This allowed them to feel that they had some control over their own destinies. The incentive plan, the perfect-attendance plan, the quality circles, the computer-aided training, and the fact that we made no differentiation between union and non-union training, all sent the same consistent signal to the employees. This message was that every individual has value and wants to do well. This consistent signal allowed us to develop and sustain momentum."

But specific to the program results, how effective was it? According to Phil, "It got us into the game. Performance results went well into the 90th percentile, and in production we had never been there before. We gained a 20-percent market share, and as a result of this and other pressures in the market, the IBM ball passed into history." From a direct-investment viewpoint, the plan provided a return on investment of over nine to one.

Were there other, ancillary benefits to installing a noncash, behavior-based incentive compensation plan? Phil believes so. "The incentive plan helped set the tone that manufacturing could build anything," he says. "In addition, it helped us establish better relations with employees who belong to the union."

When asked about any lessons to be gleaned from the experience, he replies, "It's obvious that everyone is motivated by an opportunity for gain. The lessons to be learned are that leadership and communications will have a definite impact on results. The program worked primarily as the result of the leadership. It takes someone to stand up and say, 'We are going to do this.' More importantly, the leadership has to stay consistent in the face of the ongoing criticism that will be present in any difficult effort. You will always receive criticism when you put resources at risk, but you must have the determination to stay the course. Leadership is critical and well worth the effort."

The noncash behavior-based incentive plan was in place for two years. During that time, the performance and business issues changed, and then a change of management brought in different ideas. The use of noncash incentives was phased out, and management decided not to replace it with a permanent cash-based incentive plan.

The Total Effectiveness Rating

Using the technology we have developed in earlier chapters, let's evaluate the effectiveness of the program design. Figure 9-2 shows that the extrinsic factors of why-pay, what-pay, and how-pay each maintained their normal values. The performance objectives were

Figure 9-2. Total effectiveness rating for Xerox OPD.

Extrinsic Factors		Intrinsic Factors		Subtotal Rating	How-Pay Modifier	Total Rating
Factor	Weight	Weight	Factor			
Why-Pay	1 +	1	Focus	= 2	+ 3	= 5
What-Pay	2 +	2	Positive Reinforcement =	4	+ 3	= 7
(strong) How-Pay	3 +	3	Empowerment	= 6	+ 3	= 9
					Total Points	21

well defined, and for the most part, each had the ability to be measured. Due to the use of noncash media, the incentive opportunity was perceived by the participants as being sufficient. The fact that the thresholds were based on performance plan rather than on history appears to have been offset by the use of noncash media as well. Each of these factors added their value to the intrinsic factors with which they are linked. The intrinsic factor of focus was strongly supported by the factor of why-pay. Each group knew exactly what objectives they were responsible for and how they fit into the overall picture. Positive reinforcement was provided by measured performance improvement communicated on a timely basis in a highly visible format.

What really made the difference was the modifying element of how-pay. The emphasis and training on behavioral skills to managers encouraged them to deliver both intrinsic and extrinsic compensation. The delivery of intrinsic compensation became a daily affair, and the delivery of extrinsic compensation, in the form of monthly performance point checks, was timely and unique, separating the incentive earnings from other forms of compensation. This emphasis on the factor of how-pay enabled it to enhance the intrinsic factor. Focus was maintained and positive reinforcement was provided on a daily basis. The training that management received enabled them to facilitate the empowerment of the employees. As a result of all this, the program's total effectiveness rating is twenty-one points, a perfect score for a behavior-based incentive compensation plan.

Why Aren't You Using It?

That's great, you say. Merchandise, travel, and other noncash media have proven themselves effective in motivating employees to contribute more of their potential to addressing the needs of the organization. But your chosen field is human resources (or Finance, or Operations . . .), not retail sales. And you're not about to get entangled in the giant hassles involved in purchasing, warehousing, shipping, order entry, warranty returns, customer service, travel negotiations, or any of the other elements required to fulfill the promises of a noncash incentive plan. Indeed, you probably don't have the expertise or the staffing to do this.

Relax. You don't have to do this by yourself. There is an entire industry out there waiting to provide the goods and services necessary to initiate a quality noncash incentive plan.

The Noncash Incentive Industry

The noncash incentive industry consists primarily of merchandise and travel providers. Each year *Incentive* magazine, a Bill Communications publication, conducts a survey of the state of the incentive industry. The December 1990 issue states that incentive spending for 1990 was at an all-time high of $17 billion. That's not to say that this is incentive compensation as we have been discussing it, but it does tell us that there is a well-established industry providing noncash incentives to the sales, distribution, and consumer markets. This industry is showing a keen interest in the nonexecutive, nonsales employee environment as a viable new market.

The survey by *Incentive* magazine shows that close to 30 percent of the respondents indicate expenditures for nonsales employee programs. Interestingly, the survey results show that more mature incentive compensation plans are using tangible awards. The budgets reported for merchandise incentives increased almost 15 percent over the 1989 survey data. This increase appeared to be at the expense of the cash incentive budgets. It's no wonder that the incentive industry is paying close attention to this noncash incentive compensation movement and will respond rapidly and with great focus to your request for service.

You can obtain noncash incentives from a variety of sources that will provide an array of value-added services in conjunction with the merchandise and/or travel awards. The cost of the incentives will be a reflection of how much support you require. Each category of service agency has strengths and weaknesses that differentiate them. The service provider that you choose should work for your personal strengths.

Service Providers

A full service sales incentive/sales promotion agency that has expanded its marketplace to include the nonsales environment could provide total support should you decide to use a noncash approach as your pilot project. If you need support in the design, communications, training, performance tracking, and administration, then you need a full-service agency. These companies provide complete incentive programs focused at your business needs. They have the organization in place to successfully support your plan from start to finish.

In many instances, this is the most effective approach when first deploying incentives. Your primary role would be to provide direction and guidance to their staff in the design of the compensation structure. A full-service agency will provide the experience and staffing support during the development, implementation, and ongoing administration. More importantly, they are staffed to provide employee satisfaction services. Because of the overhead normally associated with such services, the cost of the incentive medium is often expensive.

If you have the staff that can provide the initial analysis, design, communications, and ongoing administrative support needed for a campaign, then all you need is merchandise or travel fulfillment.

Incentive distributors generally put together their own catalogue and provide tracking and administration support. They carry a lower overhead by maintaining fewer ancillary services in-house. While the element of process control becomes less direct, these distributors can provide reasonably priced incentives with various degrees of administrative value added.

The lowest product cost will be to purchase directly from a manufacturer's representative. These representatives will arrange for the products to be shipped directly from the manufacturer to a location specified on the recipient's order form. Manufacturer's reps often support more than one line of leading consumer products, but in dealing with them you will find your selection somewhat narrow. As an example, you may have to run a program that features just Sony, Minolta, and General Electric products.

A strong cost/benefit analysis should be performed before you cast your lot with the lowest bidder. For a first-time program it may be prudent to purchase the support services to ensure the smooth operation of the campaign. There is an adage in the incentive industry that says: "The most expensive program is the one that fails." While it is necessary to maintain fiduciary responsibility, don't let cost be the critical factor in the decision process. If it costs too much to do correctly, then you can't afford to do it.

Incentive Industry Associations

While the incentive industry has many associations, the ones that we are interested in will be those that are focused on the employees rather than the consumer. These associations can be very helpful in providing information concerning their members.

The Incentive Manufacturers Representatives Association (IMRA) in Naperville, Illinois, is an association for those sales organizations that represent manufacturers. In general, members of this organization will be able to obtain low prices for the end user, but are normally not staffed to provide ancillary services such as design and development of incentive compensation.

The Association of Incentive Marketing (AIM) in New Jersey was founded almost thirty-five years ago as an association of incentive merchandise professionals dedicated to the growth, education, quality, and ethical standards of the incentive marketing industry. The association conducts meetings and seminars on topics affecting the incentive merchandise industry. It provides updated communications to its members and conducts public and industry relations to maintain and enhance the industry's image. It acts as a clearing house for communications between and among manufacturers wanting to enter the incentive marketplace, sales organizations that bring merchandise to the incentive marketplace, and the customers that purchase merchandise for incentive purposes.

AIM conducts two industry seminars each year as well as an annual probe conference, where issues affecting the growth and direction of the incentive industry are discussed. AIM represents the organization and its members at the key incentive trade shows that are conducted annually.

In recognition of the important role that incentives play in commerce and industry, the AIM Education Committee plans and conducts incentive seminars at the university level. As with more traditional forms of compensation design, there is a conspicuous lack of formal education concerning incentives available on the secondary level. The AIM Education Committee is working to address that issue.

The Marketing Practices Committee is responsible for the implementation of the standards of marketing practice by AIM members. The association also defines the curriculum whereby an incentive professional can earn certification as a Certified Incentive Professional (CIP).

Annually, AIM conducts the University of Incentives training program. At the University of Incentives, attendees have the opportunity to learn the incentive basics from seasoned professionals. New marketplace opportunities, such as noncash incentive compensation, are often showcased at this time.

The Society of Incentive Travel Executives (SITE) in New York is an association that represents those organizations that provide incentive travel services to end user companies. SITE describes itself as an organization established to develop a better understanding of and appreciation for the value of incentive travel in the modern business community. SITE members have the knowledge, staffing, and skill levels to conduct a full-service incentive travel program on either a group or individual basis. Travel, because of its experiential nature, can be a very powerful incentive offering. If your incentive compensation planning includes the element of travel, members of this association can support the delivery once the employee has earned the incentive.

Publications

There are several magazines and periodicals that serve the incentive industry. One of the more widely distributed magazines and one that provides a good focus on the direction and growth of the industry is *Incentive* magazine published monthly by Bill Communications of Akron, Ohio. It is in its eighty-sixth year of publication and presents as its purpose: "to cover the methods used by organizations to motivate customers at all levels to buy and employees to work more effectively." Annually, it publishes directories of incentive companies, retailers, representatives and distributors, and merchandise and travel suppliers. Contacting a local representative to discuss your business objectives will be time well spent, even if you decide to take a different approach.

Business & Incentives magazine is published monthly by Gralla Publication of New York. Its stated purpose is the coverage of incentive strategies for business managers. As part of this coverage, it reports on the use of merchandise and incentive travel in nonsales employee incentive plans.

Shows and Expositions

If you really want to gain insight as to the depth and breadth of the noncash incentive industry, you should attend one of the two national merchandise and travel shows that are held annually. This will firmly establish in your mind the idea that merchandise and travel incentives are mainstream compensation.

What is billed as the largest general merchandise trade show in America is held at the Javits Convention Center in New York. The other main show is held in Chicago and includes both the National Premium Incentive Show and the Incentive Travel and Meeting Executives Show.

At these shows, you will meet prime source suppliers who can give you the best value for your dollar from purely a cost perspective. You will see the new and motivationally exciting items that are being introduced into the incentive industry for the first time. These shows are geared toward sales and marketing professionals and you can't help but benefit from the awareness they generate. Even if your incentive compensation plans do not include the use of merchandise or travel, a trip to one of these shows would be time well spent. The synergy that is developed during the show has a tendency to break down barriers and cause the attendees to rethink old preconceptions. That's one of the prime purposes of the shows. They are examples of American creative entrepreneurialism at its best, and the environment is contagious.

Notes

1. "Forget Cash, Give Me the TV," *Newsweek*, October 31, 1988, p. 58.
2. William H. Wagel, "Make Their Day—the Noncash Way," *Personnel*, May 1990, pp. 41–44.
3. Greg Trauthwein, "FP&L Premium Use Results 'Shock' Management" ("Incentives in Action" Column), *Premium/Incentive Business*, April 1990, pp. 22–26.
4. Carla O'Dell and Jerry McAdams, *People, Performance, and Pay,* a report on the American Productivity Center/American Compensation Association national survey of nontraditional reward practices, American Productivity and Quality Center, 1987, p. 82.

10

Problems and Opportunities

There are situations in which incentives, either cash or noncash, will not be effective. The lack of performance is not because the basic laws of human behavior are no longer in effect in these situations. When incentives fail to act as a stimulant to performance improvement, the reason can most often be traced to the environment that has been created as the result of the program design or a failure to conform to the guidelines of behavior-based incentive compensation. The BBIC Fishbone and the effectiveness rating model are good tools for the analysis of program design. Prior to implementation of your program, it's a good idea to have one last review of the relationships between employee needs and organizational needs and the interactions of intrinsic and extrinsic compensation as they conform to the factors of behavioral psychology. Such a review can avert implementing a design fraught with problems.

A Checklist for Action

The following checklist of items can serve as a quick review to see if additional analysis is required. It is by no means comprehensive, but by answering these questions, you will be in a good position to initiate your pilot plan.

☐ Are all levels of management committed to the success of the incentive compensation plan? Will they provide the visibility necessary to reassure the employees?

☐ Is the plan coordinated with other systems such as total quality management and just-in-time manufacturing?

☐ Has a good start already been made toward changing the organization's culture into one that emphasizes employee involvement?

☐ Are the rewards contingent upon results? Will the program pay the participants only if improvement is realized, or can they "game the system" and earn incentive in ways that will not result in real, measurable gains to the organization?

☐ Are the rewards clearly linked to specific actions and activities, or are they vaguely linked to business objectives by personal behavior or some other subjective indicator?

☐ Is the program structure simple to understand? There is a fine line of balance here that requires insight and judgment. On one hand is the necessity to "cover all the bases" and make provisions for contingencies in the program plan design. On the other hand, a program that appears to the employees as a complex legal document will often remain unread or be misunderstood by everyone except the author. Care must be taken not to fall into the trap of managing for the exception. There will always be that "10 percent" where circumstances fall outside the design. A good rule of thumb is to design for the majority and plan to address the exceptions as they occur.

☐ Did the designer(s) of the plan think like an employee-participant or like a manager-accountant? Since the accountant's job is to keep costs to a minimum, the accountant's design will lack motivational appeal every time. We have seen that behavior-based incentive compensation is more of an investment than a cost and should be designed with that in mind.

☐ Are the performance improvement payout plans realistic? Don't shoot for the stars in setting the goals for the plan. Evaluate historical performance in light of the competition and market conditions. Does the plan design deal in the reality of improving performance over what it is rather than what management would like it to be?

☐ Does the design of the plan closely follow the tenets of behavioral psychology? From the point of view of the participant, is the incentive opportunity positive?—is the budget sufficient to present an attractive opportunity to earn intrinsic and extrinsic compensation? Is it immediate?—will the participant receive the incentive compensation today? this month? this year? When? Is it certain? If participants increase their efforts and contributions to the organization, will they benefit?

☐ Is the design structure inflexible or cast in stone? Remember that employees are a key component in an incentive compensation plan, and to accommodate them, the plan must be dynamic. As such it will require periodic maintenance.

☐ Does the design try to do too many things? Has input from various sources within the organization turned the performance-improvement design into a program to address all the issues in the organization? Keep a singular focus to the plan, and ensure that the objectives are something that the employees have control over.

☐ Is there a well-established communications system in place?

☐ Are the communications designed to match the incentive media? A cash incentive compensation plan will require an entirely different approach to communications and promotional activity than will a noncash plan.

☐ Is the base compensation sufficient to build upon? Employees who are underpaid, or who perceive they are underpaid, will respond poorly to an incentive compensation plan until the disparity is resolved.

☐ Has the proper training been designed and delivered? Do employees understand what they need to do in order to earn the incentive compensation? Does management understand the program and how to use it as a tool to encourage improvement? Does management understand how to deliver intrinsic and extrinsic incentive compensation to make the most out of the program?

☐ Is there overall equity in the process? Is everyone included in the plan? Are the groups of a size where the employees still maintain "line-of-sight" focus on immediate and local objectives? Are the earning opportunities of all groups equal?

☐ Do the objectives generate a positive competition, such as against historical performance or against the performance of the competition? Will the objectives have negative effects on other areas of the organization? Will unwanted internal competition be the result? Does the plan design encourage teamwork and the sharing of information?

☐ Does the program include both financial objectives and nonfinancial objectives such as quality and customer satisfaction? Do the plan objectives take advantage of the opportunity to address both economic needs and organizational effectiveness needs?

☐ Are the measurement and control systems in place to report performance improvement and the associated incentive earnings to the participants on a timely basis? Can the systems provide timely feedback?

☐ Will program reporting be communicated as "incentive compensation expense YTD," or will it be positioned as the performance improvement that has been achieved and the improved financial position that occur as a result? Reporting on the program as a compensation expense will soon color management's perception of the program.

☐ Has the legal department had an opportunity to review and comment on the plan?

☐ Does the employee-performance appraisal process support or undermine the objectives of the incentive compensation plan? If the incentive plan emphasizes teamwork, are the performance-approval criteria set up to encourage individual effort or to support teamwork?

☐ Do the employees understand that this is a good-faith effort to improve the competitive position of the organization by empowering the employees and allowing them to share in the gains of the results? Do they understand that the systems, objectives, and payout structures will be fine-tuned until this objective is realized?

Taxes and the Budget

There is one more question that should be added to the checklist prior to startup of the incentive compensation plan. That is the question of taxes: income taxes, sales taxes, service taxes, and gratuities.

At this point, it is necessary to enjoin the disclaimer that the following information in no way should be considered as tax advice. The author is not an expert on the issue of taxes, and any advice on the issue of taxes should come from a qualified source. The important thing is to develop an awareness of the issue of taxes as it applies to the incentive compensation budget.

The issue of taxes on cash compensation is quite straightforward and well established. The incentive compensation is either added or not added to the base. Similarly, it is either figured into or is not figured into total benefits and retirement costs. The employee pays the taxes on the compensation, and the company pays its associated share of Social Security and other costs. With their years of experience in cash compensation, the accountants should have no trouble with including tax issues in the budget planning.

What about noncash incentives? Are they taxed? The fact is that noncash media are so different from cash that there is an opportunity to address the issue of taxes in a variety of ways. First of all, it must be established that noncash awards, items such as merchandise or travel, are taxable. There is no dispute or gray area about this. But who should pay the various payroll taxes? If an award were in cash, the employee would pay the income taxes and accept this liability as the cost of receiving cash compensation.

On the other hand, a color TV and home entertainment center or an all-expenses-paid trip to Hawaii are perceived quite differently than is cold cash. Noncash compensation is outside the established realm of monetary thinking and is perceived as a singular entity, detached from cash compensation. If the employee is assigned to pay the taxes on the noncash award, the fair market value of the award shows up on the pay stub and the associated taxes are removed from the base compensation. The net result is that the incentive compensation has a negative effect on the base compensation. This develops a unique form of stress in the minds of many employees, especially those who are tightly budgeted to their base compensation. The positive impact of the incentive compensation is replaced with the negative impact of a lower paycheck. Even employees who are told that this will happen never totally accept it. They perceive the taxes as an intrusion, a takeaway from base compensation.

Some employee populations can live with this tax impact, but many cannot. For those who cannot, the organization should pay the taxes on the noncash incentive award. This provides a much greater value to the employees because they are receiving what to them is tax-free compensation. In combination with the perceived value of merchandise or travel, this represents a powerful incentive offering to the employees. As we have seen, the stronger the incentive opportunity, the greater impact it will have on performance.

Budgetary Considerations

If an organization decides to use noncash incentives and pay the various payroll taxes for the employees, the additional cost must be calculated into the incentive compensation budget in order to avoid an unpleasant budget overage at the end of the year. Most payroll departments are in fact familiar with a process called "grossing up," where the organization pays the associated taxes on an award. Unfortunately, the IRS considers such payment of taxes as compensation and, as such, taxable income. Sounds like an ever decreasing spiral of cost, doesn't it? Fortunately, at some point the computation becomes so small that the IRS concedes the point. This point can be anywhere from 35 percent to 48 percent of the fair market value of the award.

An organization may choose to pay all of the associated payroll taxes, just the income tax, or just the FICA taxes. If an organization chooses to pay the taxes, you will want to know what the gross amount of the award will be so that the budget can be established accordingly. Here is one formula that can be used to compute the gross amount of the award when all the taxes are paid:

$$g = n + wg + sg + lg + fg$$

where

g = gross value of award

n = net value of award provided to employee

w = federal income tax rate

s = state income tax rate

l = local income tax rate

f = FICA rate

The following example of using this formula to calculate the gross value of a $100 award received by an employee (assuming a federal rate of 20 percent, state rate of 6 percent, city rate of 1.5 percent, and a 1990 FICA rate of 7.65 percent):

$$g = \$100 + 0.20g + 0.06g + 0.015g + 0.0765g$$
$$g = \$100 + 0.3515g$$
$$0.6485g = \$100$$
$$g = \$154$$

Reg. 30.3402(g)-1 and Rev. Rul. 66-190, Employers Tax Guide, allows an organization to withhold a flat 20 percent in lieu of using the graduated withholding rates for income tax. Rev. Proc. 81-48, 1981-2 C.B. 623, contains a formula for computing the Social Security tax liability for an award. The formula is $w = s/1-r$, where w is the employee's total after tax FICA wage, s is the employee's wages, and r is the employee's FICA tax rate.

Using the formula to calculate the gross amount of the award is useful when developing the budget. First, determine n, the net value of the incentive award, at goal and then add the payroll taxes to n for a gross value that would be the incentive element of the total budget. In this example, a payout of $100 would cost the organization $100 plus $54 in taxes.

The reality of the business world is that you may need to consider g, the gross value of the incentive award, as the value of the incentive compensation opportunity at goal. This approach provides the employee with the incentive opportunity at goal equal to the amount net of taxes of the gross award. For example, if your budget is fixed at $100 at goal, then the employee would receive performance points equal in purchasing power of $64.85.

Gross award:	$100
Less federal income tax:	20
Less state tax (6%):	6
Less city tax (1.5%):	1.5
Less FICA (7.65%):	7.65
Employee's net purchasing power:	$64.85

Using the net-purchasing-power approach would provide you with the budget data from which to back into the value of each increment of improvement. The total increments at the performance-improvement goal should equal this net number. This approach ensures that the total budget will remain intact for performance up to goal. Don't forget that the opportunity must appear attractive to the employees! All too often a budget is established that, after taxes, does not provide an attractive enough award for the employee. If the organization is going to pay the taxes, it is recommended that they be viewed as a cost of the program, much like the fixed costs of communications and administration and not as part of the employee's incentive opportunity.

Fair Market Value and Taxes

There are ways to reduce the tax burden, no matter who pays the tax. When the incentive consists of goods or services, the fair market value of the goods or services is what is considered as compensation and therefore taxable income. If, in the case of a custom trophy or plaque, the award has no market value, then it could probably be considered nontaxable. In the case of merchandise and travel, the fair market value is considered the price that the employee would typically pay for similar items in the marketplace.

This is a valuable concept to keep in mind if you are using a full-service incentive house to handle the fulfillment of your noncash incentive compensation. These agencies and, to a lesser extent, other middle-man operations add a cost to the price of the goods and services in the form of value-added services, such as financial analysts, program design specialists and other consulting oriented services (you use these companies if you need these services). This markup is, in reality, a service fee that may not be subject to tax. As an example, the fair market value of a $100 item could be established at $75 if, say, the local discount house is selling it as a loss leader for that price. Then $75 is used in the formula to calculate the tax liability. Using this approach could mean a substantial savings in payroll tax expense. This does not mean that you have to establish a fair market value for each item in the catalog. The representatives of these various service agencies will provide you with an indication of what value to use.

Other Budget Considerations

There are other nontraditional budget items in a noncash incentive compensation program. If your merchandise program has a significant budget, then such things as shipping and sales tax will be a consideration. But if you use an outside supplier to provide fulfillment, the merchandise will be shipped directly to the employees as it is ordered by them. Some catalogs include the cost of transportation in the price of the merchandise, others add it to the invoice. If you hadn't planned on an additional transportation cost of, say, 8 percent in your budget, you could be in for an unpleasant surprise.

The same awareness applies to state and local sales taxes. Merchandise and travel awards will have the cost of sales tax associated with them; this should be taken into consideration in budget planning. Now the compensation professional must don the hat of the tax expert.

Is It Worth It?

The use of noncash incentives is a cost-benefit tradeoff. If the company pays the taxes, will the budget be too big? The answer to that question varies from situation to situation, but the general answer is no. If the budget for the program is significant enough, and if you are judicious in your choice of suppliers so that you pay for those services that you cannot perform, then it is possible to obtain pricing at a lower rate than the individual employee could for the same selection of merchandise. With this pricing, even if the employees pay taxes on the incentive, they are getting something for less than its retail value that they would have paid for with after-tax dollars.

Perhaps the size of the incentive opportunity at goal can be smaller because of the element of perceived value. Perhaps the amount of performance improvement that can be gained with the use of merchandise will offset the increased size (if that is the case) of the budget. In addition to all the other pros and cons for the use of noncash, the somewhat subjective question of impact should be asked. Thus, "If $1 in cash will get me a 2-percent improvement, will $1.45 in merchandise get me 4-percent improvement"?

There is a financial benefit for giving noncash awards to employees in recognition of length of service or a good safety record. These awards are not subject to payroll taxes, as noted in Sec. 274(b) of the Tax Reform Act of 1986. It would be a good idea to obtain a copy of this document as part of your incentive compensation planning. It could save the organization and the employees some money. Naturally, there are limits to the value that can be bestowed. Under the tax law, the organization with an unwritten plan can give merchandise awards of up to $400 in value to each employee. If the plan is "qualified"—that is, a written plan that does not discriminate against or in favor of any employee—the award value can be up to

$1,600, but the average cost of all items awarded must not exceed $400.

There are other restrictions, definitions, and conditions that apply to awards for safety and length of service. The point to realize here is that noncash awards, given to the employees under these circumstances, present a better value because neither the employee nor the company has to shoulder the tax burden. A cash award of $400 given to an employee would result in an actual award closer to $300 after taxes, or a cost to the organization of closer to $600 if it pays the taxes.

As you can see, there are several ancillary costs to be aware of in the use of noncash incentives. Issues such as sales tax and transportation should be considered as a cost of the incentive compensation and included in the cost-benefit analysis. Payroll taxes are a complicated issue and impact intrinsic compensation as well as extrinsic compensation. You may find that the negative impact on the extrinsic incentive budget (if there is one) for payment of payroll taxes is more than offset by the positive impact on the intrinsic incentive budget and the overall impact on performance improvement. If you decide to pay the taxes, don't overlook the opportunity to promote this fact as additional proof of management's good-faith position. The tax issue, rather than being a liability, can be viewed as an opportunity to act as a bridge between behavioral psychology and incentive compensation.

Career Path

What, then, becomes of the compensation professional in this evolutionary process? What are the duties of the compensation professional in the world of behavior-based incentive compensation? Ideally, when the power of incentive compensation is accepted as a strategic process for guiding the organization, the compensation professional should be considered more of a strategic planning executive. In this position, when designing or managing the compensation strategy, he or she begins to think like the chief executive officer. In order to develop a reward philosophy that reinforces and supports the organization's strategies, it is necessary that the designer(s) have access to, and be involved in, the communications flow from such areas as marketing, human resources, quality, operations, finance, and administration.

But information is power, and those who have it may be reluctant to share. In the world of behavior-based incentive compensation, information hoarding is damaging to the organization. If an organization's success is based on achievement of the business plan or adherence to the budget, then the compensation professionals will need to be well versed in the financial aspects of the organization. Only with this knowledge can they design the most effective motivational structures.

If the organization's success is based on achieving strategic objectives, then the compensation professional should be involved in the strategic planning process. If an organization's success is based on improvement over historical performance, then the compensation professional should be closely associated with the operations end of the business. Technology will soon provide access to this fount of information; it will be up to executive management to permit access to it.

Remember, the design of a behavior-based incentive compensation plan is not just a payout matrix. It is the assimilation of a payout matrix into a structure of employee involvement. To effectively develop such a design, the incentive compensation professional will have to be omniscient . . . or lead a cross-functional team of senior management that can provide such knowledge.

An Encouraging Word

For many of you, this book has covered a lot of new ground. It has addressed the disquieting position that the discipline of compensation is in a state of change. This change will accelerate as technology provides the wherewithal for business to change and adjust more rapidly to economic and competitive situations.

The human resources of an organization have become and will continue to become the most important element in the resource mix. The discomfort in this reality is that human resources are the most volatile resource to manage. The needs that drive this area of business seem to change on an almost daily basis, fueled and directed as they are by the rapid advance of communication and computer technology.

The upside of this reality is that the potential of the human resources to impact the economic value and organizational effectiveness of an organization has largely been untapped. To the organizations that master the skills of tapping into human potential will go the spoils of victory, for they will stand as leaders in the marketplace.

Recommended Reading

Blinder, Alan S. *Paying for Productivity: A Look at the Evidence.* Washington, D.C.: Brookings Institution, 1990.

Cannellon, Thomas K. *How to Improve Human Performance: Behaviorism in Business and Industry.* New York: Harper & Row, 1978.

Deming, W. Edwards. *Out of the Crisis.* Cambridge, Mass.: Center for Advanced Engineering Study, Massachusetts Institute of Technology, 1986.

Drucker, Peter F. *Innovation and Entrepreneurship: Practice and Principles.* New York: Harper & Row, 1985.

Fukuda, Ryuji. *Managerial Engineering: Techniques for Improving Quality and Productivity in the Workplace.* Stamford, Conn.: Productivity, Inc., 1983.

Garvin, David A. *Managing Quality: The Strategic and Competitive Edge.* New York: Free Press, 1988.

Heckscher, Charles C. *The New Unionism: Employee Involvement in the Changing Corporation.* New York: Basic Books, 1988.

Herzberg, Frederick. *Work and the Nature of Man.* Cleveland: World Publishing, 1966.

Hopeman, Richard. *Production: Concepts, Analysis, Control.* Columbus, Ohio: Merrill, 1976.

Hunnius, Gerry, editor. *Workers' Control: A Reader on Labor and Social Change.* New York: Random House, 1973.

Imai, Masaaki. *Kaisen: The Key to Japan's Competitive Success.* New York: Random House, 1986.

Johnson, Perry L. *Keeping Score: Achieving Integrated Quality Management.* New York: Ballinger, 1989.

Juran, J. M. *Juran on Planning for Quality.* New York: Free Press, 1987.

Kanter, Rosabeth Moss. *The Change Masters: Innovations for Productivity in the American Corporation.* New York: Simon & Schuster, 1983.

Lawler, Edward E. III. *High-Involvement Management.* San Francisco: Jossey-Bass, 1986.

Levering, Robert. *A Great Place to Work: What Makes Some Employers So Good, and Most So Bad.* New York: Random House, 1988.

Lynch, Dudley, and Paul L. Kordis. *Strategy of the Dolphin.* William Morrow and Co., Inc., 1988.

McAdams, Jerry. "Communications: Critical to Performance Improvement Efforts." *Password* (American Hospital Supply Co.), Winter 1984, pages 8–10.

Maccoby, Michael. *Why Work?: Leading the New Generation.* New York: Simon & Schuster, 1988.

Maslow, Abraham H. *Motivation and Personality*, 2nd edition. New York: Harper & Row, 1970.

Peters, Thomas J., and Robert H. Waterman, Jr. *In Search of Excellence: Lessons From America's Best-Run Companies.* New York: Harper & Row, 1982.

Riggs, James L. "Matrix Family of Measures." *Industrial Engineering*, January 1986. (Published by the Institute of Industrial Engineering, Atlanta, Ga.)

Rock, Milton L., and Lance Berger. *The Compensation Handbook: A State of the Art Guide to Compensation Strategy and Design.* New York: McGraw-Hill, 1991.

Skinner, B. F. *Contingencies of Reinforcement: A Theoretical Analysis.* New York: Appleton-Century-Crofts, 1969.

Szilogyi, Andrew. *Management and Performance.* Glenview, Ill.: Scott, Foresman, 1988.

Thompson, Phillip C. *Quality Circles: How to Make Them Work in America.* New York: AMACOM, 1982.

Tregoe, Benjamin. *Vision in Action: Putting a Winning Strategy to Work.* New York: Simon & Schuster, 1989.

Ulrich, David. *Organizational Capability: Competing From the Inside Out.* New York: John Wiley & Sons, 1990.

Zuboff, Shoshana. *In the Age of the Smart Machine: The Future of Work and Power.* New York: Basic Books, 1988.

Index